# Sexuality Education for Students with Disabilities

## Special Education Law, Policy, and Practice

**Series Editors**
Mitchell L. Yell, PhD, University of South Carolina
David F. Bateman, PhD, Shippensburg University of Pennsylvania

The *Special Education Law, Policy, and Practice* series highlights current trends and legal issues in the education of students with disabilities. The books in this series link legal requirements with evidence-based instruction and highlight practical applications for working with students with disabilities. The titles in the *Special Education Law, Policy, and Practices* series are designed not only to be required textbooks for general education and special education preservice teacher education programs but are also designed for practicing teachers, education administrators, principals, school counselors, school psychologists, parents, and others interested in improving the lives of students with disabilities. The *Special Education Law, Policy, and Practice* series is committed to research-based practices working to provide appropriate and meaningful educational programming for students with disabilities and their families.

**Titles in Series:**

*The Essentials of Special Education Law* by Andrew M. Markelz and David F. Bateman

*Special Education Law Annual Review 2020* by David F. Bateman, Mitchell L. Yell, and Kevin P. Brady

*Developing Educationally Meaningful and Legally Sound IEPs* by Mitchell L. Yell, David F. Bateman, and James G. Shriner

*Sexuality Education for Students with Disabilities* edited by Thomas C. Gibbon, Elizabeth A. Harkins Monaco, and David F. Bateman

# Sexuality Education for Students with Disabilities

Edited by

Thomas C. Gibbon, Elizabeth A. Harkins Monaco, and David F. Bateman

ROWMAN & LITTLEFIELD

Lanham • Boulder • New York • London

Published by Rowman & Littlefield
An imprint of The Rowman & Littlefield Publishing Group, Inc.
4501 Forbes Boulevard, Suite 200, Lanham, Maryland 20706
www.rowman.com

6 Tinworth Street, London SE11 5AL, United Kingdom

British Library Cataloguing in Publication Information Available

**Library of Congress Cataloging-in-Publication Data**
Names: Gibbon, Thomas C., editor. | Monaco, Elizabeth A. Harkins, 1981– editor. | Bateman, David, 1963– editor.
Title: Sexuality education for students with disabilities / edited by Thomas C. Gibbon, Elizabeth A. Harkins Monaco, and David F. Bateman.
Description: Lanham, Maryland : Rowman & Littlefield, 2022. | Series: Special education law, policy, and practice | Includes bibliographical references and index.
Identifiers: LCCN 2021005846 (print) | LCCN 2021005847 (ebook) | ISBN 9781538138526 (cloth) | ISBN 9781538138533 (paperback) | ISBN 9781538138540 (epub)
Subjects: LCSH: Sex instruction for people with disabilities. | Students with disabilities.
Classification: LCC HQ30.5 S485 2022 (print) | LCC HQ30.5 (ebook) | DDC 306.7087—dc23
LC record available at https://lccn.loc.gov/2021005846
LC ebook record available at https://lccn.loc.gov/2021005847

♾️™ The paper used in this publication meets the minimum requirements of American National Standard for Information Sciences—Permanence of Paper for Printed Library Materials, ANSI/NISO Z39.48-1992.

# Contents

# CHAPTER 1

# Introduction

### David F. Bateman

Why is this important?
In a span of just a few years, adolescents transition dramatically in almost all realms of their lives: they mature physically, their ability to analyze and reason develops, and their social relationships are redefined. Key social and emotional milestones during adolescence are often directly related to the abilities to initiate and maintain intimate relationships (Perkins & Borden, 2003), maintain physically maturing bodies, and manage personal sexuality (Murphy & Elias, 2006). A problem is that adolescents with disabilities may have difficulty expressing sexuality in satisfying ways, consequently facing issues such as limited intimate relationships, low self-esteem, increased social isolation, deregulated emotional maintenance (Sabornie et al., 1989), reduced sexual functioning, and limited sexual health (Blum, 1997).

Finding ways to express sexuality is a key part of functional development and a formal education in sexuality is critical for all students but is often neglected for students with disabilities (Neufeld et al., 2002). Appropriate sexual knowledge not only assists in achieving personal fulfillment and addressing problems of loneliness and self-esteem, but also provides protection from mistreatment, abuse, unplanned pregnancies, or sexually transmitted diseases (STDs; Murphy & Elias, 2006).

## Who Should Be Taught?

Effective sexuality education for students with intellectual and developmental disabilities (IDD) and autism spectrum disorder (ASD) must involve the student and stakeholders. Too often, sexuality instruction focuses solely on the individual with a disability, but due to the nature of the possible need for long-term supports, others should be included in this education. For many, the education of family and caregivers is just as important and necessary to help the individual with disabilities to develop.

## Family Members

Family members are the primary stakeholders in this developmental arena in the earlier ages, but many need assistance when establishing appropriate expectations for their children in relation to cognitive levels, functional abilities, and ages. Many family members have experienced the various stages of development as the individual with a disability matures, but sexual awareness brings with it other issues, topics, and concerns. Family members often are not prepared to address these concerns and also are unsure about where to go for help (Murphy & Elias, 2006).

Much of the instruction for family members has to address preconceived notions and stereotypes. Sexuality instruction should help them understand that, while their family member with a disability may seem to be functioning academically like a first- or second-grade student, significant hormonal changes occur during adolescence. Additionally, adolescents with disabilities, like all adolescents, have near constant exposure to mass and social media including sexually provocative images and associations. It is not uncommon for family members to talk about the "childlike" behaviors, which could still include fascination with children's television shows, games, dolls, pets, and even clothing. These activities often preclude thinking about their family member with a developmental disability growing up, getting older, and especially wanting to express himself or herself sexually (Murphy & Elias, 2006). Parents also may assume their children are too young or immature to explore appropriate personal sexual preferences or gender norms. Children with disabilities can—and have the right to—identify on the gender or sexuality continuum beyond heterosexual or cisgender, but heteronormative assumptions may prevent this.

Families need help to realize their family member will change, that support will need to be provided, and they will need to address sexuality issues in a way that does not prevent development. In many respects, the support and acknowledgement of the need for appropriate sexuality education for their family member is one of the most important parts of this process. The attitudes, statements, and subsequent actions can have a short- and long-term impact on the ideas and behaviors of the individual with a disability. Additionally, the opportunities (or nonopportunities) provided by families for spending alone time with a person who may be a sexual partner also will have a long-term impact on the individual with a disability.

As has been pointed out in many places, the long-term care and support of individuals with some disabilities often becomes the responsibility of family members as the parents either become too old or pass away (Brown et al., 2015). Including the family members helps to ensure a smooth transition and a consistent message. The support of siblings and other family members can be crucial for everyone involved. If home and school share the responsibilities for appropriate sexuality functioning, students are more apt to adhere to appropriate expectations while maintaining personal safety (Murphy & Elias, 2006).

Just about any parent will tell you how difficult it is to get an adolescent to delay gratification. Think about adolescent requests for a video game, movie, concert tickets, or even the latest phone, or especially the persistent repeated desire to hang out unsupervised with friends or ride with other young drivers. Parents of children and young adults with disabilities face an even more challenging task. As noted above, having a disability does not typically diminish normal biological human development. Just about all adolescents with disabilities develop physically and have sexual desires (Murphy & Elias, 2006). Parents and family members of individuals with disabilities often want their children to have as normal a life as possible, while knowing that their children are more likely to be victims of sexual assault. Teaching children with disabilities to negotiate the increasingly complex interaction between their desires while providing skills for self-protection is particularly problematic if the children have impaired cognitive functioning, emotional instability, impulsivity, or authority aversion.

Balancing a need for development along with the need to help the individual prevent sexual harassment should be an important part of any educational curriculum that is geared toward an individual's needs and ability level. There are programs, agencies, and advocacy groups that provide free information for parents and educators of individuals with disabilities on this topic. One example, the Florida Developmental Disabilities Council, Inc., provides free educational resources that address topics such as identifying basic body parts, understanding development, and identification of appropriate and inappropriate actions on a level that is easy for students with IDD to understand (Baxley & Zendell, 2005). The Center for Parent Information and Resources (2018) also provides links to information directly related to various disabilities, such as ASD, deaf-blindness, IDD, learning disabilities, emotional disturbances, physical disabilities, and traumatic brain injuries. These two resources are just a few of the programs and informational guides provided free of charge. It is important such information is sought out and delivered to parents and families in a way that will meet their specific needs. The more the parent, caregiver, and family know about development, appropriate ways to show affection, and the right to say no, and teach ways the individual with a disability can protect themselves from being harmed and/or telling a trusted adult when something inappropriate does occur, the more successful we can be at preventing and stopping sexual assault of individuals with disabilities.

Finally, parents of any adolescent face the multipronged challenge of educating their children about normal biological and human sexual development while warning them about the potential dangers of others. Impulse control in the adolescent brain occurs after brain stem development. The frontal lobes, which also develop later, control impulses and help us to manage behavior; the brain stem sends out messages for the body to act. Communication between these two parts of the brain is required for carefully considered decision making. Some researchers have suggested that the means of communication between the frontal lobes and brain stem are not completely formed until an individual reaches his or her mid to late 20s (Marshall & Neuman, 2011), further exacerbating the education period related to sexual education.

## The Staff

We acknowledge that the first teachers and long-term caregivers and supporters are often family members of the individual with disabilities; however, individuals with some disabilities require long-term support and care by paid staff. The same statements made about attitudes and perceptions for family members relating to the discussing, instructing, and providing alone time need to be addressed with staff members. Although individuals with disabilities often may not require a residential placement and concomitant staff assistance until they are older, the perceptions about childlike behaviors must be addressed as well.

It is an undisputed problem that we often do not provide sufficient monetary compensation for staff who work with individuals with disabilities. The role they play in loco parentis is a valuable one; however, we need to realize all of the other demands we often place on them. The other realization that needs to be addressed is the awareness of the frequency of staff turnover that often makes consistent programs and services very difficult.

Staff training must address the needs of the individuals with disabilities. A vital component of training for staff is ensuring all individuals under their care are treated as individuals. Based on the history of the person with the disability, expectations and comments the individual makes, the expectations and comments made by family members, the location of the services provided, the number of individuals being served, and the interaction with others all provide settings and opportunities that need to be addressed and individualized.

In addition to all the other staff responsibilities that require training, from billing to confidentiality, from providing appropriate medications to documenting behaviors, staff will also need training about issues of sexuality education. This training should include terms to use, expectations, and how to respond to certain circumstances. The problem is that training often needs to be provided about the individual needs and expectations for each person with whom they will be working.

## The Student

Finally, the needs and desires of the student must be addressed. Like the discussion regarding training the parents and the staff, training about issues of sexuality needs to be individualized to the student. This training needs to address the individual's desires, functioning levels, religious beliefs, and opportunities that will be presented. There is no one level of education and support appropriate for every individual with a disability, just as there is no one level of education and support appropriate for individuals who do not have a disability.

Given the need to individualize the training based on the above descriptors, it is also important to individualize the training based on the comfort level of the student in addressing these issues. For some, the issues are so embarrassing and uncomfortable to talk about that attending or participating in a large-scale class or group on the topic would not be considered an option. Others may be more comfortable and may be more willing to participate in a class and be willing to engage in an open discussion about topics related to sexuality and relationships.

Finally, planning for discussions related to this important topic should include—and this will be mentioned repeatedly in later chapters—the need for continuing support to provide information and be available to answer questions as they arise. As will be noted, one-time efforts without follow-up opportunities are inappropriate for topics as important as this. Plan the instruction for the student to include repeated sessions of information (which may be on the same topic) along with continued availability for questions.

Finally, given all the factors described above related to family desires balanced out with individual desires, education surrounding issues of sexuality may not necessarily occur in schools. For some it may occur in places of worship. Clearly not all individuals participate in regular worship services; therefore it is inappropriate to assume this is a sole place of instruction, but for some it is a very important part of their family life.

# History

As unpleasant as it is, it is important to address the history of issues related to sexuality for individuals with disabilities. Some of the attitudes related to sexuality, of which many may be wrong or impractical, may still need to be addressed to help convince family or staff members of the need for education. There is a lot of stigma related to education on issues of sexuality for individuals with developmental disabilities, and much of that stems from historical misconceptions.

The history of sexuality for individuals with disabilities will be covered more extensively in other parts of this book, but they should be a part of any training program that teaches family members and staff. The following is a brief background about **eugenics**, institutionalization, and sexual assault for people with disabilities in order to provide context for the move toward a more comprehensive approach to sexuality education for people with a wide range of disabilities.

# Eugenics

Although unpleasant, it is important to discuss the Eugenics Movement. For decades the Eugenics Movement steered much of the discussion related to how we think about individuals with disabilities. This was not just for professionals but pervaded much of the popular media and dramatically altered popular thinking about individuals with disabilities.

The Eugenics Movement and its ideas started to flourish in the late 1800s and clearly remained popular until well after World War II, and was in many respects still part of the discussion for individuals with disabilities well after that (Allen, 2012; Lombardo, 2012). The basics of eugenics stemmed from ideas related to how farmers dealt with livestock, where there was a culling of the herd to make the animals stronger by removing the weaker animals, and applying that logic and belief system to humans (Allen, 2012). Specifically, if reproduction could be controlled so that unfit stock (humans with "problems") could either be eliminated or at least controlled, society would, as a whole, benefit (Allen, 2012). The result would be that we would improve future generations and be able to get rid of undesirable traits (Lombardo, 2012).

The observable application of eugenics to people has much more deep-seated roots than simply a relation to farming practices. It was also based on a very narrow and xenophobic interpretation of the Bible

(Allen, 2012; Lombardo, 2012; O'Brien & Bundy, 2009). This was used extensively to justify propaganda for years to come. As the United States went through a series of immigration waves, xenophobia was very present. Along with xenophobia existed a prejudice about people with disabilities.

Based on the above, advocates for eugenics increasingly pushed for laws supporting their ideas. In turn, state legislatures started to pass laws based on eugenics with the first one enacted in 1907 (Lombardo, 2012). Increasingly, states passed laws sanctioning involuntary sterilization, restricted marriage, and forced institutionalization, with some legislation that supported euthanasia (O'Brien & Bundy, 2009).

The main target group for the Eugenics Movement were those who were "feebleminded"; the group we now refer to as individuals with IDD. Other disability groups were also targeted, but to a lesser extent. Those groups included individuals with emotional and behavioral disorders, epilepsy, and sensory impairments (O'Brien & Bundy, 2009). People who were considered feebleminded were the target group because it was believed that all or most cases were due to genetic causes. The intellectual characteristics of individuals who were feebleminded were the ones thought to be undesirable to continue on to other generations. About the same time, large institutions to house people with disabilities grew rapidly.

It is sad to point out that, from the 1900s and running through the 1980s, the most common housing placement for people with intellectual disabilities was large state-run institutions. These institutions often resembled hospital campuses and became holding centers. In general, these large institutions did not educate or advance the development of the people with disabilities who lived there. These institutions and their practices were an important outgrowth of the Eugenics Movement. Families who had children with clearly identifiable disabilities were often told to send their children to the institutions and not encouraged to maintain normal familial connections. There was often no education related to sexuality. There were frequent forced sterilizations, which were easier to carry out in an institutional setting (O'Brien & Bundy, 2009).

For our purposes, it is important to point out these facts to highlight how far society has changed (in most places) related to sexuality education for individuals with disabilities. It is estimated 65,000 Americans with disabilities were legally sterilized by 1970 (Powell, 2014). That number is probably a gross understatement of the true number. North Carolina recently enacted legislation to compensate the 7,600 residents forced to be sterilized (Thompson, 2013). This is the first state to set up this type of compensation system; however, many of the earlier victims are likely deceased. The prevailing thinking was people with disabilities who were institutionalized were not capable of normal human interaction with the opposite sex.

Clearly times have changed, but it is also clear there is a lot of work still left to do.

## Sexual Assault

Just like the section on eugenics, it is important to point out that sexual assault of individuals with disabilities is all too common. A study released by the U.S. Department of Justice found close to 82,100 cases of rape and/or sexual assault of persons with disabilities were reported each year from 2008 to 2012 (Harrell, 2014). The sad part of the study shows the number of reports more than doubled from 2010 to 2011 and the numbers continued to exceed 80,000 reports in 2012 (Harrell, 2014). Another survey, the 2012 National Survey on Abuse of People with Disabilities, found 90% of individuals with disabilities who reported some abuse stated that the abuse was often repeated. Shockingly, 57% of these individuals who reported abuse also reported the abuse occurred on more than 20 occasions (Baladerian et al., 2013).

In January 2014, media attention was generated when the White House Council on Women and Girls recognized the increased risk of becoming a victim of sexual assault for individuals with disabilities. This report cites sources indicating individuals with disabilities are three times more likely to experience sexual assault and women with severe disabilities are four times more likely to be sexually assaulted, when compared to their typically developing peers (White House Council on Women and Girls, 2014).

Furthermore, Sullivan and Knutson (2000) found children with disabilities were more than three times more likely to be the victims of sexual abuse than children without disabilities.

Krohn (2014) recognized this variability in the increased risk across disability groups, age, and gender of individuals with disabilities. Krohn also noted studies have overwhelmingly found women and girls with disabilities show some of the highest percentages of sexual assault victims, stating most females with disabilities experience sexual abuse at some time in their lives. This statement is supported by evidence from the U.S. Department of Justice reports and in a study by Baladerian (1991): 68% to 83% of women, 39% to 83% of girls, and 16% to 32% of boys with developmental disabilities experience sexual assault in their lifetime.

The problem with this data is that it is classically underreported (Wissink et al., 2015). The 2012 National Survey additionally found

41.6% of individuals who took the survey reported sexual abuse, while 41% of these victims did not report these incidents to authorities (Baladerian et al., 2013). Krohn also emphasized cases go unreported, relaying many survivors with disabilities never report the sexual abuse compared to the survivors without disabilities (Krohn, 2014).

Some children who reported sexual assaults said that no action was taken as a result of reporting (Wissink et al., 2015). Also, when incidences were reported to authorities, studies have found low percentages of arrest rates and a high likelihood that no action would be taken as a result of the report. Of all sexual assault and/or rape cases reported in the United States, only 12% became investigations between 2005 and 2010 and one study found that cases had been dismissed 75% of the time with 80% disapproval from the victim (White House Council on Women and Girls, 2014).

Getting an accurate actual number of the risk to people with disabilities is difficult due to the variety of studies on this topic. It is safe to say children with disabilities are at an increased risk of sexual assault. This is all the more reason for appropriate and comprehensive education on this topic.

## Curriculum

The importance of the content of this book cannot be overstated. Individuals with IDD and ASD not only deserve an opportunity to receive a free appropriate public education while they are in school, but they should also receive an education that will help them understand sexual needs and how to act. As mentioned above, there needs to be a concerted effort from all parts to help, and that is what this book offers.

It is important to highlight the different expectations for the education of students with disabilities in different grades. Sexuality education for students with disabilities is not just a task or responsibility as a part of a secondary education curriculum. Just like other parts of transition instruction, the attitudes and words chosen by elementary teachers also can play a very important role in setting the stage for more direct and explicit instruction later.

As will be presented in this book, sexuality education for students with disabilities should be part of a comprehensive curriculum plan, and will have four important points guiding all of the chapters because teaching about sexuality is more than just sex education.

1. *Relationships are important.* It is more than just sex. It is about being an important part of someone else's life, which can include living with others.

2. *Respect.* Treating others with respect should be integrated into all training programs, whether relating to sex education or not, but especially when sex is involved. This includes not only respecting others, but also respecting oneself and learning to advocate for one's own interests and rights.
3. *Dealing with emotions.* Sex is an emotional response, not just a physical one. This book includes discussion items to help individuals with disabilities to address the emotions that come with sex and to help realize this is a very important and often forgotten aspect of the need for training.
4. *Honoring others.* This will build on the ideas of respect but will also ensure others' opinions and values are treated with dignity and that we do not embarrass others.

While these four points may seem simple, they are actually very important to the overall sexuality education curriculum that needs to be emphasized for all students, not just those with disabilities. All educators have the additional responsibility of working to provide an appropriate education for individuals who have historically been discriminated against, legally sterilized, and prevented from engaging in sexual activities.

Not only is the movement of sexuality education for people with disabilities wrestling with the past; it needs to move forward and help pave the way for the future. The various chapters of this book will clarify this work.

Specifically, the current best practices in sexuality education for individuals with disabilities will be highlighted. This will include topics about relationships (of which there are many facets), appropriate sexual development/urges, public versus private behaviors, safety and personal rights, and curricular adaptations. All of these are very important.

This book will also highlight the changes in adolescent physical and cognitive development, how cognitive development can affect sexual development, family and parent considerations, and information available to parents and families for sexuality education. The text covers information about disability studies and intersectionality as it relates to students with disabilities. It will highlight recommendations for teachers and other human services providers, discuss special considerations for group home and recreational facilities, and discuss the similarities (and differences) between different disability categories. This text covers consent, issues of self-determination, and dealing with uncertainty, and will conclude with a list of additional resources. Individuals with disabilities need our support—not restrictions—to lead a full and engaged life. This book seeks to provide supports so that individuals with disabilities can not only access society, but also express their preferences.

# Disability Studies

Elizabeth A. Harkins Monaco

*What if we looked at "disability [as] a social enigma" (Berger, 2013, p. 1)? This way, we can challenge "the widespread belief that having an able body and mind determines whether one is a quality human being."*

(Siebers, 2008, p. 4)

## Overview

Chapter 2 will review how disability studies provides a theory for understanding how disability helps us understand humanity. The reader will explore social elements such as the language used when discussing disability, the defining features of disability, and how these concepts connect to ableism and disability rights advocacy. In addition, this chapter will discuss how these considerations affect access to sexuality education for people with disabilities and the societal consequences of disability rights in this area. Perspectives of individuals with disabilities will be included.

Readers will

- explore a disability studies lens and evaluate how it aims to improve disability advocacy;
- analyze theoretical approaches to disability and person-first perspectives;
- critique cultural and political influences on disability theories and sexuality education;
- evaluate how sexual identity, sexual development, and sexual relationships interconnect for people with disabilities; and
- investigate current and future issues in disability studies.

# Introduction to Disability Studies

Historically, individuals with disabilities have not been fully included in society; they are devalued, underrepresented, or ignored. Additionally, nondisabled people don't necessarily notice this issue. **Disability studies,** an interdisciplinary field of study, aims to combat this. Disability studies examines perspectives of disability from the social sciences, humanities, medical, rehabilitation, and educational lenses. It seeks to incorporate disability when "understanding humankind" (Berger, 2013, p. 3) by emphasizing the importance of the disability rights movement to promote the voices of people with disabilities. Disability studies aims to identify society's responsibilities to be inclusive by defining disability as a social difference rather than a medical or cognitive condition (Berger, 2013). Reframing disability as this kind of construct shows that having a disability does not limit one's quality of life, and that "people with disabilities have a better chance of enjoying a fulfilling life if they accept their disability as a positive aspect of their identity that provides them with a unique and at times contentious way of being in and viewing the world" (Berger, 2013, p. 14).

Disability studies emphasizes the importance of language around disability. Shifting language around disability is one way to reduce social discrimination and marginalization faced by people with disabilities. First, consider if labels and terms are current. Then, gauge whether they make negative assumptions. For example, consider the word **handicap;** handicap implies something is inherently wrong and therefore is considered outdated. Recommended terms include "**impairment[s]** ... [or the] biological or physiological conditions that entail the loss of physical, sensory, or cognitive function, and **disabilit[ies]** ... inability[ies] to perform a personal or socially necessary task because of that impairment or the societal reaction to it" (Berger, 2013, p. 6). These terms have more positive connotations. Disability studies also encourages people to consider how people with disabilities prefer to be labeled. Some prefer **person-first language** (people with disabilities) while others prefer **identity-first language** (disabled people). Person-first language labels the person prior to the disability (boy with autism) while identity-first language puts the disability in front of the person (autistic boy). *See Chapter 13 for more information on person-first and identity-first language.* This chapter will use both terms accordingly, but overall this text uses person-first language to acknowledge our roles as faculty, teachers, and advocates.

Disability studies asks us to consider how people with disabilities are marginalized in society. For example, when buildings are not architecturally accessible, people with wheelchairs are not able to enter. The lack of accessibility impacts their abilities to access certain activities in these environments, which in turn limits their independence, contributions to society, and abilities to make and keep relationships in these spaces. Other exclusionary examples extend beyond the physical environment and manifest through the attitudes or judgments of society; people without disabilities have reported feeling uncomfortable or fearful around people with disabilities. This **stigma,** or attitude, reduces people with disabilities as "less than," and has had long-term effects because of **institutional discrimination** (Linton, 1998; Papadimitriou, 2001), or recurring political, economic, cultural, and social discrimination (Berger, 2013; Nowell, 2006).

The intersection of language and stigma around disability amounts to a form of discrimination known as **ableism.** Ableism assumes that some people are "normal" and superior while other people are "abnormal" and inferior. "Ableism is so taken for granted that it remains unconscious and invisible to most people, even though it constitutes an overarching regime that structures the lives of people with disabilities" (Berger, 2013, p. 15).

## Theoretical Approach

Disability studies utilizes specific frameworks, or disability models, to organize disability-specific concepts into social constructs (Berger, 2013). There are many models, but we are focusing on three of the more common ones. The first is the **medical model of disability,** which approaches disability through a rehabilitative lens. The medical model promotes using etiology, diagnosis, or preventative measures to treat or cure those with impairments (Berger, 2013; French & Swain, 2001; Shakespeare, 2006; Siebers, 2008; Turner, 2001; Wendell, 1996). This essentially is an "ableist view that depicts people with disabilities as deficient and inherently inferior to nondisabled people, and thus it is they, not society, who are most in need of change" (Berger, 2013, p. 27). Ultimately, the medical model supports grieving or fixing an impairment rather than honoring the individual who has one.

Another common model is the **social model of disability,** which emphasizes society's responsibilities in ensuring accessibility and acceptance. The social model claims that society limits those with disabilities through its very infrastructure, systems of privilege and oppression, or through the attitudes and judgments of the nondisabled. This model tends to dismiss or remove the impairment itself, however, something essential to the core of the disability experience.

The **cultural model of disability** encourages people with disabilities to "come together to assert an affirmative identity and community of like-minded people" (Berger, 2013, p. 30) by highlighting the relationship between society and the experiences of individuals with disabilities. It shifts the narrative that disabled people should be pitied *(see Rhetoric in Chapter 13)* into the belief that they are "normal" humans who lead enriched lives and contribute to society. In fact, "some scholars have drawn on the tradition of phenomenology . . . [or] the lived experience of . . . human beings [as] the starting point for understanding disability" (Berger, 2013, p. 28). The cultural model has "a number of complex issues regarding the tenuous nature of solidarity among people with disabilities" (Berger, 2013, p. 31). Despite this challenge, however, this is a strong framework that seeks to honor people with disabilities through a cultural lens. Let's explore the Deaf community as an example.

## Disability Culture

The Deaf community defines Deafness as a way to highlight a group of people—a "linguistic minority"—who use sign language as their primary form of communication. They do not consider Deafness an impairment or disabling condition and they openly oppose the medical model by rejecting the use of technological aids (e.g., cochlear implants) to "correct" their Deafness. Rather, the Deaf community views Deafness as an asset that makes the members of their community unique. This community honors and preserves their linguistic traditions as cultural norms in the same way other groups do (Aronson, 2001; Barnes & Mercer, 2001; Lane, 1995) by maintaining separate environments in their schools, social gatherings, athletic events, or places to worship, to honor and preserve their culture (Barnes & Mercer, 2001; Berger, 2013; Groch, 2001; Lane, 1995; Tucker, 1998).

The very idea of a disability culture brings about questions of solidarity, cultural identification, and shared experiences and outlooks, but various disability communities do not share the same views. Some people with disabilities do not identify their disability as important parts of their identities (Watson, 2002; *see Intersectionality in Chapter 4*), while others are less likely to develop pride for it. This is quite common when disabilities are developed later in life (Darling & Heckert, 2010). Ultimately, most people with disabilities differ considerably in the following areas: (a) the degree of their impairments; (b) their attitudes about their impairments; and (c) their responses to technological, medical, or instructional supports (Berger, 2013).

## Disability Studies and Politics

The **political economy** is rooted in the relationship between societal contributions and access to resources, which is an important part of disability studies. In the United States, one third of disabled people live in poverty and less than 40% of the general population aged 18 to 64 who work have disabilities (Pincus, 2011; Stodden & Dowrick, 2000). Further complicating this is the societal attitude that people with disabilities are draining public resources because they are not productive contributors to society. This is very complicated when one considers the increased struggle people with disabilities face in gaining access to opportunities alongside necessary economic resources. Albrecht and Bury (2001) suggested that while those with disabilities who have insurance or financial resources are able to access necessary medical services, therapies, and assistive technologies, many with disabilities experience poverty and have little social privilege. These differences distinguish between those who can live independently and those who cannot (Berger, 2013).

## Disability Studies and Feminist and Queer Theory

**Feminist theory** is one way to frame disability studies. Feminist theory intersects gender, sexuality, and disability by taking the concept of gender away from one's biological sex. In fact, it defines gender through social statuses and symbols assigned to women and men through their expression, appearance, and personality traits. Typically, men are granted more power, prestige, and privilege than women (Jaggar, 1983; Oakley, 1972). This kind of social construct is complicated for people with disabilities because (a) people with disabilities are typically viewed as sexually undesirable or asexual (Gerschick, 2000; Gerschick & Miller, 1995; Rainey, 2011); (b) disabled men are perceived as feminine and denied a sense of masculinity; and (c) disabled women are doubly oppressed.

Feminist theory also links disability with gender through the **politics of appearance,** which connects to the [lack of] desire attributed to the disabled's physical appearances. Feminist theory discusses the reproductive rights movement with genetic testing and selective abortion *(see later in this chapter)* and **intersectionalities,** "or the ways in which different social statuses—such as gender, race/ethnicity, class, sexual orientation, and (dis)ability"—intersect with one another *(see Intersectionality in Chapter 4;* Berger, 2013, p. 39).

Disability studies borrows from **queer theory,** which critiques the concept of "normal" sexuality the same way disability studies critiques the "normal" body *(see LGBTQ+ Considerations in Chapter 4).* This, known as **crip theory,** focuses on the "parallel[s] between **compulsory heterosexuality** and **compulsory able-bodiedness**" (Berger, 2013, p. 40). "Similar to the way in which gay, lesbian, and transgendered people appropriate[d] the term 'queer' as an affirmative identify, disabled people appropriate[d] such terms as 'gimp' or 'crip' in an affirmative way" (Berger, 2013, p. 5).

## Why Disability Studies Matters in Sexuality Education

Sexuality is a basic human right and all people are entitled to "a positive and respectful approach to sexuality and sexual relationships as well as the possibility of having pleasurable and safe sexual experiences, free of coercion, discrimination, and violence" (World Health Organization, 2012). Personal matters of sexuality are considered private, but sexuality is actually highly controlled by the institutional policies and values that have historically excluded people with disabilities. Ableist institutional barriers largely exclude disabled people from mainstream sexual health supports (Hernon et al., 2015). "Both sex and disability threaten to breach certain bodily boundaries that are essential to categorical certainty and, as such, they provoke widespread anxiety" (Shildrick, 2013, p. 3). This restricts people with disabilities' physical, emotional, and social health and well-being. This is especially problematic for those who have increased needs for comprehensive healthcare or for those who are dependent upon others for personal needs. These situations are "fraught with potential dilemmas, not the least of which is the absence of privacy regarding an individual's most personal bodily functions—eating, dressing, and undressing, toileting, bathing, and so forth" (Berger, 2013, p. 138). This means people with disabilities are more susceptible to abuse or violence; in fact, recent studies show that children with disabilities are three to four times more likely to experience sexual violence or abuse than their nondisabled peers (Jones et al., 2012; Sullivan & Knutson, 2000).

Many people with disabilities are dependent on people without disabilities for their basic personal needs (Thomas, 2004). These **systems of supervision** mean that people who are considered socially dominant are in charge of personal care decisions. This can get tricky; medical and health professionals typically operate through the medical model and **diagnostically overshadow,** or blame the person's impairment for the caregiver's increased stress. Ultimately diagnostic overshadowing runs the risk of not acknowledging sexual violence or abuse as crimes against people with disabilities and excuses any violence or abuse (Kennedy,

1996; Taylor et al., 2015). It also minimizes any protective systems that are in place (Jones et al., 2012; Murray & Osborne, 2009).

Systems of supervision have prevented people with disabilities from developing their sexuality at the same rates as their nondisabled peers (Morris, 1997; Shah, 2005). Those responsible for coordinating resources—typically educators, parents, and health professionals—tend to not accommodate different learning, communication, or behavioral needs (Shah, 2017) and often operate under the belief that disabled people are incapable of healthy sexual expression. Furthermore, those who do teach don't necessarily offer comprehensive sexuality programs or modify the curriculum (East & Orchard, 2014). This indicates that most resource providers are unprepared to teach about sexuality (Shah, 2017).

Additionally, systems of supervision increase risks of sexual abuse and violence. For example, when people with disabilities are unable to use traditional communication methods, they depend on communication proxies or assistive communication devices. The communication proxies could be abusers themselves and oftentimes these devices do not include the vocabulary for sexual acts or violence (Shah, 2017; Westcott & Cross, 1996).

Because people with disabilities do not have the same social connections as their nondisabled peers, they are not able to develop positive sexual identities at the same rate (Shah, 2017). Couple this social segregation with the pervasive **societal devaluation of disability,** or the stigma that portrays disabled people as asexual beings (Payne et al., 2016), and people with disabilities end up being viewed as eternal children (East & Orchard, 2014) or unworthy of having healthy sexual identities. People with disabilities then can have a lack of knowledge of personal safety or legal rights regarding their sexual selves (Hernon et al., 2015). They may not be prepared to protect themselves from sexual violence, abuse, unplanned pregnancies, and sexually transmitted diseases (Shah, 2017); they may not even recognize they are victims (Jones et al., 2012; Shah et al., 2016b; Taylor et al., 2015); or they may not know how or when to advocate for themselves.

## Disability Studies and Sexual Identity

Societal attitudes are a major factor in whether people with disabilities have the abilities and access to healthy sexual relationships. Society doesn't attribute sexually desirable attributes to disabled people and may even view them as asexual (Shah, 2017). Despite these challenges, we recognize that all human beings experience "physical sexual development [that] follows a typical neurophysiological progression" (Niles,

2018, p. 69). According to the National Child Traumatic Stress Network (2009) and the Society of Obstetricians and Gynecologists of Canada (n.d.):

> As sexual beings, human sexual development manifests anatomically, physiologically, psychologically, and cognitively. Sexual development consists of four interrelated components including emotional, social, cultural, and physical development. The four components of sexual development influence three aspects of sexuality, including sexual attraction, sexual arousal, and sexual behavior. (Niles, 2018, p. 70)

Interestingly enough, there is evidence that societal attitudes also influence disabled men's relationship preferences. Disabled men tend to seek relationships with nondisabled partners (Berger, 2013), but "it is more common for nondisabled women to partner with disabled men than for nondisabled men to partner with disabled women, and this is a likely consequence of the more nurturing aspects of conventional female socialization" (Rainey, 2011; Shakespeare et al., 1996, as cited in Berger, 2013, p. 132). *(See more about Sexual Identity in Chapter 4.)*

## Disability Studies and Development

Childhood is an arena of development where all children—those with and without disabilities—explore their sexual and gender identities. *(See Chapter 4.)* "Children begin to form gender segregated small cliques that set themselves apart from other youths" (Berger, 2013, p. 114), which continues to develop through adolescence. During adolescence, social cliques become more exclusive, social status is more important, and social approval and personal validation are priorities. Adolescents with disabilities face even more challenges because they also crave status recognition (Berger, 2013), but they are more at risk because they face increased hostility or pity from their peers. They are more vulnerable to peer pressure, and sometimes due to disability-dependent needs, they experience strange social boundaries. Marchak et al. (1999) explained: "For me, one of the hardest things . . . was that I wanted to challenge and defy my parents, as many teenagers do. However, because I was physically dependent on them for personal care, my desire for independence seemed thwarted" (p. 123, as cited in Berger, 2013, p. 114).

The complete transition to adulthood takes longer for adolescents now than it has historically; today, it extends into one's 20s, but "the extended transition period characteristic of all youths is even longer for disabled people" (Berger, 2013, p. 125). While typically developing young adults are often able to exhibit full autonomy by living independently or with friends, they are also able to balance their relationships with working full time or going to school. Opportunities in colleges and universities are more challenging for people with disabilities due to environmental or architectural challenges, the need for personal care assistance, or a lack of learning accommodations. Moreover, "the employment prospects for people with disabilities are much lower than for nondisabled workers" (Berger, 2013, p. 125). These factors only further prevent people with disabilities from achieving autonomy in their lives. In fact, the more significant the disability, the "less likely [people with disabilities will] establish independent households, marry, and have families of their own" (Berger, 2013, p. 125).

### Disability Studies and Sexual Satisfaction

People achieve sexual satisfaction in different ways, and this isn't different for the disability community. One study showed that a paraplegic's sexual and emotional awareness and intimacy was actually improved because of his paralysis. In his case, sexual satisfaction was possible with parts of the body other than his genitalia, something he may not have discovered had he not been paralyzed (Berger, 2013; Rainey, 2011; Shapiro, 1993; Zola, 1982). Other ways people with disabilities have achieved sexual satisfaction are when their nondisabled partners are also their caregivers. There are examples of how having disabilities routinely brings people together in intimate ways; in fact, research suggests that acts of service are another way to express love and increase sexual intimacy and satisfaction (Berger, 2013; Rainey, 2011).

## Disability Studies: Current and Future Issues

Understanding appropriate sexual behavior requires consistent, explicit direct instruction, but perhaps even more critical is to develop an understanding of sexual health and happiness. Comprehensive, inclusive sexual education is the best way to help individuals understand the physical, emotional, social, and cultural aspects of sexual development (Harkins Monaco et al., 2018). We recommend sexuality education begin in early childhood. *(See Chapter 9 for teaching strategies.)* "As children approach puberty, specialized instruction is needed . . . to understand the physical development of secondary sex characteristics that emerge during puberty." Table 2.1 (p. 76 in Harkins Monaco et al.) "provides developmentally appropriate guidelines for supporting sexual development"

**Table 2.1 Developmentally Appropriate Guidelines for Supporting Sexual Development**

| | Neurophysiological Sexual Development | Neurocognitive Sexual Development |
|---|---|---|
| Preschool children (less than 4 years) should: | • Know that boys and girls have different body parts.<br>• Know accurate names for body parts of boys and girls.<br>• Know that private parts are your body parts that are covered by a bathing suit or underwear.<br>• Know that babies grow inside mommies first.<br>• Receive simple answers to questions about the body and bodily functions. | • Know the difference between "okay" touches (which are comforting, pleasant, and welcome) and "not okay" touches (which are intrusive, uncomfortable, unwanted, or painful).<br>• Know that your body belongs to you.<br>• Know that no one—child or adult—has the right to touch your private parts.<br>• Know that it is okay to say "no" when adults ask you to touch their private parts, or for them to touch or kiss your private parts.<br>• Know who to tell if people do "not okay" things to you, or ask you to do "not okay" things to them. |
| Young children (4–6 years) should: | • Know that boys' and girls' bodies change when they get older.<br>• Receive simple explanations of how babies grow in their mother's womb and about the birth process. | • Know that there are different types of hugs and kisses.<br>• Know that you have the right to say no to anyone who tries to hug you, kiss you or touch your private parts.<br>• Know that touching your own private parts can feel nice; it is okay in private and when you are alone. |
| Older children/ Pre-teens (Ages 7–12) should: | • Know what to expect and how to handle changes of puberty (including menstruation and wet dreams).<br>• Know the basics of reproduction, pregnancy, and childbirth.<br>• Know the risks of sexual activity (pregnancy and sexually transmitted diseases). | • Know that there are different types of relationships (family, friendships, romantic relationships).<br>• Know that hugs and kisses, even with family members, change as you get older.<br>• Understand sexual attraction and arousal.<br>• Understand how clothing and social interactions relate to attraction. |

| | Neurophysiological Sexual Development | Neurocognitive Sexual Development |
|---|---|---|
| Teens (13–18) should: | • Understand the processes of sexual behaviors.<br>• Have a person who they are comfortable asking questions about sexual attraction, arousal, and behavior. | • Have social opportunities to explore potential romantic relationships.<br>• Have opportunities to talk about and explore sexuality.<br>• Understand how to seek consent and how to give consent. |
| Young Adults (19–21) should: | • Have the ability to self-determine sexuality.<br>• Have continued support for questions about sexual attraction, arousal, and behavior.<br>• Have opportunities for privacy and intimacy. | • Have the ability to explore and pursue romantic relationships.<br>• Have inclusion in social and cultural aspects of sexuality, relationships, and family planning. |

Niles, G. Y. (2018). No one can escape puberty: Physical and cognitive development. In E. A. Harkins Monaco, T. Gibbon, & D. Bateman (Eds.), *Talking about sex: Sexuality education for learners with disabilities*. Rowman & Littlefield.

(Niles, 2018, p. 75). Oftentimes, however, sexuality instruction is based on the special education program and curricula policies in the schools.

## Disability Studies and Special Education

Special education aims to help school-aged, disabled children cultivate strategies that will help them develop alongside their peers and become successful in postschool endeavors. There is evidence, however, that the very nature of special education is actually exclusive in nature.

> The existence of segregated provisions, catering for "special" pupils taught by "special" teachers supported by "special" courses in teacher training, has all contributed to the legitimation of values, attitudes, and practices that are inimical to the realization of an inclusive society and educational system. (Barton & Armstrong, 2001, p. 707; Lipsky & Gartner, 1997, as cited in Berger, 2013, p. 107)

Separate services are often needed because general education teachers are not equipped to teach skills to students with disabilities alongside content. Other exclusionary factors include the perspectives of parents. Parents of both nondisabled and disabled children fear inclusion. Although it is important to note that many parents *do* believe in special education, the reality is that for some, "special education is both a service and a disservice" (Connor & Ferri, 2007, p. 74, as cited in Berger, 2013, p. 109).

## Disability Studies and Selective Abortion

There is a general issue in using prenatal genetic screenings when a woman is pregnant. These tests are often part of typical routine visits to determine if there are any genetic disabilities detectable in a fetus. These are often used to guide parents into deciding whether to execute a selective abortion, something legal under current abortion law (*Roe v. Wade*, 1973). In fact, research shows that these screenings ultimately put pressure on parents to make these kinds of decisions; the medical and societal perspective often revolves around how people with disabilities are burdensome to their finances, on their family members, and on society as a whole. There is also an international discussion of "the new reproductive and genetic technologies [that] are promising to eliminate births of disabled children" (Saxton, 1998, p. 375, as cited in Berger, 2013, p. 214). What kind of messages are being sent? This has the potential of drastically reducing certain disabilities in society, as evidenced in the Down syndrome community. Zuckoff (2002) claimed that already "about 90 percent of pregnant women who learn they are carrying a child with Down syndrome choose abortion" (as cited in Berger, 2013, p. 38).

Disability studies recognizes the "divide between the feminist reproductive rights/choice movement and the disability rights movement" (Berger, 2013, p. 214). Feminist scholars have gone back and forth on this particular issue; generally speaking, feminists want to preserve women's rights to choose whether to get an abortion, but disability advocates argue that there should not be a choice to abort a fetus because of a disability. In other words, if the fetus was wanted, should a disability be a contributory factor in choosing to keep the baby?

## Summary

Disability studies emphasizes the importance of exploring firsthand accounts of the experiences and needs of disabled people (Jones et al., 2012; Shah et al., 2016a; Taylor et al., 2015). This cannot be overstated when considering healthy and happy sexuality. As Finger (1992), a female disabled sociologist, said,

> Sexuality is often the source of our deepest oppression; it is often the source of our deepest pain. It's easier for us to talk about—and formulate strategies for changing—discrimination in employment, education

and housing than to talk about our exclusion from sexuality and reproduction. (p. 9)

Schools are in a position to help shape societal perspectives on disability
by teaching children the positives of disability culture and how societal
supports should be available to everyone. If disability studies were more
at the forefront of special education, perhaps schools would better be
able to promote a **celebration agenda,** which celebrates the integration
of disabled people into mainstream society and the cultural development
of disability. School programming itself can better adjust to the particular needs of the disabled student alongside the appropriate cultural
perspectives of the family and individual themselves. With appropriate
resources and education dedicated to healthy and safe sexuality, people
with disabilities will better be able to develop their **sexual citizenship**
and fully have access to all of their legal and social rights to develop a
sexual identity (Bacchi & Beasley, 2002; Shah, 2017).

# Resources

## Internet Resources

*SexEd Library:* https://www.sexedlibrary.org
>    Sexuality Information and Education Council of the United States (SIECUS)
>    provides the SexEd Library, which is a comprehensive online sexual educa-
>    tion resource on human sexuality. Resources in the SexEd Library include
>    lesson plans, information and statistics, and professional development
>    opportunities related to human sexuality.

## Books/Articles and Other Resources

Berger, R. J. (2013). *Introducing Disability Studies.* Lynne Rienner Publishers,
Inc.

Harkins Monaco, E. A., Gibbon, T., & Bateman, D. (2018). *Talking about sex:
Sexuality education for learners with disabilities.* Rowman & Littlefield.

The *Sexuality and Safety with Tom and Ellie* series by Kate E. Reynolds:

* *Things Ellie Likes:* A book about sexuality and masturbation for girls and
young women with autism and related conditions.
* *Things Tom Likes:* A book about masturbation for boys and young men
with autism and related conditions.
* *What's Happening to Ellie?* A book about puberty for girls and young
women with autism and related conditions.
* *What's Happening to Tom?* A book about puberty for boys and young men
with autism and related conditions.

## Organizations

- American Association of Sexuality Educators, Counselors, and Therapists: https://www.aasect.org
- Kinsey Institute (Indiana University): https://kinseyinstitute.org/
- Planned Parenthood: https://www.plannedparenthood.org
- Society for Disability Studies: http://disstudies.org/
- Society for the Scientific Study of Sexuality (SSSS): https://sexscience.org

## Suggestions for How to Maintain Current on This Topic

- Remain current on your state laws and policies related to disability rights, advocacy, and sexuality education.
- Advocate for inclusive sexuality education in your school district.
- Follow the organizations listed above on social media, and sign up for Kinsey Institute newsletter to remain current on research related to human sexuality.

# CHAPTER 3

# Ethics

Chelsea VanHorn Stinnett, Rebecca Smith-Hill, and David F. Bateman

*Kianna is an 18-year-old college student attending an inclusive postsecondary education (**IPSE**) program for students with intellectual and developmental disabilities (IDD). As an individual with an intellectual disability, Kianna has support needs specific to understanding social situations, processing verbal information, and problem solving in everyday life. She is navigating college life as a freshman and is interested in exploring dating and her identity as a bisexual woman. She comes from a very traditional family that fears that Kianna will be coerced into a sexual relationship that she is not ready for. They also do not believe that Kianna understands what it means to be bisexual and that she's saying this for shock value. Are there ethical issues in providing support for Kianna in exploring her sexual identity in college? Kianna has her first date with a woman next week, whom she met online and is not a woman with an intellectual disability. Are there ethical issues in Kianna going to meet this woman or dating women who do not have an intellectual disability? She is her own guardian, yet her family is opposed to any sexual relationship, let alone a homosexual relationship. Are there ethical issues regarding what professionals in her IPSE program need to consider when supporting Kianna in navigating this situation?*

## Overview

Achieving **sexual agency** for adults with disabilities begins with developing sexual knowledge. Many young adults with disabilities are often denied sexuality education during their youth due to misconceptions regarding their ability and interest in sexuality. For those with a physical disability, sexual activity is often portrayed as predatory given individuals' inability to physically "fend off" unwanted physical contact. For those with an IDD, their ability to consent to sexual activity is often in question given their cognitive support needs. However, sexual satisfaction is a basic human need and right for all people, including those with disabilities and across all categories. People with disabilities are not unlike their nondisabled peers and desire meaningful sexual relationships. For this reason, we must examine the ethical responsibility that families, adult service providers, and educators have to provide effective sexuality education for people with disabilities to ensure they are equipped with the knowledge to consent to a healthy sexual relationship. The treatment of individuals with IDD is used as an example throughout this chapter to highlight the need for ethical treatment of all people with disabilities.

Readers will

- establish sexuality as a basic human need and right for individuals with disabilities, especially those with cognitive support needs specific to intellectual and developmental disabilities;
- review the ethical responsibility to provide sexuality education for adults with disabilities;
- define capacity, sexual consent, and elements of sexual consent;
- review types of guardianship and support provided by families and the implications for developing sexual agency;
- provide an overview of the perceptions of capacity for sexual agency and consent for individuals with disabilities in the legal, medical, and social worlds; and
- describe the impact of the #MeToo movement on individuals with IDD.

## Sexuality: A Human Right and Ethical Responsibility

Societal misconceptions have placed individuals with disabilities on opposites sides of the sexuality spectrum: either asexual or oversexed. According to Brodwin and Frederick (2010) some common misconceptions include the idea that people with disabilities lack certain biological functioning such as ovulation, menstruation, or the ability to orgasm. Other inaccuracies include the idea that adults with disabilities lack the social skills or desires to participate in a sexual relationship (Brodwin & Frederick, 2010). For those with a physical disability, they may be viewed as incapable of having "traditional" vaginal intercourse; therefore they don't need to know about sexuality (Rohleder et al., 2018). Comprehensive sexuality education speaks to the need to educate all individuals on the many avenues through which they could experience sexual agency, including alternative sexual practices and lifestyles.

Sexual exploration could be made difficult for those with physical disabilities due to the need for specialized physical supports or "props" and the presence of support staff. Further, while there may be some concern with the inability of people with a physical disability to distance themselves from unwanted sexual advances, they lack the cognitive support needs that call into question their ability to willingly consent to a sexual encounter. Misconception regarding consent could be to any individual across disability categories, yet is often applied to individuals with IDD, given their cognitive support needs. Like other adults with disabilities, those with IDD express a desire for sexual intimacy (Gil-Llario et al., 2018). In fact, the level of sexuality interest of young adults with IDD is no different from their peers without disabilities (Castelão et al., 2010).

Interest in engaging in sex implies a need for sexuality education; however, this instruction is not always comprehensive or effective (McDaniels & Fleming, 2016). More than half of young adults with IDD report that they did not receive sexuality education in high school (Barnard-Brak et al., 2014). Most report that they also do not broach this topic with their parents (Isler et al., 2009). Adults with IDD want to have sex, yet often lack the comprehensive sexuality education needed to prevent negative consequences of engaging in unsafe sexual practices, which could result in sexual abuse, unwanted pregnancy, and/or contraction of sexually transmitted disease (STD) or infection. Additionally, sexual and gender identity exploration are other topics within sexuality education that are rarely broached with individuals with IDD (Dinwoodie et al., 2016).

Barriers to accessing sexuality education include a general perception from parents of individuals with IDD on their inability to consent to a healthy sexual relationship or understand their sexuality (Sinclair et al., 2015). In an effort to protect their child, parents or caregivers may deny them from accessing sexuality education or engaging in sex, especially those parents who retain guardianship over their child. Parents may perceive their child with IDD as an **"eternal child"** (Parchomuik, 2012), deeming sexuality education unnecessary and inappropriate. Essentially, parents act as gatekeepers to the level of sexual agency their child can achieve. Adults with IDD live with less autonomy and increased oversight from parents and service providers, who may encourage friendships, but oppose intimate relationships (Healy et al., 2009). These "caretakers" exert control over many aspects of their lives, including money to purchase birth control and condoms, transportation to access healthcare and visit a sexual partner, and general privacy to engage in sexual acts (Azzopardi-Lane & Callus, 2014).

Despite these barriers and perceptions, people with IDD are entitled to experience sex and access sexuality education. According to a joint position statement of the American Association on Intellectual and Developmental Disabilities (AAIDD) and the Arc, an organization serving individuals with intellectual and developmental disabilities in the United States (AAIDD, 2013), individuals with IDD have a right to

- sexual expression and education, reflective of their own cultural, religious, and moral values and of social responsibility;
- individualized education and information to encourage informed decision making, including education about such issues as reproduction, marriage and family life, abstinence, safe sexual practices, sexual orientation, sexual abuse, and sexually transmitted diseases; and
- protection from sexual harassment and from physical, sexual, and emotional abuse. (AAIDD, 2013, p. 1)

Sexual desire and expression is a basic human right. People with any disability are entitled to the same dignity of risk as their peers without disabilities. The example of people with IDD can be extended to those with other disabilities. Engaging in a healthy sexual relationship is correlated with better quality of life and happiness for people with IDD, despite the potential for negative consequences (Arias et al., 2009). Inability to access comprehensive sexuality education can increase the risk of STD contraction, unwanted pregnancy, and abuse for people with IDD (Gougeon, 2009). People with disabilities want to have sex, benefit from having sex, and have the right to have sex; therefore there is an ethical responsibility to provide sexuality education while navigating the nuances of the characteristics of individuals with disabilities and the perceptions of their families to ensure capacity to engage in and consent to safe sex.

## Capacity to Provide Consent

There is no internationally accepted definition of legal capacity. The need for understanding capacity reflects an individual's ability to make binding decisions. Legal capacity is a particularly challenging and complex issue because it affects all areas of life, including where to live, whether and whom to marry, signing an employment contract, having property, or casting a vote. The right to legal capacity is, therefore, closely entwined with equality and nondiscrimination. At the center of this discussion is a person, and there needs to be discussions related to the implications for legal capacity legislation and its implementation for each individual.

Individuals may lack the capacity to make some decisions but not to make others (Herring, 2012). Does an individual with IDD have the capacity to give consent to sexual relations? The capacity to consent is situation and person specific. Sexual consent remains a nebulous construct that is subjective and based on an individual's personal experiences and communication style (Beres, 2007). In order to establish **consent**, an individual needs to (a) understand the information relevant to the decision, (b) retain that information, (c) use or weigh that information in the process of making the decision, or (d) communicate this decision (Herring, 2012).

How do we determine whether an individual has the capacity to consent to a sexual relationship? Herring (2012) reports that most court cases have used a medical model focusing on the capacity to understand the physical act, health risks, and consequences such as pregnancy or contracting a sexually transmitted infection (STI). However, what about the capacity to understand the emotional risks? Additionally, circumstances surrounding the sexual act must be considered. How was the encounter negotiated? Are there steps taken to ensure it was an act respecting their mutual interests (Herring, 2012)? Does Kianna in the above case understand something as subtle as the level of commitment to the relationship? Does she understand whether she is being lied to? Does she understand the difference between someone being tender and someone being exploitative? These are all nuances that can be difficult to understand, even without cognitive support needs.

**With whom?** There are unique considerations to be made regarding sexual consent. For example, sex with one in a position of power is determined exploitative. It is clear sexual relations with a boss/supervisor, a caregiver, a doctor/psychologist are not acceptable. But what about sex between two people with IDD? In 2002, Spiecker and Steutel asked the question: is sex between adults with mild or moderate IDD morally permissible and, if at all, under what conditions? They noted that a distinctive characteristic of IDD is practical rationality, which is the "capacity of determining and weighing the pros and cons of different actions one might perform under the circumstances, with the intention of determining which alternative is the right, most desirable or virtuous one" (p. 160). Their argument is that individuals with IDD lack the deliberative capacity to think of long-term welfare of self or others and they lack the practical rationality implied in adult status. This is why they are "permanently dependent on the paternalistic guidance and moral supervision of adult caregivers" (p. 162). "If valid consent is taken as a necessary condition of moral permissibility, many cases of sexual interaction between people with [IDD] should be deemed morally wrong, not because they are coerced or deceived, but because their capacities of judgement are deficient" (p. 164). Spiecker and Steutel's (2002) conclusion was that sexual interaction between people with IDD is only morally permissible under adult supervision with the permission of caregivers.

Stephen Greenspan (2002) countered Spiecker and Steutel's 2002 argument by stating that giving caregivers substitutive consent and control over the **presumed incompetents** based on their best interest perpetuates the eternal child stereotype. This approach denies people with IDD the opportunity to make, and learn from, their mistakes. Another problem may involve which caregiver was in charge. One caregiver may allow sex and another may not. Spiecker and Steutel's argument was based on a broad generalization that all individuals with IDD have the same characteristics, personality traits, and support needs. People with IDD have historically lost their individual identity to the generalizations of their disability. Once a person is known to have IDD, general incompetency has been assumed with little or no investigation of their actual capabilities. A change in thinking has evolved among professionals in the field, based on an increase in knowledge and the development of advocacy groups. Best practice requires the use of assessment to determine the actual capabilities of the person with IDD before consideration of any of the general manifestations of the disability. This is required due to the wide range of abilities and individual personality traits exhibited by people with IDD. Greater awareness of the range and nature of IDD is required by all professions to ensure the treatment or services provided are based on the needs of the individual, and not diluted by generalities of the disability (Greenspan, 2002).

## Guardianship

**Guardianship** may be viewed as a mechanism of control or as a device to support the individual. The way it is viewed is significant when the adult with IDD is given more opportunity to make choices. If society deals with IDD by broad strokes and lacking individualization, it exercises maximum control in that form. Guardianship, if used at all, is often invoked only when there are considerable assets to manage. In contrast, social integration of citizens with IDD into society is characterized by choices and opportunities for all citizens and presents more significant and difficult questions concerning the proper use of guardianship. If community-based services are available to assist, guardianship should be viewed as a mechanism of support for the individual in making his or her own choices. A completely supportive structure of community-based services would drastically reduce the need to use guardianship at all.

An individual with IDD can experience both formal and informal restrictions on decision making. Formal restrictions of legal capacity are those in which an individual loses his or her power to make decisions recognized by law, wholly or in part, because of legal measures. This usually involves a court decision to deprive someone of his or her legal capacity, followed by the appointment of a guardian who makes legally binding decisions on his or her behalf. Substituted decision making is where the legal representative, guardian, or tutor has court-authorized power to make decisions on behalf of the individual without necessarily having to demonstrate that those decisions are in the individual's best interest or according to his or her wishes. Additionally, there is a wide range of different terms used to discuss the issues surrounding legal capacity, in particular, issues involving who is legally empowered to make decisions on another's behalf. The loss of legal capacity is, for example, distinct from the introduction of a protective measure that refers to the placement of an individual under guardianship and not to the loss of the person's legal capacity. Under guardianship, a legal representative makes binding decisions for the person placed under a protective measure.

Informal restrictions of legal capacity are often independent of any formal legal measure. They include factors and practices restricting the ability of a person to make decisions about his or her life. They assume that persons with disabilities cannot make decisions for themselves because they do not understand the likely consequences of their actions, and it is therefore in their best interest if decisions are made on their behalf. Lack of access to decision making leads individuals with IDD to become risk averse and vulnerable. Therefore, guardianship, substitute decision making, and informal restrictions are not ideal.

As an alternative to guardianship and substitute decision making, supported decision making enables a person with a disability to make and communicate decisions with respect to personal or legal matters. With supported decision making, the presumption is always in favor of the person with a disability who will be affected by the decision. The individual is the decision maker; the support person explains the issues, when necessary, and interprets the signs and preferences of the individual. Even when an individual with a disability requires total support, the support person should enable that person to exercise their legal capacity to the greatest extent possible, according to the latter's wishes and/or best interests.

An individual with IDD may be prevented from accessing sexuality education if their guardian or support system does not believe in their ability to develop sexual agency. If they are not provided the opportunity to learn from experience or provided sexuality education, this limits their ability to be the sexual decision maker in their own lives. They are then deemed incapable of consent due to the lack of knowledge they have no control over receiving.

## Perceptions of Capacity for Sexual Agency and Consent

**Legal.** There are many inherent flaws regarding the established practice of determining the ability to consent for people with IDD. Harris (2018) critiques four major claims in what is considered outdated literature pertaining to people with disabilities consenting to sex that is still used in the legal world. Upon examining all states' statutes, Harris describes them as vague in defining disability, usually over- or underemphasizing disability status and its implications on ability to consent. Non-consent must be proven beyond reasonable doubt and include incapacity "on the basis of age, consanguinity, mental disability, physical helplessness, or intoxication" (Harris, 2018, p. 494); however, state law is inconsistent in defining incapacity and/or mental disability. Additionally, these statutes are inherently risk averse. The state has an ethical obligation and predisposition to "protect" people with IDD, prohibiting sexual agency in fear of the risk of engaging in intimacy resulting in negative consequences (Harris, 2018).

Second, Harris (2018) argues that factfinders (e.g., lawyers and judges) in the court system should look more at adaptive skills instead of standardized IQ scores when judging functional capacity to consent. New regulations and normative ideas have led to a need to consider how sexual consent and capacity for people with IDD are interpreted in the eyes of the law. In an attempt by states to explicitly define disability and capacity to consent, the medical definition of intellectual disability has been used, which diminishes the ability to define capacity and consent based on adaptive skill level rather than IQ level. Courts are focusing more on adaptive skills to supplement IQ scores; however, factfinders may focus on skills not related to the capacity to consent to sex such as self-care, hygiene, toileting, verbal communication, etc. In doing so, these factfinders may over- or undervalue certain evidence of adaptive functioning over others. Third, upon review of 172 sexual assault and rape decisions spanning the past 20 years, Harris (2018) found that a majority of complainants with disabilities in sexual assault cases were people living in the community, while the literature base focuses primarily on individuals in an institutional setting. In fact, 76% of cases were initiated by individuals who live independently in the community. These data provide a need to address consent in informal, community-based settings. The focus may remain on formal care settings because they are traditionally regulated by a state agency. Lastly, Harris questions the ability of others to truly examine matters of consent when an individual with a disability testifies, stating that it is difficult to see beyond one's disability to determine capacity. Eighty-eight percent of people with IDD in sexual assault cases do not testify. In 87.2% of cases, the victim is deemed incapable of consent. She refers to this phenomenon as "the aesthetics of disability" (Harris, 2018). Testifying in court opens cases to bias; factfinders often cannot see beyond disability.

During the past 40 years, society has become more aware of the capabilities of people with IDD and their entitlement to basic human and legal rights (AAIDD, 2013). With the growth of knowledge in the field of IDD and the development of advocacy groups, the public awakened to the fact that people with IDD have long been denied full citizenship status guaranteed to them by the Constitution (Shogren & Wehmeyer, 2017). This awareness has resulted in judicial decisions and legislative mandates that seek to correct past deficiencies. There are still, however, areas of the law requiring revision to reflect the change in attitudes and to ensure theoretical legal victories are established in practice. To do this, statutes should be revised so people with IDD and varying levels of support needs are able to live as independently as possible. Legislators and members of the legal community must become aware of the nature of IDD, consider the personhood of each individual, and devise a legal framework with flexibility enough to accommodate the individual.

**Medical.** Only in the past few decades has there been a shift from institutionalization to community living, and primary care providers are still not prepared to meet the growing needs of individuals with IDD as a result of this societal shift (Greenwood & Wilkinson, 2013). Outdated knowledge of the capacity of individuals to consent to a sexual relationship may still exist within the world of medicine. In compliance with the Americans with Disabilities Act (ADA), medical care providers are required to provide access to services, including sexual healthcare. In an article published in the *American Medical Association Journal of Ethics*, Silvers and colleagues (2016) discuss mistaken assumptions within the medical community regarding the sexuality of patients with disabilities and the need to remove "paternalistic judgment" (Silvers et al., 2016, p. 341) regarding patients' ability to consent to sex and reproduction. Within the medical community, there may be an assumption that people with disabilities don't have the same ambition for an intimate family life. When seen merely as a population in need of protection from sexual violence, rather than an individual who desires sexual intimacy, individuals with disabilities may receive less access to care (Silvers et al., 2016). Access to such care may be denied if it is not the wish of the guardian. Extreme measures, including sterilization, are decisions placed in the hands of parents who have medical power of attorney.

Practice recommendations for primary healthcare providers include creating safe environments for conversations regarding sexuality, scheduling an appropriate amount of time for an appointment, including family members in sexuality, and/or excluding family members when appropriate to respect the privacy of the individual (Greenwood & Wilkinson, 2013). Anyone who has limited experience in sexuality may have a difficult time asking their doctor for sexuality education materials, let alone an individual with IDD who may have support needs specific to verbal expression. Creating a safe and welcoming environment allows patients to feel confident in broaching difficult topics such as preventatives and sexual healthcare. People with IDD may also require more time for an appointment to discuss sexual education and healthcare. This may be due to time to develop rapport with the patient for them to feel comfortable addressing this topic. It could also be due to the need for more time for an individual with IDD to verbalize their experiences and needs. The inclusion of family members with or without guardianship may prove beneficial to all parties understanding and normalizing the sexual needs of people with disabilities. However, primary care providers should be cognizant of the need to exclude family members from the conversation if they are prohibiting the patient from disclosing the full extent of their interest and needs. Primary care providers may feel compelled by their need to protect individuals with IDD but must approach this topic with patients without the assumption that sexual experience is the result of abuse (Greenwood & Wilkinson, 2013).

**Social.** According to the World Health Organization, expression of and enjoyment from sexuality is a core component of the human experience; all humans have the right to "the possibility of having pleasurable and safe sexual experiences, free of coercion, discrimination and violence" (2012, para. 1). Historically, this right to sex as it pertains to people with disabilities has been largely ignored in society. Vehmas (2019) points out that the traditional and safe way to deal with the possible erotic desires of individuals with IDD is to ignore them. This kind of precautionary policy conflicts with the view of sex as a right. In a recent film review, Adams (2015) identified an overall theme of the capacity of individuals with IDD to establish and sustain committed and mutually satisfying relationships. In all three films analyzed, Adams (2015) discovers that "sex is shown as a kind of social justice index" (para. 29) for people with disabilities. Overall, she likens the sexuality of people with disabilities to that of all other human beings—"determinations about consent are messy and complicated in all sexual encounters, given that pleasure often exists in tension with reasoned considerations of risk, consequence, and voluntariness" (Adams, 2015, para. 30). In reference to the scenario at the beginning of the text, Kianna as a young adult with IDD, if informed about consent and the realities of sexual relationships, has the right to the same dignity of risk as her peers without disability. If she makes an informed decision to enter a sexual relationship and it results in a negative outcome, Kianna is entitled to that experience and the risks therein as a human being.

Ditchman and colleagues (2017) conducted a study to determine the impact of individual and societal characteristics on attitudes toward sexuality for people with IDD. Cultural orientation plays a significant role in societal attitudes toward the sexuality of individuals with IDD and accounts for 27% of the variance in attitudes. Females and people with more familiarity with intellectual disability have a more positive attitude regarding the rights and sexuality of adults with IDD and their ability to parent (Ditchman et al., 2017). Societal attitudes and perceptions of sexuality and disability are difficult to improve without the knowledge that people with IDD are capable of and interested in sex (Esmail et al., 2010).

There is a way in which people with IDD can access relationships and sexuality education with less societal stigma; however, it comes with challenges and concerns. Access to the internet and the world of online dating has opened the door to immeasurable data and opportunity, where anyone can access information about sex, view pornography, and participate in relationships without even leaving their home. In this sense, people with IDD can access sexuality education more freely, yet this information is not always correct or thorough. Within the past decade, online dating has become a mainstream phenomenon, where a person with a disability can often delay revealing their disability to their partner. Individuals with IDD are having to understand and interpret a whole new set of societal norms that exist in an online dating culture where they are more susceptible to cyber bullying and sexual solicitation (Normand & Sallafranque-St-Louis, 2015). While the internet presents its own challenges in navigating online dating and relationships, it also allows for people with disabilities to gather and share common experiences and needs.

An example of this is the #MeToo movement. According to the movement's official website, the "Me Too" movement was founded in

2006 to help survivors of sexual violence, particularly young women of color from low-wealth communities, find pathways to healing. Although the inception of the movement was in 2006, it gained greater traction in 2017 following the use of the #MeToo hashtag after the Harvey Weinstein sexual abuse allegations. As of October 2018, the #MeToo hashtag had been tweeted over 19 million times (Brown, 2018).

Included in the #MeToo movement's website is a list of statistics, including sexual abuse rates of individuals with disabilities. In an op-ed for *The Guardian* in 2018, Anne Wafula Strike, a writer who identifies as a black disabled woman, laments the fact that women with disabilities have been largely left out of the #MeToo movement. She offers the phenomenon of disabled persons' sexuality being "shrouded in taboo" as an explanation for the omission. Further, she posits that it is this willful ignorance of the sexuality of those with disabilities that puts them in even more inherent danger when it comes to sexual assault, as well as woeful lack of the knowledge and skills related to effectively recognizing and reporting such an assault (Strike, 2018). Brown & McCann explore this idea in their 2018 review of the literature surrounding sexuality issues for adults with IDD. The authors conclude that individuals with IDD face challenges when invoking the right to express their sexuality and to access the education and support necessary to achieve agency (Brown & McCann, 2018).

The #MeToo movement could be a powerful tool for empowering people with disabilities in their quest for recognition as sexual beings. The movement serves as an avenue for galvanizing survivors for systemic change. It serves as a tool for better access to supports after a sexual assault and demands for comprehensive and commensurate sexuality education for people with disabilities. The official #MeToo movement website proclaims that their "goal is also to reframe and expand the global conversation around sexual violence to speak to the needs of a broader spectrum of survivors. Young people, queer, trans, and disabled folks, Black women and girls, and all communities of color" (MeToo-Movement.org, para. 4). If this broader spectrum is to be effectively empowered and include sexual assault survivors with a disability, a shift must occur in society to acknowledge people with disabilities as sexual beings in the first place. In a 2019 participatory observation of Chinese women with disabilities' involvement in the online #MeToo movement, Lin and Yang found that the movement has been empowering on an individual level for these women. They describe women using the platform to reject the social stereotypes about themselves and to become intolerant of social biases. As alluded to in other research and activism surrounding the sexual assault of people with disabilities as it fits into the larger framework of the #MeToo movement, "we must change the subconscious biases present in the dominant discourse" (Lin & Yang, 2019, p. 846). People with disabilities must be seen as sexual beings with the same rights to sex as every other human being. And inherent in that right is access to appropriate and comprehensive sexuality education.

Ethically, those individuals supporting people with disabilities should acknowledge sexuality as a basic human need. In doing so, they should feel compelled to support all individuals with disabilities to develop sexual agency by building sexual knowledge. Guardianship and level of comfort and experience of support team members with sexuality in general may affect whether an individual with a disability receives comprehensive and timely sexuality education. If this information is not provided, it could increase the likelihood of negative outcomes. Misconceptions that an individual with a disability is uninterested in or incapable of a healthy and fulfilling sexual life should not deter the provision of comprehensive sexuality education; doing so may prohibit those individuals from understanding and providing consent.

# Resources

## Internet Resources

*American Association of Intellectual and Developmental Disabilities*: https://www.aaidd.org/news-policy/policy/position-statements/sexuality
Position of AAIDD and the Arc on sexuality.

*Andrew Gurza: DisabilityAfterDark*: http://www.andrewgurza.com/homepage
A brand aimed at talking about sexuality and disability.

*Disability and Sexuality Access Network*: https://dasanetwork.org/about/
"A community of disabled peers, researchers, practitioners, activists, allies, students, artists, and others who believe that access to sexuality, pleasure, and intimacy is a fundamental human right."

*JU Gosling*: http://www.ju90.co.uk/
Disability rights activist in the United Kingdom.

*Kay Ulanday Barrett*: http://www.kaybarrett.net/
Poet, performer, and educator, "navigating life as a disabled pin@y-amerikan transgender queer in the U.S. with struggle, resistance, and laughter."

*Outsiders*: https://www.outsiders.org.uk/outsidersclub/
Outsiders is a social, peer support, and dating club, run by and for socially and physically disabled people in the United Kingdom.

*Rooted in Rights*: https://rootedinrights.org/

"Nothing about us without us."

*Sexuality and Disability*: https://sexualityanddisability.org/

The site operates under the premise that people with disabilities are sexual beings; "answers to a bunch of questions a woman with a disability might have—about her body, mechanics of sex, intimate relationships, fears, and more."

*Sexuality and Disability Resources*: https://www.disability.illinois.edu/sexuality -resources

A collection of resources.

*Susan's Sex Support Site*: https://www.sexsupport.org/

Facts about sex and support for people of all abilities, ages, and sexual orientations.

## Additional Reading and Resources

Gill, M. (2015). *Already doing it: Intellectual disability and sexual agency*. University of Minnesota Press.

*Impact* Feature Issue on Sexuality and People with IDD:

https://ici.umn.edu/products/impact/232/

Quarmby, K. (2015). Disabled and fighting for a sex life: How misperceptions about disability can prevent people with physical and cognitive impairments from being able to express their sexuality. *The Atlantic.* https://www .theatlantic.com/health/archive/2015/03/sex-and-disability/386866/

*RAPP New Hampshire newsletter, Spring 2020*

The latest in disability research, advocacy, policy, and practice; the intersection of disability and sexuality: https://drcnh.org/rap-sheet/spring-2020 -disability-sexuality/

*Sexual Respect Toolkit*

Resources and information for general practitioners and other health and social care professionals to feel more comfortable initiating discussions about sex: http://www.sexualrespect.com/

Shakespeare, T., Gillespie-Sells, K., & Davies, D. (1996). *The sexual politics of disability: Untold desires*. Burns & Oates.

# Intersectionality

## Elizabeth A. Harkins Monaco

*Understanding "how converging identities contribute to inequality" (Museus & Griffin, 2011, p. 10) has historical importance for certain groups of people who have a need to "frame their circumstances [but also] to fight for their visibility and inclusion."*

(Crenshaw, 2015, para. 6)

## Overview

Chapter 4 will discuss intersectional considerations (race, ethnicity, language, religion, norms, etc.) for people with disabilities. While the intersection of all social identities is important, this chapter will focus on the intersection of disability with gender and sexuality. It will also focus on the intersectional perspectives of a comprehensive sexuality education as well as LGBTQ+ considerations, including the sexuality and gender spectrums. Individuals with disabilities' perspectives will be included.

Readers will

- explore concepts in intersectionality,
- identify how intersectionality impacts individuals with disabilities and comprehensive sexuality education considerations,
- evaluate the importance of including gender and sexuality considerations alongside issues of disabilities, and
- identify ways to incorporate intersectional pedagogy in personal practices.

## Intersectionality

One way to understand how social inequalities affect certain groups of people more than others is through **intersectionality theory,** or intersectionality. Intersectionality acknowledges how multiple overlapping social identities impact and oppress certain populations (Weber, 2007). Social identities, or race, class, gender, sexual orientation, religion, and [dis]ability, among others, "interpenetrate one another" (Berger, 2013, p. 39) and support larger social structures that determine social power and inequality (Dill & Zambrana, 2009; Weber, 2007; Wijeyesinghe & Jones, 2014). Intersectionality exposes social norms that support structural and systemic discrimination (Cooper, 2015; Niles & Harkins Monaco, 2019; Wijeyesinghe & Jones, 2014).

Intersectionality impacts individuals with disabilities who, in addition to identifying as part of the disability community, also hold identities of race, socioeconomic status, religion, gender, and sexuality among others. These identities shape their experiences in life. For example, a Black, female student with a disability will have different school experiences from her peers who are White, male, and nondisabled. Each social identity—race, gender, and [dis]ability—places her at higher risk of discrimination or oppression (National Association of School Psychologists, 2017; Proctor et al., 2017). Additionally, when we consider how women have less social power than their male peers, we also need to consider how women with disabilities have less social power than women without disabilities, which essentially doubly oppresses them. The same rules would then increase the oppression for women of color with disabilities, gay women with disabilities, or women of color who are disabled and gay; these women are triply or quadruply oppressed for each of those additional identities (Niles & Harkins Monaco, 2019). These systems of oppression propagate "ever-present social jeopardy" toward people with **multiple minoritized identities** (Cooper, 2015, para. 13). While the intersection of all social identities is important, this chapter will focus on the intersection of disability with gender and sexuality.

## LGBTQ+ Considerations

The links between all of the communities in the lesbian, gay, bisexual, transgender, and queer (LGBTQ+) community and the disability rights movement cannot be overstated. Compulsory heterosexuality is "the manner in which heterosexuality as a social institution establishes itself as the dominant or hegemonic sexuality, relegating other sexualities to marginal status that are at best tolerated as "alternatives" to the normal but which are still subordinated" (Berger, 2013, p. 40). This closely connects with the concept of compulsory able-bodiedness, which is when an absence of a disability is considered the dominant trait; disability in this case is an "alternative" to the "normal."

The LGBTQ+ community's continual evolution (Dresher & Pula, 2017; Freeman & Knowles, 2012; Harkins Monaco et al., 2018) can be particularly tricky for people with disabilities, in the realms of gender and sexual identity. Terminology around gender and sexual identity are often in a state of fluctuation (Azzopardi-Lane & Callus, 2015), which can be confusing. This gets even more complicated when gender and sexual identities are assumed by others. Ableist assumptions are already directly impacting people with disabilities and gender or sexual assumptions can be even more problematic.

## How Intersectionality Affects Sexuality Education

There is an increasingly large disparity between the social identities of K–12 school practitioners and K–12 students (Niles & Harkins Monaco, 2019). Sources cite that 83% of school psychologists are female, 87% are white, and 86% speak only English (National Association of School Psychologists [NASP], 2016; Walcott et al., 2016), while 86.4% of special educators are female and 81.3% are white. Only 10.4% of special educators are Black or African American (U.S. Census Bureau, 2016). There is a lack of data regarding how many educators are members of the LGBTQ+ community; we believe that a lack of safety or job security may contribute to that.

Almost 50% of K–12 students, on the other hand, identify in racial or ethnic groups; 9.4% are English language learners, and 13% have disabilities (Proctor et al., 2017; National Center for Education Statistics [NCES], 2017). Recent surveys indicate there are inaccurate reports of "disparities between LGBTQ and non-LGBTQ youth [because] . . . youth may hold back sensitive information, which can lead to under- or over-estimates" (Strauss, 2017, para. 13). Other reasons for this inaccuracy are that students don't take these surveys seriously or that the "tremendous amount of diversity among LGBTQ youth [makes] it . . . unclear how survey data errors affect the findings about subgroups within the LGBTQ youth community" (Strauss, 2017, para. 16).

Practitioners are not necessarily prepared to face these intersectional challenges in their work with students (Darling-Hammond, 2002; Gay & Howard, 2000; Owen, 2010) because (a) they may not be aware of their unconscious biases (Gay & Howard, 2000; Owen, 2010); (b) they may not be willing to examine them (Darling-Hammond, 2002); and (c) they may not understand the layered actions, feelings, and needs of their multiple minoritized students (Carroll, 2009; Proctor & Meyers, 2015). This is because practitioners do not subscribe to these identities personally, they have never experienced systemic oppression themselves, or they have never been taught how these complex issues apply to education.

> School systems have historically ignored or erased aspects of identity (Bazerman & Tenbrunsel, 2011; Chugh et al., 2005), and preservice programs [and school districts] typically regulate diversity to awareness days, weeks, or months, the curricula, or discuss it diagnostically (Linton, 1998). . . . While this does not necessarily mean that school practitioners are ineffective, it is important they are equipped to mutually serve all populations. (Niles & Harkins Monaco, 2019, p. 116)

Sometimes practitioners view all children as being the "same"—"to some, being 'colorblind' [is] valuing diversity" (Owen, 2010, p. 18), but "when practitioners do not recognize these nuances or counteract them in their daily interactions, they are inadvertently contributing to further oppressive acts" (Niles & Harkins Monaco, 2019, p. 116). This can have drastic, long-term consequences (Brown, 2007) for people with disabilities. Consider the patterns of domestic abuse and violence. Children with disabilities experience physical, emotional, and sexual abuse more than their nondisabled peers, and disabled girls experience rates higher than disabled boys (Sobsey, 1994; Sobsey et al., 1997; Sullivan & Knutson, 2000). Disabled women experience more domestic battery than both disabled and nondisabled male peers (Berger, 2013, p. 39; Sobsey, 1994; Thiara et al., 2011). These kinds of statistics show how important even just a few intersectional considerations are for children with disabilities. If practitioners are able to infuse intersectionality in their work with people with disabilities, they will better be able to recognize and incorporate multifaceted lived experiences of their students.

## Disability and Gender Identity

**Gender** is defined as "society's constructed roles, expectations, behaviors, attitudes, and activities that it deems appropriate for men and women" (Niles & Harkins Monaco, 2018, p. 80). **Gender identity** further defines gender as inherently diverse and reflects both biological and psychological considerations. Gender and gender identity are different from **assigned biological sex,** which refers to the anatomical and physical traits of male and female bodies. This means one's gender identity may be different from their assigned biological sex. Niles (2018) clarified it further:

> As soon as the biological sex of a fetus is assigned either from a uterine ultrasonic examination during pregnancy or from observation of the neonate's external genitalia at birth, the tendency is for parents

and others to begin to make gender-based decisions for their child. For example, the parents select a name for their daughter or son, purchase gendered clothing, furnishings, and decoration. Toys and gifts for the baby align to the societal assumptions of the preferences of either boys or girls. [These kinds of] gender expectations also influence how infants are perceived soon after birth. Boys are perceived as strong and masculine, while girl infants tend to be perceived as fragile and dainty. (Niles & Harkins Monaco, 2018, pp. 80–81)

By age two, most children are aware of their own gender; most of the time they imitate gendered behaviors and show preference for gendered items or clothing (Bryan, 2012; Niles & Harkins Monaco, 2018), like when little girls wear pink dresses and play with dolls, or when young boys are dressed in blue. Other times, children show signs if their gender identities do not align with their assigned biological sex. This is also apparent at a very young age (Niles & Harkins Monaco, 2018).

## Gender Binary and Gender Dysphoria

Westernized society typically acknowledges two biological sexes—those with male genitalia and those with female genitalia—that directly correspond to two genders—male and female. This is known as the **gender binary** (Bryan, 2012). Growing research indicates gender is not a binary; however, it is actually a spectrum that encompasses a variety of gender identities and expressions. The **gender spectrum** is evolving at a rapid pace, which has resulted in a struggle to understand "alternatives to the gender binary . . . new terminology has emerged including gender expansive, gender fluid, gender variant, gender creativity, genderqueer, bigender, and agender" (Dresher & Pula, 2017; Freeman & Knowles, 2012; as cited in Niles & Harkins Monaco, 2018, p. 82). The terminology is also changing in the medical field; in 2015, the *Diagnostic and Statistical Manual of Mental Disorders (DSM-5)* first introduced the term **gender dysphoria** as the replacement of gender identity disorder. Gender dysphoria is the medical term for **transgender,** or someone whose assigned biological sex is not the same as their gender identity (Richards & Barker, 2015). The name of the diagnosis now implies that being transgender is no longer considered a disease or impairment, but it is a diverse concept in gender and sexuality. This change is important and attributed to the successful advocacy of the LGBTQ+ rights movement (Niles & Harkins Monaco, 2018).

## How Impairments Affect Gender Development

Children navigate their environments by observing and emulating cultural and societal expectations, which includes gender roles (Bryan, 2012; Kothlow & Chamberlain, 2012). Typically, as children use pretend and imaginary play, they show preferences for playing with peers who share their interests and their genders (Niles & Harkins Monaco, 2018). Because these developmental stages are delayed or altered for children with disabilities, their gender roles and gender preferences may be influenced. Children with disabilities may not be able to intuitively observe differences in gender or recognize gender roles, behaviors, or capabilities. Additionally, children with disabilities who express alternative gendered statements "I am a boy (or girl)" may be corrected due to an assumption that the child is not capable or perhaps confused about gender terminology (Sherer et al., 2015). This is exacerbated for children with more significant cognitive impairments, whose parents or caregivers may make more decisions based upon perceived gender assumptions, such as what clothing to wear, or what toys, books, or movies to engage with.

**Down Syndrome drag controversy.** One such example is the recent controversy with a successful drag group from the United Kingdom, called Drag Syndrome. Drag Syndrome's performers have Down syndrome and believe in healthy gender and sexuality expression; they stream live shows and offer sensory friendly screening rooms for their patrons (*Disability Drag Show*, 2019). The members of Drag Syndrome have stated, "We deserve to do what we want with our lives, and to give ourselves more power" (Bond, 2019) on the Drag Syndrome Facebook page and "we're going to continue doing it whether you like it or not" (Jacobs, 2019) to the *New York Times*. After all,

> People with Down syndrome are people. Some people are queer. Since people with Down syndrome are people, some people with Down syndrome are queer. People with Down syndrome have the same variety of sexuality and gender expression everyone else has. The members of Drag Syndrome celebrate that, and they do it in glittery stiletto heels. (Luterman, 2019, para. 4)

In September of 2019, Drag Syndrome booked a show in Michigan, but the owner of the venue canceled their performance to "protect people with Down syndrome from being 'exploited' onstage" (Luterman, 2019, para. 1). This reaction indicated that people believed these particular adults with Down syndrome needed protection from nonbinary gender or sexual expression. Unfortunately, these kinds of ableist responses are quite common, but in this case Drag Syndrome booked another site in Michigan and sold out two shows (*Disability Drag Show*, 2019).

# Disability and Sexual Identity

Everyone has a **sexual orientation,** or the "attractions, arousal, and behavior . . . demonstrated through emotional and physical attractions (Bryan, 2012). **Sexual arousal** is the physical response to an attraction that leads to **sexual behavior,** or the physical actions of sexual activity with oneself (masturbation) or with a sexual partner. While sexual arousal occurs without awareness or control, sexual actions or behaviors can be controlled (Niles & Harkins Monaco, 2018). Neurological control over sexual behaviors is especially important considering the intricacies of obtaining consent, ensuring privacy, or of generalizing skills and strategies (Niles & Harkins Monaco, 2017).

Sexuality is a continuum that is similar to gender; it is fluid and constantly evolving. Some people identify with **heterosexuality** and are attracted to people of the opposite sex; some people identify with **homosexuality** and are attracted to people of the same sex. **Bisexuality** is when people are attracted to both sexes, and **pansexuality** is when people are attracted to all forms of gender expression. Those who identify as **asexual** are not sexually aroused by any gender, and those who "**question**" may not know who they are attracted to (Planned Parenthood, 2017).

## How Impairments Affect Sexual Development

People with disabilities struggle with their sexuality, sometimes because of their limited sexual maturity, other times because of a lack of relationship exposure, limited or no healthy sexual encounters, or a lack of sexual partners *(see Chapter 2)*. Research indicates disabled people are more likely to be overlooked as viable candidates for relationships and may have limited abilities to form their own unique gender or sexual behavior (Planned Parenthood, 2017). Parents and caregivers may also attempt to protect their disabled children by avoiding or rejecting their child's sexual development. As Niles (2018) stated, "This ultimately results in individuals . . . lacking education and opportunities to use self-advocacy skills to explore and define their unique sexuality and gender" (Niles & Harkins Monaco, 2018, p. 80). This can have lasting effects for certain people with disabilities and may even result in what Niles coined as **sequestered sexuality** (Niles & Harkins Monaco, 2018).

# Intersectional Considerations in Schools

While some may think schools are environments that do not include elements of gender and sexuality, there is actually evidence that LGBTQ+ considerations are purposely ignored (Niles & Harkins Monaco, 2018). Only four states—California, Colorado, New Jersey, and Illinois—have laws that require schools to teach LGBTQ+ history, and six states—Alabama, Louisiana, Mississippi, Oklahoma, South Carolina, and Texas—have **no promo homo laws** that ban the "promotion of homosexuality" through teaching:

> Some states even require teachers to speak about LGBT people in a negative light, according to GLSEN, an education organization fighting for LGBT cultural inclusion and awareness in K–12 schools. Alabama law, for example, states that when discussing sexual health education, "classes must emphasize, in a factual manner and from a health perspective, that homosexuality is not a lifestyle acceptable to the general public and that homosexual conduct is a criminal offense under the laws of the state." (Leins, 2019, para. 12–13)

Schools also don't typically ask students to help establish inclusive policies or specifically outline intersectional considerations. This means that "just as individuals who experience marginalization based on disability, race, ethnicity, religion, individuals are also marginalized based on heteronormative assumptions of gender identity or sexual diversity" (Niles & Harkins Monaco, 2018, p. 85). For example, when school clubs and activities do not specifically include students who have flexible sexual or gender expressions or identities, they are marginalizing these students. When schools do not offer training for students, parents, faculty, and staff in these concepts, they are not explicitly including members of the community who subscribe to the LGBTQ+ community. This may further isolate students with disabilities who are part of this population and has ultimately elevated exclusion for the LGBTQ+ community:

- Approximately 75% of transgender students feel unsafe at school (Gender Spectrum, 2016);
- Almost 50% of gay students face verbal harassment in schools; and
- 83.7% of transgender and 69.9% of gender nonconforming students were bullied or harassed at school because of gender. (GLSEN, 2019)

These statistics can be compared to the social isolation and harassment of students with disabilities (Harrison, 2007). According to Harkins Monaco (2019), "the U.S. Government Accountability Office (2018) [reported] ... students with disabilities face disproportionate rates of discipline, suspension, and expulsion regardless of schools, income, or disciplinary guidelines, which have devastating social consequences" (Bateman & Cline, 2019, p. 108). National data does not discuss the experiences of students who are part of both the LGBTQ+ community and the disability community, but we believe that disabled students who are part of the LGBTQ+ population are doubly marginalized in schools. More research is needed in this area.

## Bathroom Laws

One example of double marginalization is around the inclusivity in school bathrooms. Sixty percent of transgender students avoid going to the bathroom in schools (Gender Spectrum, 2016). The most pressing case to date regarding school bathroom inclusivity is Virginia's *G.G. v. Gloucester County School Board*. Gavin Grimm, a transgender senior at the time, was no longer allowed to use the boys' bathroom at school. He sued his school district, and in May 2018, Virginia's court system ruled that Grimm had suffered from sex discrimination and stereotyping. While this ruling will most likely strengthen other issues of bathroom assignments across the nation, the reality is that there are opposing policies state-to-state and the federal government's lack of support is a significant challenge (American Civil Liberties Union, 2017; Harkins Monaco & McCollow, 2019). In fact, recent federal legislation mandates people:

> to only use facilities consistent with their biological sex. The reality is these bills will affect the transgender community and they will also affect students and adults with disabilities because they do not accommodate for people who need assistance using restrooms . . . individuals with disabilities who require assistance in restrooms are faced with a choice: use the bathroom aligning with their physical anatomy and potentially expose their assistants to fines or criminal penalties, or use the bathroom consistent with their assistants' physical anatomy and incur fines or penalties themselves. (Harkins Monaco & McCollow, 2019, p. 3)

This is also problematic when people with disabilities do not identify according to the gender binary (Sager, 2017).

## Intersectional Pedagogy

In order to fully engage doubly or triply marginalized students in schools, programs must foster **intersectional pedagogy** through developing awareness around intersectional concepts and the impact this has on students with marginalized identities. This begins when school professionals acknowledge that others' intersectional identities—and consequently their experiences—are different from their own (Proctor et al., 2014). If practitioners are able to recognize intersected structures of inequality in the classroom, they can better reduce systems of oppression to improve social conditions in schools.

## Intersectional Context and Climate

To begin, school norms must include intersectional considerations. Harkins Monaco (2019) advised that the "the administrator is on the front line to determine . . . intersectional social constructs [to] best equip teachers to create daily practices in cultural reciprocity (Scharf, 2016)" (Bateman & Cline, 2019, p. 110). School policies should support and enhance diversity, promote equity, social justice, and intersectionality, and minimize discrimination. "When transgressions occur, there must be effective enforcement of policy and supports provided to those victimized" (Appreciating the Impact of Intersectionality, n.d., p. 4).

## Intersectional Self-Reflection

Intersectionality "requires introspective reflection for confronting assumptions and stereotypes" (Niles & Harkins Monaco, 2019, p. 113). There are several steps in achieving this in schools. First, administrators and practitioners must intentionally seek to deconstruct and develop an understanding of their own multifaceted identities. They must fully examine their experiences so they can identify how others' experiences are different and how biases worked against minoritized groups of people. Then they can attempt to understand the complexity of another person (Howard-Hamilton et al., 2011). Only after this kind of self-reflection becomes part of their daily practices are they equipped to guide the school community in exploring their identities (Shriberg, 2016; Spring, 2000).

## Intersectional Curriculum

An intersectional curriculum must support individual experiences and how these experiences connect to the "why" of one's beliefs. Intersectional curricula should include societal and communal considerations and emphasize the need for continuous self-reflection. In this way, it reduces bias by recognizing systemic barriers and reducing discriminatory practices (NASP, 2016; Niles & Harkins Monaco, 2019).

**Bias and privilege.** Individuals must "recogniz[e] and accept biases exist" (Niles & Harkins Monaco, 2019, p. 119), particularly their **implicit biases,** or unconscious feelings or inclinations toward or against people or ideas. Implicit bias is rooted in the very constructs of one's subconscious thoughts and most people are unaware of it (Choudhury, 2015). Brains are constantly developing patterns of subconscious thought or **schemas** that ultimately operate life habits (Murray Law, 2011). This means that people are not necessarily aware when schemas are making decisions or choosing preferences for them. "For example, individuals may not purposely discriminate against others and may even actively identify as inclusive, but they may offer preferential treatment to certain social groupings, like when a woman is not offered a job interview due to a fear of not fitting into a male-dominated workforce or when one assumes that a colleague is married to a member of the opposite sex" (Harkins Monaco, 2020). The individuals in question are most likely oblivious that their actions are based on these preferences. In fact, some may be so unaware and consciously believe they are actively unbiased (Murray Law, 2011).

Opportunities to explore how belief systems are influenced by **social privilege** (Bell, 2016), the social power held by identities considered the "norm" (Crenshaw, 1989; Roysircar, 2008), can set the foundation for individuals to recognize the ethical consequences of long-term implicit biases (Banaji et al., 2003; Chugh et al., 2005; Tenbrunsel & Messick, 2004). When students are given "opportunities to practice 'constructive uncertainty'. . . [they will] naturally promote self-reflective feedback, like 'am I biased' or 'am I missing something?'" (Niles & Harkins Monaco, 2019, p. 119).

**Minority rhetoric.** Students need opportunities to develop positive connections about and with people who subscribe to other social identities. This is especially important for people with disabilities. Many times, **rhetorics,** or subliminal messages, send powerful messages that "idealize or medicalize the challenges inherent to the diagnosis rather than promoting a multifaceted approach to human diversity" (Niles & Harkins Monaco, 2019, p. 118). For example, "individuals with autism are often portrayed through a disability-first perspective with the focus on scientific, clinical, or savant-like characteristics in popular media" (Maich & Belcher, 2014; Niles & Harkins Monaco, 2019, p. 118). Positive rhetorics can be incorporated into the curriculum. Ask yourself the following questions to get started:

1. "What kind of characters, pictures, and texts are used in teacher-provided resources?

2. Do they positively represent multiple minoritized identities, or perhaps they do not represent them at all?" (Harkins Monaco, 2020)

Examples in English Language Arts include choosing literature or films that show realistic and appropriate representations of marginalized groups. Discussions should include the implications and ethics of positive and negative messaging, especially if using examples that do not have realistic or any representation. The science and math disciplines naturally lend themselves to the discussion of how technologies have benefited people with disabilities or a lack of representation in the field altogether (Bialka, 2017). *(For more information on various disability rhetorics, see Chapter 13.)*

## Summary

"The importance of creating a climate of understanding and acceptance in a [school] environment extends beyond the four walls of the classroom, as the social implications are far-reaching" (Bialka, 2017, p. 172). Shifting demographics in schools means that school practitioners must develop their understandings of how to address the increased risks of the students they serve. We recommend that practitioners integrate multidimensional aspects of intersectionality directly into educational policies, school cultures, and curricula.

## Resources

### Internet Resources

*The Ackerman Institute for the Family: The Gender and Family Project:* www
.ackerman.org/gfp/

> This has gender-inclusive resources; trainings; curricula for elementary, middle, and high school classrooms; and resources for families and caregivers. It also provides literature that explores more gender diversity across a variety of reading comprehension levels.

*Planned Parenthood:* www.plannedparenthood.org/learn/teens/lgbtq/

> This nonprofit organization delivers reproductive health care, sexuality education, and sexual orientation and gender identity resources.

*The Gender Spectrum:* https://www.genderspectrum.org/

> This website offers trainings, books, multimedia resources, and additional conference opportunities that support gender-sensitive and gender-inclusive environments.

## Books/Articles and Other Resources

Berger, R. J. (2013). *Introducing disability studies.* Lynne Rienner Publishers, Inc.

Harkins Monaco, E. A., Gibbon, T., & Bateman, D. (2018). *Talking about sex: Sexuality education for learners with disabilities.* Rowman & Littlefield.

Niles, G., & Harkins Monaco, E. A. (2019). Privilege, social identity and autism: Preparing preservice practitioners for intersectional pedagogy. *DADD Online Journal (DOJ),* 6(1), 112–123.

There are various books that support sexual and gender exploration for children:

- *King and King* by Linda de Haan and Stern Nijland (2004). A prince reluctantly agrees to marry but none of the eligible princesses strikes his fancy . . . and then he meets Prince Lee. Gr. 2–5
- *Mommy's Family* by Nancy Garden (2004). When a classmate tells her, "No one has two mommies," Molly is upset and confused. But as her mommies and teacher help her understand that all families are different, she becomes proud of her own family. Gr. K–3
- *Antonio's Card/La Tarjeta de Antonio* by Rigoberto Gonzalez (2005). With Mother's Day coming, Antonio has to decide what is important to him when his classmates make fun of the unusual appearance of his mother's partner, Leslie. Gr. 2–5
- *Daddy, Papa, and Me* and *Mommy, Mama, and Me* by Leslea Newman (2009). This board book with rhyming text shows a toddler spending the day with his/her daddies or with her/his mommies. Gr. preK–1
- *In Our Mother's House* by Patricia Polacco (2009). The oldest of three adopted children recalls their childhood with their mothers, Marmee and Meema. Gr. 1–6
- *A Tale of Two Daddies* by Vanita Oelschlager (2010). A young girl describes how her two daddies help her through her day. Gr. 1–4

## Suggestions for How to Maintain Current on This Topic

- Remain current on your state laws and policies related to disability rights, advocacy, and sexuality education.
- Advocate for inclusive sexuality education in your school district.
- Follow the organizations listed below on social media, and sign up for Kinsey Institute newsletter to remain current on research related to human sexuality.

## Associations

- American Association of Sexuality Educators, Counselors, and Therapists: https://www.aasect.org
- Kinsey Institute (Indiana University): https://kinseyinstitute.org/
- Planned Parenthood: https://www.plannedparenthood.org
- Society for Disability Studies: http://disstudies.org/

# CHAPTER 5

# Students with High- and Low-Incidence and Physical Disabilities

Anne O. Papalia and Willa Papalia-Beatty

*Young people with disabilities are no different from other kids in their need to understand their bodies and relationships: they, too, need to understand how their bodies work, and may have romantic longings and sexual interests.*

(University of Michigan Health System, 2010, p. 1)

## Overview

Within this chapter various disability categories and their implications for comprehensive sexual education are presented. The importance of understanding the nuances between high-incidence and low-incidence disabilities and physical impairments is explored and the effects of these elements on comprehensive sexuality education are discussed.

## Advanced Organizer

- Understanding the impact of a disability on the person has implications for providing sexuality education.
- **High-incidence disabilities** are the most prevalent disability categories within the Individuals with Disabilities Education Act (IDEA, 2004). They tend to require less intensive interventions and directly impact learning.
- Sexuality education instruction for individuals with high-incidence disabilities must be adapted to address learning difficulties. Support for social pragmatic skills, social skills, community involvement, and

executive functioning are needed to foster safe and meaningful sexual relationships.

- **Low-incidence disabilities** are less frequent, require more intensive interventions, and affect an individual across various areas (i.e., physical, sensory, and intellectual). Most, but not all, low-incidence disabilities impact a person's cognitive functioning.
- Important topics for sexuality education with individuals with low-incidence disabilities include sexual hygiene and health information, as well as social and relationship skills. Self-determination and self-advocacy skills are needed to promote access to intimate and meaningful sexual encounters.
- Physical disabilities are conditions that incapacitate skeletal, muscular, and/or neurological systems of the body. They tend to be visible and result in medical conditions, health problems, and physical limitations. Many individuals with physical disabilities have no cognitive mental disability but typically experience mobility issues.
- Sexuality education implications for individuals with physical disabilities involve the need for accurate information regarding sexual functioning and a redefinition of sexual activity and intimacy due to the anatomical impact of the disability. Stigmatization may be an issue due to the visibility of a physical disability.

The purpose of this chapter is to review the impact of high-incidence and low-incidence disabilities and physical impairments and discuss implications for delivering comprehensive sexual education for these individuals. Within the chapter, high-incidence disabilities, low-incidence disabilities, and physical disabilities are defined, characteristics of specific disabilities included in each category are explained, and the general impact of these disabilities as they relate to comprehensive sexual education are discussed.

Persons with disabilities, like all individuals, are sexual persons. Students with disabilities have the right to the same education about sexuality as their nondisabled peers, but they may require interventions that are beyond what is typically available in the **general education curriculum** (Landrum et al., 2003). Understanding the impact of a disability on the person overall has implications for providing sexuality education. The nature of the disability affects the content included and how it is taught. Sexuality education content must be individualized to address the specific behavioral, social, and physical implications of a student's disability. Curricular adaptations and modifications may be necessary to ensure content is presented in a way the student understands. Nuances associated with characteristics of high-incidence disabilities, low-incidence disabilities, and physical disabilities will inform content, curriculum, and instructional methods to be included in comprehensive sexual education for each group.

# Overview of Disabilities

## Definition of a Disability

A disability is defined within two pieces of legislation with two distinct purposes. The Americans with Disabilities Act (ADA, 1990), civil rights legislation that prohibits discrimination based on disability in programs or services, defines a disability as a physical or mental impairment that substantially limits one or more major life activities. Individuals with disabilities are protected by ADA across their lifespan. The Individuals with Disabilities Education Act (IDEA) (2004) regulates educational services provided to children with disabilities and their families and only applies while students with disabilities are in school. Under IDEA, a child or adolescent can qualify as a student with a disability under one of 13 categories. Table 5.1 contains a list of the 13 disability categories within IDEA.

Table 5.1  **Thirteen IDEA Disability Categories**

| Categories |
| --- |
| Autism |
| Deaf-Blindness |
| Deafness |
| Emotional Disturbance |
| Hearing Impairment |
| Intellectual Disability |
| Multiple Disabilities |
| Other Health Impaired |
| Orthopedic Impairment |
| Specific Learning Disability |
| Speech Language Impairment |
| Traumatic Brain Injury |
| Visual Impairment |

*Note.* Individuals with Disabilities Education Act, 20 U.S.C. § 1400 (2004).

## High-Incidence Disabilities

In addition to legal definition, disability is often categorized using broad, preference-based terms. The term *high-incidence disability* is used to identify the more prevalent IDEA disability categories that account for more than half of all students served in special education and approximately 8% of the school population (Bryant et al., 2019). Examples of high-incidence disabilities in the order of prevalence include specific learning disabilities (LD), mild autism, mild intellectual disabilities (ID), and emotional and behavior disorders (EBD). Along with prevalence, several other common factors exist among students with high-incidence disabilities. First, high-incidence disabilities tend to be considered mild, meaning they have a mild impact and require less intensive interventions (Boyle & Scanlon, 2019). Second, high-incidence disabilities tend to directly impact an individual's ability to learn. Information processing is impacted in some way that results in learning difficulties in one or more areas (Bryant et al., 2019).

## Low-Incidence Disabilities

In contrast to high-incidence disabilities that tend to be prevalent and mild, low-incidence disabilities occur less frequently yet have a more significant effect on an individual. Low-incidence disabilities tend to affect an individual across various areas (i.e., physical, sensory, and intellectual) and require more intensive interventions. Most, but not all, low-incidence disabilities impact a person's cognitive functioning (Westling et al., 2015).

The characteristics of individuals with low-incidence disabilities vary greatly; however, one major commonality exists—the need for ongoing support in more than one major life activity in order to participate in an integrated community setting and enjoy the quality of life available to individuals with fewer or no disabilities (TASH, 1991). Individuals with low-incidence disabilities are served within a variety of IDEA disability categories. Examples of categories include moderate to severe autism, moderate to severe intellectual disabilities, traumatic brain injury, multiple disabilities, and deaf-blindness (Bryant et al., 2019).

## Physical Disabilities

A **physical disability** is defined as a condition that incapacitates skeletal, muscular, and/or neurological systems of the body to a degree that impacts one or more major life functions (Hallahan et al., 2019). IDEA uses the term *orthopedically impaired* to describe students with physical disabilities. The primary distinguishing characteristics of physical disabilities are medical conditions, health problems, and physical limitations. Many individuals with physical disabilities have no cognitive mental disability but typically experience mobility issues. Few commonalities exist among individuals with physical disabilities. The type and impact of physical disabilities varies greatly, ranging from mild and transitory to profound and progressive conditions. As a result, the needs of individuals with physical disabilities tend to vary greatly and must be considered on an individual basis (Hallahan et al., 2019). This notion of individualization is also true when exploring implications for comprehensive sexual education for individuals with physical disabilities.

The characteristics of individuals with high-incidence disabilities, low-incidence disabilities, and physical disabilities have an impact on sexuality education. In general, the features of each group and their impact on sexuality education differ regarding the impact of the disability, but some common effects exist. In the following sections, characteristics, impact, and implications for sexuality education for individuals with high-incidence disabilities, low-incidence disabilities, and physical disabilities are presented and discussed.

## Individuals with High-Incidence Disabilities

As previously stated, the term *high-incidence disabilities* is used to describe the more prevalent disability categories under IDEA. Examples of these categories include LD, mild autism, mild ID, and EBD. These disabilities tend to have a less intense impact on the person and directly impact their ability to learn (Bryant et al., 2019). As a result, the majority of these individuals participate in general education with support (Hallahan et al., 2019). Common characteristics found among these disabilities involve deficits in (a) information processing, (b) language processing, (c) **pragmatics,** (d) behavior, (e) social skills, and (f) executive functioning (Hallahan et al., 2019; Hunt & Marshall, 2015). These deficits directly impact comprehensive sexuality education because they affect the individual's ability to learn sexuality education content without adaptation, initiate and sustain social and romantic relationships, interpret social cues, and realize and evaluate the impact of their actions and decisions within a social context (Rowe et al., 2018; Sinclair et al., 2015). Despite these commonalities, the nature and subsequent impact of each high-incidence disability vary slightly. In the next section, the IDEA definitions, impact, and implications on sexuality education for LD, mild autism, mild ID, and EBD are outlined.

## Individuals with Learning Disabilities

A higher percentage of students ages 3–21 (34%) received special education services under IDEA for LD than for any other type of disability (McFarland & Hussar, 2019). According to IDEA:

> [A specific learning disability is defined as] a disorder that impacts in one or more of the basic psychological processes involved in understanding or using language, spoken or written, that may manifest itself in an imperfect ability to listen, think, speak, read, write, spell, or do mathematical calculations. Disorders include such conditions as perceptual disabilities, brain injury, minimal brain dysfunction, dyslexia, and developmental aphasia. The disorder does not include a learning problem primarily resulting from visual, hearing or motor difficulties, intellectual disabilities, emotional and behavior disorders, and environmental, cultural or economic disadvantages. (Individuals with Disabilities Education Act, 2004)

This complex definition can be broken down into three distinct components. First, it implies that a student with LD has difficulty with **information processing,** the ability to take in, store, and retrieve information. Language, both verbal and nonverbal, is the avenue in which information is shared, stored, and retrieved. Deficits in information processing result in learning difficulties in the areas of language (i.e., oral expression, written expression, and listening comprehension); reading (i.e., basic reading skills and comprehension); and math (i.e., mathematical calculations and reasoning). Second, the information processing difficulties result in an achievement-ability discrepancy. Individuals with LD have the potential to learn as evidenced through an average to above average IQ score, but demonstrate deficit-specific content areas (i.e., reading, written expression, language, or math) while performing at an average to above average level in other areas. Third, learning difficulties cannot be due to other known causes, such as a sensory disability (i.e., visual or hearing impairment), or the presence of another disability recognized under IDEA (i.e., intellectual disability or emotional behavior disorders), or no opportunity to learn (i.e., environmental, cultural, or economic disadvantage; Hunt & Marshall, 2015).

### Implications for Comprehensive Sexuality Education

The impact of a learning disability has several implications for sexuality education. First, students with LD tend to have difficulty with reading-based coursework. Most students with learning disabilities have a learning disability in reading (Hunt & Marshall, 2015). As a result, academic learning is directly impacted. After grade 3, students move from learning to read to reading to learn (Chall, 1996). As a result, students with LD will have difficulty in any academic area that relies heavily on reading and is textbook based. Health education in general, and comprehensive sexuality education in particular, can be textbook and lecture based. Teachers rely on the text as a means for students to acquire basic information.

In addition to relying heavily on reading, comprehensive sexuality education includes some content-specific vocabulary that students may not understand. Words referring to reproduction, (e.g., menstruation, copulation, nocturnal ejaculations), anatomical terms within the reproductive system (e.g., metrium, fallopian tubes, epididymides, ductus deferens), and names of contraception methods (e.g., intrauterine device, tubal ligation) are content specific, and may not be easily understood by students with LD. Additionally, teachers may be reluctant to define them in specific, overt terms due to awkwardness with teaching sexuality-based content. As a result, euphemisms and figurative language is often used to describe sexually related content in everyday language. This leads to an additional issue: difficulties comprehending figurative language. As mentioned previously, students with LD, as indicated in the definition of learning disabilities, have difficulty processing language in abstract. They are likely to experience difficulty with abstract, inferential terms associated with sexuality education. For example, the overall content area is often referred to as learning about "the birds and the bees." The connection between this phrase and sexuality education may escape some students with LD, and an overt explanation may be necessary. Other figurative terms include a "monthly visitor" or "Aunt Flo" for menstruation, and a variety of terms used to describe specific sex acts (i.e., making love, hooking up, etc.). Given these difficulties with reading, text-based instruction, and language processing, students with LD are likely to require specific adaptations during comprehensive sexuality instruction. *(This topic is discussed in depth in Chapter 9 of this text.)*

As noted in the definition, individuals with learning disabilities may have difficulty interpreting nonverbal language such as gestures, facial expressions, and proximity cues. These misinterpretations can lead to issues with social pragmatics. These difficulties have implications for sexuality education because social skills and communication are impacted. Social skills and relationships are fundamental aspects of comprehensive sexuality education. Students with learning disabilities may struggle with interpreting the nuance of a friendship or romantic relationship, expressing intense intimate emotions, and interpreting the subtleties of giving and receiving consent (Sinclair et al., 2015).

Many of these implications for comprehensive sexuality education that impact students with learning disabilities will also impact individuals with other high-incidence disabilities such as mild intellectual disabilities. However, the impact will vary slightly due to the nature of the specific disability. For example, individuals with learning disabilities have an unexplained difficulty processing information that results in variable academic performance in an individual who is otherwise capable of learning. In contrast, an individual with mild ID experiences learning difficulties across all areas due to subaverage intellectual function.

## Students with Intellectual Disabilities

Approximately 6.4% of students who received special education services under IDEA have intellectual and developmental disabilities (IDD; McFarland & Hussar, 2019). According to IDEA, an individual with an intellectual disability has "significantly subaverage general intellectual functioning, existing concurrently with deficits in adaptive behavior and manifested during the developmental period, that adversely affects a child's educational performance." This definition consists of three distinct components: (a) subaverage intellectual functioning, (b) adaptive behavior, and (c) age of onset. Subaverage intellectual function is operationally defined by a total IQ score of 70 or below, indicating the person is scoring in the below average range. Additionally, an individual must demonstrate difficulty interacting with their environment, otherwise known as adaptive behavior. Adaptive behavior skills are based on the typical performance of individuals in meeting environmental expectations. Although no single, universal definition of adaptive behavior exists, it is typically defined as effectiveness and degree to which an individual meets social and cultural standards of personal independence and social responsibility (Gresham & Elliot, 1987). The nature of adaptive behaviors for an individual varies with age, development, and cultural context. Examples of behavioral domains addressed when assessing adaptive behavior include social skills, communication skills, self-care, daily living skills, community use and access, employment, leisure skills, and functional academics. Furthermore, intellectual disabilities occur during a child's developmental period prior to the age of 18, in order to distinguish intellectual disabilities from other disabilities acquired in adulthood that also may affect intellectual functioning and adaptive behaviors (Hunt & Marshall, 2015).

Intellectual disabilities are typically classified according to IQ scores. Individuals are classified as mild (IQ of 50–70), moderate (IQ of 30–50), severe (IQ of 20–35), and profound (IQ score is 20 or below). Most individuals with ID fall within the mild range. As a result, the characteristics of individuals with mild ID are discussed in the following section. Characteristics of people with more moderate and severe ID are included in the discussion of individuals with low-incidence disabilities (Hallahan et al., 2019).

## Impact of Mild Intellectual Disabilities

The presence of a mild intellectual disability impacts a person's academic, behavioral, and social emotional abilities. Individuals with intellectual and developmental disabilities experience low levels of cognitive ability across all academic areas due to a reduced capacity to learn. These learning difficulties are due to a limited capacity to process information. Individuals with intellectual disabilities process smaller amounts of information, resulting in a restricted range of learning. More specifically, persons with mild IDD can master basic concepts from the general education curriculum and acquire a basic understanding but may experience difficulty mastering more complex, in-depth concepts (Hunt & Marshall, 2015).

Restricted cognition and limited information processing ability contribute to difficulty across several areas. Information processing is a language-based system. Language, both verbal and nonverbal, is the vehicle for transporting information. Individuals with mild IDD experience difficulty processing **expressive** and **receptive language,** resulting in a restricted vocabulary that creates a barrier to understanding content and conversation and expressing what they have learned. People with IDD have a limited range of problem-solving skills and experience difficulty applying these skills to novel situations. They tend to employ the same limited range of problem-solving strategies across situations rather than developing situation-specific strategies. Attention also is impacted. Attention is vital to the acquisition of information. Individuals with IDD may have difficulties coming to attention, maintaining attention, and/or paying selective attention to critical content, blocking their ability to acquire new information. Memory is impacted as well. Memory difficulties affect content retention, thereby impacting the ability to remember complex directions and complete tasks. Difficulties with problem solving, attention, and memory culminate in generalization issues. **Generalization** is the ability to transfer learning from one setting to another. It is a complex process that requires the learner to determine when and how to apply previous learning information to a novel setting. Generalization requires the effective use of executive function skills. Executive functioning skills are also affected by the restricted cognitive ability associated with intellectual disabilities. Metacognition is an example of specific executive function often impacted by an intellectual disability. Metacognition refers to one's ability to identify how one learns and to evaluate, monitor, and adapt the learning process. People with mild IDD often experience difficulties assessing their own thinking. Self-regulation is a component of metacognition. Self-regulation refers to the ability to regulate one's own behavior. As a result, an individual with IDD may experience behavioral and social skills difficulties due to an inability to interpret the impact of their own actions and behavior, leading to self-regulatory issues such as impulsivity, risk taking, and relationship issues (Hallahan et al., 2019).

Social and relationship skills are impacted by an intellectual disability. People with mild IDD often lack awareness of how to respond in social situations. Difficulties with expressive and receptive language impact social pragmatics and cause difficulty in interpreting the subtleties of verbal and nonverbal language and the ability to interpret them in novel situations. Restricted vocabulary makes it difficult for an individual with IDD to understand degrees of emotion or issues involved in communicating feelings involved in relationships. These relationship challenges can cause frustration and contribute to low self-esteem. Consequently, individuals with mild IDD often experience social problems. They tend to exhibit immature or maladaptive behaviors and have difficulty making friends. The restricted range of problem-solving skills can contribute to over trying in a relationship or the repetition of ineffective social behavior that leads to peer alienation (Hunt & Marshall, 2015).

Individuals with mild ID may require some support for adaptive behavior as well. Overall, they tend to blend in with the school and work environments but may require assistance with tasks or situations that are complex and abstract such as social skills, community use (e.g., using public transportation), leisure activities, self-care, and self-direction. Challenges experienced by individuals with mild ID in these areas can create barriers to building friendships and intimate relationships (Hunt & Marshall, 2015). (*Additional information about developmental issues and relationships is discussed in Chapter 9.*)

## Implications for Comprehensive Sexuality Education

The impact of mild ID has several implications for comprehensive sexuality education. Presentation and delivery of content must be adapted due to the restrictive range of cognitive functioning experienced by individuals with mild ID. The curriculum must be analyzed to highlight the most essential information. Emphasis should be placed on fundamental, high-utility content. Content-specific and figurative language must be simplified and concrete examples used. *(More detailed information about adapting comprehensive sexuality curriculum and instruction for individuals with ID is included in Chapter 9.)*

Difficulties with adaptive behavior, communication, and generalization also have implications for comprehensive sexuality education. Each of these areas impacts social skills and the ability to establish relationships. Direct instruction may be necessary in skills such as initiating friendships, mores of dating, and dynamics of a romantic relationship. Individuals with mild ID may require practice and systematically planned opportunities for generalization in implementing these skills, as well as coaching and reflection on their actual implementation of social and dating skills (Rowe et al., 2018).

Social skills, involvement with peers, and community interactions form a foundation for healthy and meaningful sexual interactions. Inherent in sexual development is interaction and connection with other people, and social skills are the foundation for these connections. Individuals with mild ID may experience difficulty performing these skills independently due to deficits in adaptive behavior. They may require explicit instruction on how to access and participate in social events. Specific skills include planning the event (e.g., accessing websites and community organizations to find out about the event, arranging transportation, fees involved), securing admission (e.g., whether tickets are required and how to purchase them), any special skills or equipment required for an event (e.g., bowling ball and specialized shoes), and expected behaviors or interpersonal skills needed to be an effective friend or partner during the event (e.g., staying together, starting conversation, paying attention to your companion rather than others, etc.) need to be taught (McDaniels & Fleming, 2018).

Limitations of individuals with ID in problem-solving skills and the ability to self-monitor can make them vulnerable in sexual relationships. Safety skills should be addressed directly. These skills include overtly discussing boundaries, and understanding the aspects of consent (i.e., no means no, the right to change your mind). Individuals with ID may need to rehearse language involved in giving or denying consent during instruction and may benefit from overt discussions regarding personal boundaries in relationships in general and within sexual relationships. Consequences of risky behavior associated with drug and alcohol use as they relate to personal boundaries and consent should be addressed directly as well (Wolfe & Blanchett, 2003).

## Students with Emotional and Behavior Disorders

Approximately 5.3% of students ages 3–21 received special education services for emotional and behavior disorders (McFarland & Hussar, 2019). The term *emotionally disturbed* is used within IDEA to describe this category. However, within the following section, EBD is used to describe this disability category to avoid the negative connotation derived from the term *disturbed*. According to IDEA (2004),

> *An emotional and behavior disorder refers to a condition exhibiting one or more of the following characteristics over a long period of time and to a marked degree which adversely effects educational performance: (a) An inability to learn that cannot be explained by intellectual, sensory, or health factors, (b) an inability to build or maintain satisfactory interpersonal relationships with peers and teachers, (c) inappropriate types of behaviors or feelings under normal circumstances, (d) a general pervasive mood of unhappiness or depression, or (e) a tendency to develop physical symptoms or fears associated with personal or school problems. The term does include children who are schizophrenic but does not include children who are socially maladjusted, unless it is determined that they are seriously emotionally disturbed.*

Based on the definition, it can be inferred that an EBD is determined by time (e.g., age depending on the condition) and degree of behavior rather than kind. Individuals with EBD tend to perform behaviors that could be considered normal and acceptable to greater intensity or rates, or before or after the expected age. For example, most young children tantrum, but if a child's tantrums over time are longer, louder, more self-injurious, or occur after an age when tantrums are expected, the behavior is problematic. The absence of a behavior as evidenced through withdrawal also indicates degree. The behaviors must meet at least one of the five components in the definition, including learning difficulties not explained by other reasons, to qualify for special education within this category (Kauffman & Landrum, 2018).

A wide range of disorders is encompassed within the EBD category. Several classification systems are used to classify these disorders. The clinical classification system is used frequently by mental health professionals to describe childhood, adolescent, and adult mental health disorders. It is derived from sources such as the *DSM-5* that groups behavior into diagnostic categories and systems and provides criteria for making a diagnosis. However, a diagnosis does not automatically assure that the child will qualify for special education as EBD. A second classification category relies on dimensions of behavior. Two global dimensions typically used are externalizing and internalizing behaviors. Externalizing, or overt, behaviors include disruptive or acting-out behaviors that are disturbing to others. Internalizing, or covert behaviors, reflect an individual's internal state. Examples include anxiety, withdrawal, fearfulness, and phobic behaviors (Gargiulo & Bouch, 2019).

## Impact of Emotional and Behavioral Disorders

As evidenced by the complex nature of the emotional and behavior disorder definition, individuals with EBD are a heterogeneous group. Individuals with EBD tend to experience academic, social, and communication difficulties; however, the way in which the problems manifest will vary. Each individual will differ based on the strengths, weaknesses, and intensity exhibited within each area (Kauffman & Landrum, 2018).

People with EBD typically have average to low average intelligence but tend to demonstrate below-average academic achievement across all areas. Individuals with EBD experience information processing problems. These difficulties are not as extreme as individuals with learning disabilities but contribute to the decreased academic performance. Information processing deficits can contribute to executive functioning difficulties similar to those found in students with learning disabilities, modulating emotional responses, resulting in impulsivity, lack of empathy, and misinterpretation of the behavior or intent of others. The executive function deficits contribute to the hallmark characteristic of individuals with EBD: difficulty building and maintaining social relationships. These interpersonal challenges also may be due in part to difficulty processing expressive and receptive language, resulting in communication difficulties. Behavior is a form of communication and may be used by individuals with EBD as a substitute for language. The extreme presence or absence of behavior is seen with both internalizing and externalizing disorders. In addition, the language processing difficulties can contribute to social pragmatic challenges (Hunt & Marshall, 2015).

Individuals with EBD also experience executive function deficits. Executive functioning encompasses a variety of cognitive processes that permit individuals to make decisions, organize their thoughts, prioritize tasks, and problem solve. Problems associated with executive functioning deficits include difficulty (a) stopping one's behavior at the appropriate time including stopping actions and thoughts, (b) modulating emotional responses by bringing rational thoughts to bear on feelings, (c) self-monitoring one's own performance, and (d) understanding the behavior of others. These deficits can result in impulsivity, lack of empathy, and misinterpretation of the behavior or intent of others (Hallahan et al., 2015).

## Implications for Comprehensive Sexuality Education

Students with EBD may require adaptations within the sexuality education content and instructional delivery similar to students with learning disabilities due to underlying information processing and language processing deficits. However, given the nature of EBD, behavior and executive functioning challenges associated with EBD will have greater implications for comprehensive sexuality education. More specifically, adolescents with EBD typically exhibit characteristics resulting in early sexual activity. These characteristics include distractibility, engagement in higher-risk activities, an inability to cope with stressful situations and change, and impulsivity (Treacy et al., 2018). Early sexual activity is a concern because it is associated with a variety of physiological and health risks such as sexually transmitted diseases and teenaged pregnancy. Social impacts of early sexual activity include inadequate parenting skills and risk of sexual abuse. Early sexual activity also is associated with social and emotional maladjustment. Delinquency, sexual activity, and substance abuse are often linked activities for individuals with emotional behavioral disorders (Kauffman & Landrum, 2018).

## Individuals with Mild Autism Spectrum Disorders

Approximately 10% of students from ages 3 to 21 who receive special education are identified as having an autism spectrum disorder (ASD). Within IDEA (2004), ASD is defined as a developmental disability significantly affecting verbal and nonverbal communication and social interaction, generally evident before age 3, that adversely affects a child's educational performance. Other characteristics often associated with autism are engagement in repetitive activities and stereotyped movements, resistance to environmental change or change in daily routines, and unusual responses to sensory experiences. A child who manifests the characteristics of autism after age 3 could be identified as having autism if the criteria stated above are satisfied (IDEA, 2004).

The IDEA (2004) definition of ASD does not explicitly designate severity levels. However, the *DSM-5* (American Psychiatric Association, 2015) diagnostic criteria for ASD includes three levels of severity; these levels from mild to severe are: (a) requiring support, (b) requiring substantial support, and (c) requiring very substantial support. The severity level is determined based on the extent to which social communication impairments and restricted and repetitive patterns of behavior impact an individual's functioning. In the next section the impact of ASD is discussed. This discussion reflects individuals with mild ASD diagnosed at the required support level.

## Impact of Autism Spectrum Disorders

Individuals with ASD are likely to experience difficulties with academic achievement, communication, social skills, sensory perception, and behavior. The intellectual ability of individuals with ASD ranges across all levels. Approximately half are also diagnosed with intellectual disabilities. Most individuals with ASD, including those without significant intellectual disabilities, display uneven learning patterns, often consisting of relative strength in one or two areas of learning (Hunt & Marshall, 2015).

Individuals with ASD also experience difficulty with communication. They may lack the desire to communicate for social purposes and experience deficits in social pragmatics. For example, they may use an inappropriate tone or volume, have difficulty taking turns during conversations, engage in monologues, or repeat themselves frequently. Deficits in recognizing emotions, facial expressions, and vocal intonation may underlie the problems many people with ASD have in reading social cues. They may also have impaired understanding and use of nonverbal communication, such as eye gaze, facial expression, and gestures. They may also demonstrate a ritualized use of language when interacting with others, including focusing on specific topics of intense interest (Hallahan et al., 2019).

## Implications for Comprehensive Sexuality Education

Difficulties with academic achievement, communication, social skills, sensory perception, and behavior common to students with mild ASD have direct implication for sexuality education. Students with mild ASD need access to explicit direct instruction, picture cues, and concrete descriptions to successfully master the special education curriculum and social expectations in the general education classroom (Treacy et al., 2018). The behavior and communication deficits associated with mild ASD may cause an individual to be viewed as asexual due to a reluctance to engage in interpersonal relationships, and the need for sexuality education is ignored (Sinclair et al., 2015). These same characteristics impact social skills. An individual with ASD may be unable to accurately assess social cues from others, so they may not be able to discriminate between who is an interested partner and who is not, while conversely they may not be able to initiate the social interactions needed to lead to a relationship (Tullis & Zangrillo, 2013).

Overall, individuals with high-incidence disabilities, such as learning disabilities, mild intellectual disabilities, emotional and behavior disorders, and mild autism, have similar characteristics directly impacting sexuality education. These individuals experience difficulty with information processing. The nature, extent, and impact of the information processing deficits vary, but result in challenges in learning, communication, self-monitoring, and generalization that in turn impact social skills and interpersonal interactions (Hunt & Marshall, 2015; Sinclair et al., 2015). Overall, students with high-incidence disabilities require explicit, systematic sexuality education instruction and benefit from the use of clear, understandable language and opportunities for generalization (Rowe et al., 2018). Social pragmatic skills should be addressed to support social skills and community involvement foundational to healthy and meaningful sexual relationships (McDaniels & Fleming, 2018). Support for executive function skills is needed to promote safety and prevent high-risk behavior (Kauffman & Landrum, 2018).

## Individuals with Low-Incidence Disabilities

In contrast to high-incidence disabilities that tend to be prevalent and mild, low-incidence disabilities occur less frequently yet have a more significant effect on an individual. Low-incidence disabilities tend to affect an individual across various areas (i.e., physical, sensory, and intellectual) and require more intensive interventions. Most, but not all, low-incidence disabilities impact a person's cognitive functioning (Westling et al., 2015). The characteristics of individuals with low-incidence disabilities vary greatly; however, one major commonality exists—the need for ongoing support in more than one major life activity in order to participate in an integrated community setting and enjoy the quality of life available to individuals with fewer or no disabilities (TASH, 1991). Individuals with low-incidence disabilities are served within a variety of IDEA disability categories. Examples of categories include moderate to severe autism, moderate to severe intellectual disabilities, multiple disabilities, and deaf-blindness (IDEA, 2004).

### Impact of Low-Incidence Disabilities

Many areas impacted by high-incidence disabilities are also affected by a low-incidence disability (i.e., academic ability, information processing, expressive and receptive language, social skills, and executive function); however, the impact is more pervasive and intense. As a result, the same general implications identified for providing comprehensive sexual education for persons with high-incidence disabilities apply to individuals with low-incidence disabilities, but more intensive intervention is required. However, the more pervasive impact of low-incidence disabilities leads to implications for comprehensive sexual education that are more directly applicable to these individuals.

## Implications for Comprehensive Sexual Education

**Self-care and hygiene.** Individuals with low-incidence disabilities typically require assistance with self-care and hygiene. These skills will become especially important as they enter puberty and experience physical and emotional changes. The nature of these skills changes with age and maturity. For example, the onset of menses for young women and the introduction of nocturnal emissions for young men may be of critical importance. Sexual educators must be proactive in teaching these skills to help with the physical, emotional, and hygienic challenges. Procedures and schedules for using feminine hygiene products such as sanitary pads and tampons, frequent bathing, using deodorant, and specific grooming such as shaving must also be addressed. *(More information on developmental considerations is included in Chapter 6.)*

**Social and behavioral guidelines for sexual behavior.** In addition to addressing the social aspects of puberty and sexual maturity, individuals with low-incidence disabilities will also need support in understanding social norms. Nearly all individuals with low-incidence disabilities lack the skills and opportunities required to develop intimate relationships. Most individuals with low-incidence disabilities lack basic knowledge and personal experiences related to the physical and emotional aspects of intimacy. They may have been taught that physical feelings are bad and should be ignored or are bound by a lack of knowledge and misinformation. Additionally, they may not recognize boundaries and the need for privacy and consequently engage in inappropriate acts such as public masturbation or touching others. This lack of boundaries can make the notion of concept for self and others confusing. Consequently, instruction on intimate relationships and sexuality should begin early and be an ongoing part of learning for individuals with low-incidence disabilities. Facts and information about body parts, hygiene, and how women get pregnant should be taught directly using language that a specific individual can understand. Issues such as boundaries and types of relationships also should be taught early and incorporated into social skill instruction (Westling et al., 2015).

**Self-determination and self-advocacy.** Self-determination is defined as acting as the primary causal agent in one's life, making choices and decisions regarding the quality of one's life free from undue external influences or interference (Wehmeyer, 2007). Self-determination is fostered by providing individuals with practice making decisions and choices on a multitude of personal topics. Authentic life experience is a necessary component in the development of self-determination. It can be directly applied to comprehensive sexuality education by allowing individuals to make decisions and choices that properly address personal maturity and sexuality and problem solving through challenging moments. For example, individuals with low-incidence disabilities require authentic practice with analyzing relationships and boundaries to help incorporate these skills into their lives. Therefore, as individuals with low-incidence disabilities mature and approach adulthood, they should be presented with opportunities to make their own decisions about their feelings toward other people and how they relate to them (Harkins Monaco et al., 2018; Westling et al., 2015).

A manifestation of self-determination is the development of self-advocacy. Individuals with low-incidence disabilities must develop skills required to promote their right to relationships, marriage, and family. They must advocate for the same relationship experiences as individuals without disabilities. They must work to convince family, friends, and society that all children, *regardless of cognitive abilities*, deserve opportunities to determine personal sexuality philosophies, belief systems, and rules for personal sexuality (Harkins Monaco et al., 2018).

## Individuals with Physical Disabilities

A physical disability is defined as a condition that incapacitates skeletal, muscular, and/or neurological systems of the body to a degree that impacts one or more major life functions (Hallahan et al., 2019). IDEA uses the term *orthopedically impaired* to describe students with physical disabilities. The primary distinguishing characteristics of physical disabilities are medical conditions, health problems, and physical limitations. Many individuals with physical disabilities have no cognitive mental disability but typically experience mobility issues. Few commonalities exist among individuals with physical disabilities. The type and impact of physical disabilities varies greatly ranging from mild and transitory to profound and progressive conditions. As a result, the needs of individuals with physical disabilities tend to vary greatly and must be considered on an individual basis (Hallahan et al., 2019). This notion of individualization is also true when exploring implications for comprehensive sexual education for individuals with physical disabilities.

## Implications for Comprehensive Sexual Education

Due to the varying and individualized impact of a physical disability, implications for comprehensive sexual education for people with mild and low-incidence disabilities may apply to persons with physical disabilities. However, some common components emerge. These components are discussed in the following section.

### Impact of Physical Disabilities on Sexual Functioning

Individuals with physical disabilities are impacted by factors negatively affecting sexual health and sexuality. Individual considerations that are affected by a physical disability include changes in sexual health, understanding of the impact of physical disability on sexuality, confusion about anatomical or physiological changes, and attitudes and stigma related to individuals as they pursue a safe and pleasurable sexual life after the onset of physical disability. Additional issues such as medication management, anatomical changes, and illness and disease impact sexual functioning as well (Eglseder & Webb, 2017). As a result, individuals with physical disabilities have a desire to discuss sexuality and sexual functioning, including issues involving adjustment to a disability or its progression, help with finding a partner, and practical sexual problems (Kedde et al., 2012).

**Need for accurate information.** Individuals with physical disabilities, like other persons with disabilities, have a desire to develop skills and knowledge to build relationships and understand their sexuality. The majority of individuals with physical disabilities rely on their primary health care provider as a source of information on sexual issues. However, many health care providers do not feel adequately prepared to discuss sexual functioning and sexuality in general with patients with physical disabilities. Individuals with physical disabilities perceived that their healthcare provider had limited knowledge of the impact of their disability on sexual functioning and appeared surprised when asked about sexual health concerns (Becker et al., 1997). Therefore, a need exists to provide comprehensive sexuality education directly to individuals with disabilities, and to make comprehensive sexuality training for individuals with physical disabilities available to health care providers as well (Eglseder & Webb, 2017).

**Stigmatization.** Individuals with visible physical disabilities may be especially vulnerable to stigmatization by others, especially considering their sexuality. Individuals with physical disabilities can be perceived as asexual and less likely to develop relationships with people, especially if the conditions are visible. This stigmatization results in decreased self-perceived attractiveness, poor self-concept, diminished quality of life, and low self-esteem. Consequently, individuals with physical disabilities may benefit from both physical and emotional support during comprehensive sexual education. Along with understanding the physiological elements of sexuality, elements such as self-esteem, body image, self-acceptance, and self-efficacy may need to be addressed (Eglseder & Webb, 2017).

**Redefinition of sexual activity and intimacy.** The presence of a physical disability can impact an individual's ability to engage in sexual acts such as intercourse. It may also limit spontaneity as position and preparation is required. As a result, a component of comprehensive sexual education for individuals with physical disabilities is to redefine expectations for sexual activity and learn to explore alternatives, such as oral sex, that are pleasing to them and potential partners. Additionally, the need for prompts (e.g., vaginal lubrication or the use of a strategically placed pillow) and the use of devices (e.g., vibrators) to provide physical stimulation must also be discussed. Issues involving privacy should be considered as well. At times another person may need to be present during sexual activity due to mobility issues. For instance, a person using a wheelchair may require physical assistance transferring to transfer from the chair to a bed and vice versa (Kroll & Klein, 2001).

## Conclusion

The purpose of the chapter was to review the impact of high-incidence and low-incidence disabilities and physical impairments and discuss implications for delivering comprehensive sexual education for these individuals. Characteristics and common impacts of high-incidence disabilities, low-incidence disabilities, and physical disabilities were identified, and the general impact of these disabilities as they related to comprehensive sexual education was discussed. Although general conclusions provide an overall framework, these findings are not intended to be exhaustive. The unique characteristics of each individual, the impact of their disability, as well as their environment, family, and culture must be considered when providing comprehensive sexual education.

## Summary

Individuals with high-incidence disabilities such as learning disabilities, mild intellectual disabilities, emotional and behavior disorders, and mild autism experience difficulty with information processing. The nature, extent, and impact of the information processing deficits vary, but the impact results in challenges in learning, communication, self-monitoring, and generalization. Comprehensive sexual education for these individuals requires explicit, **systematic instruction.** Methods similar to effective teaching formats used with students with high-incidence disabilities in other academic areas are needed. Information must be presented in language they can understand, and social pragmatic skills should be taught directly to support communication and social skills. Executive function deficits also should be addressed. Individuals with high-incidence disabilities may require instruction in developing empathetic, intimate relationships and understanding of boundaries. Means for controlling impulsivity and the need for immediate gratification need to be taught. Generalization of content is likely to be an issue. Activities that promote skill transfer, such as structured practice and the opportunity to debrief interpersonal exchanges and dilemmas in a safe place, are recommended.

Many areas impacted by high-incidence disabilities also affect individuals with low-incidence disabilities. However, the more pervasive impact of low-incidence disabilities leads to implications for comprehensive sexual education that are more directly applicable to these individuals. They typically require assistance with self-care and hygiene. Sexuality educators must be proactive in teaching these skills to help with the physical, emotional, and hygienic challenges. Instruction on intimate relationships and sexuality should be early and ongoing and include facts about anatomy, hygiene, and reproduction as well as issues regarding boundaries and intimacy. Skill and activities that promote self-determination and self-advocacy should be addressed by providing opportunities for decision making and analyzing relationships in authentic situations.

Implications for comprehensive sexual education for people with high- and low-incidence disabilities may apply to persons with physical disabilities, yet some topics specifically related to physical disabilities exist. The unique impact of the physical disability on sexual function must be addressed. Accurate information about factors that impact their sexual functioning is needed but is often difficult to obtain. Individuals with visible physical disabilities may be stigmatized due to the overt nature of their disability, especially when considering their sexuality. This stigmatization can contribute to physical and emotional consequences and a diminished quality of life. Expectations for sexual activity and privacy may need to be redefined. Position needs must be considered as well.

Common characteristics and impacts of high-incidence disabilities, low-incidence disabilities, and physical disabilities exist and have implications for comprehensive sexual education. However, the unique characteristics of each individual, the impact of their disability, and their environment, family, and culture must be considered.

# Resources

## Internet Resources

Disability Visibility Project Podcast #39—Sex Education: https://disabilityvisibilityproject.com/2018/12/03/ep-39-sex-education/

## Books/Articles and Other Resources

Kroll, K., & Klein, E. K. (2001). *Enabling romance: A guide to love, sex, and relationships for people with disabilities*. No Limits Communications.
Treacy, A. C., Taylor, S. S., & Abernathy, T. V. (2018). Sexual health education for individuals with disabilities: A call to action. *American Journal of Sexuality Education, 13*(1), 65–93.

# CHAPTER 6

# Physical and Cognitive Effects of Puberty on People with Disabilities
Jacquelyn Chovanes

*I love being on stage and engaging an audience on any subject, but redefining their view of disability and sex is always a good one. The shock value is really high, especially when I talk about the practicalities of growing up disabled—how likely is a sex life when your mum has to take you to your date? [Friends] would tell me what they were getting up to with boys and it was a million miles away from anything I thought I would experience. My sex life didn't start until my mid-20s when another wheelchair-user changed everything for me by telling me that anything was possible. Why had nobody done that when I was growing up?*

—Liz Carr, comedian (*The Guardian*, August 17, 2006)

## Overview

Adolescence is a time of dynamic physical, cognitive, emotional, and social change for all young people. Individuals with disabilities typically progress through the same physiological stages of human sexual development as nondisabled peers; however, their disability may impact their cognitive and social-emotional sexual development. This chapter provides a summary of typical physical, cognitive, and social-emotional development in puberty, a discussion of the ways in which common characteristics of various disability classifications may affect the development of individuals with disabilities during puberty, and a description of the ways in which having a disability affects how students with disabilities learn about sexuality.

Readers will

- understand the physiological changes of puberty in students with and without disabilities,
- understand the cognitive changes of puberty in students with and without disabilities,
- understand social and emotional development in puberty experienced by students with and without disabilities,
- understand normative sexual development and behavior in adolescents, and
- understand the ways in which various disability classifications can impact adolescent sexual development and behavior.

# Sexual Development in Adolescence and Early Adulthood

## Physical Development

The purpose of sexual development is to achieve sexual reproduction. Neurophysiological sexual development begins before birth and guides the organization of the anatomical development of primary sex characteristics, including internal organs and external genitalia. In humans, chromosome pairs formed at the joining of the sperm and egg determine gender: females have two X chromosomes, males one X and one Y. The Y chromosome controls the development of the primitive gonads, present in both male and female embryos, into testes rather than ovaries. The testes then produce testosterone, which causes the embryo to develop male primary sex characteristics (penis, testicles) and suppresses the development of female primary sex characteristics (vagina, ovaries, uterus). Absent the Y chromosome, the embryo will develop female primary sex characteristics, although there are rare cases of errors in sexual differentiation resulting in individuals with intersex conditions (Bancroft, 2002). It is important to note that individuals with any of the possible sets of chromosomes and internal and external genitalia may identify as belonging to a gender other than the one they were assigned at birth, including both male and female, fluidity between male and female, and neither male nor female (Richards & Barker, 2015). *(See Chapter 4 of this volume for a detailed treatment of disability and gender identity.)*

During adolescence, which is generally defined as a time of transition between childhood and adulthood occurring during the teen years, children begin the process of **puberty,** which refers to physical sexual maturation. At puberty, which occurs in humans generally between the ages of 10 and 18, neurophysiological development instigated by an increase in hormone production activates the emergence of **secondary sex characteristics** in boys and girls. In males, the first sign of puberty occurs when the testes and scrotum increase in size, followed by the lengthening of the penis. Pubic, underarm, and facial hair appear. A growth spurt averaging about four inches occurs. For boys, the presence of increased levels of testosterone engenders an increase in sexual interest and responsiveness, including spontaneous nocturnal erection and emission, and **masturbation,** typically between the ages of 12 and 14. For females, breast budding is the first indication that puberty has begun, closely followed by a growth spurt averaging 3.5 inches. Pubic and underarm hair appear. Menstruation, the cycle of ovulation followed by bleeding caused by the shedding of the uterine lining, indicating that a girl is capable of becoming pregnant, typically begins when the growth spurt is nearly completed, about two years after breast development begins. In girls, the influence of hormones on sexual interest and behavior are less clear and more variable (Bancroft, 2002; Emmanuel & Bokor, 2017).

## Personal Hygiene

The development of body hair and increased production of perspiration requires that adolescents engage in a consistent regimen of personal hygiene, with frequent, regular bathing, use of deodorants, and daily brushing and flossing of the teeth. Some youth will also begin shaving. For both genders, increased oil production in the skin and scalp may lead to minor skin conditions such as pimples and blackheads, which can be treated with over-the-counter creams containing benzoyl peroxide or salicylic acid. In some cases, more severe conditions such as cystic acne can develop; these should be treated by a licensed medical practitioner (Titus & Hodge, 2012). Girls begin to menstruate and will typically use either tampons or pads. Additional cleansers beyond soap and water are not necessary for girls or women at any time during the menstrual cycle, including the bleeding phase (Kim & Choi, 2020).

## Brain Development and Cognitive Functioning

Physiological changes occur in the brain, as well. Two areas of the brain that undergo specific changes during adolescence are the **limbic system** and the **prefrontal cortex** (Paris, 2019). The limbic system is a set of structures located in the brain that identify positive and negative environmental stimuli and produce emotional responses. These structures include the hippocampus, the hypothalamus, and the amygdala, as well as neurons that connect to other parts of the brain. During adolescence, hormonal changes affecting the limbic system cause adolescents to experience emotions more intensely and intensify their perceptions of and reactions to environmental stimuli and feedback they receive from others. Perceived threats can cause adolescents to experience strong fight-or-flight responses, which may lead to behaviors such as social withdrawal or verbal and physical aggression. Other changes in the limbic system increase adolescents' desire for novelty and excitement. Increased sensitivity to the hormone dopamine intensifies feelings of pleasure. These changes provide adolescents with a high incentive to seek out rewarding experiences, including sexual activity (Paris, 2019; Shulman et al., 2016).

The area of the brain that is responsible for regulating emotion and planning behavior is the prefrontal cortex. The prefrontal cortex governs self-control, problem solving, risk assessment, and long-term planning (Paris, 2019). During puberty, the prefrontal cortex is still developing. The relative immaturity of the prefrontal cortex during the same period of heightened emotionality and pleasure-seeking experienced by adolescents makes this a challenging developmental stage. Increases in white matter and improved connections between the prefrontal cortex and other brain regions allow for improved cognitive and executive functioning (Fuhrmann et al., 2015). Adolescents are in the process of becoming more capable of regulating their emotions and engaging in thoughtful problem solving; however, the prefrontal cortex may function less efficiently when the individual is tired, stressed, upset, or overstimulated (Paris, 2019). In these instances, youth may experience difficulties in decision making and self-control, making them more likely to engage in risky behaviors (Shulman et al., 2016). Current research indicates that the prefrontal cortex may not be fully mature until early adulthood, around age 25 (Shulman et al., 2016).

**Social and Emotional Development.** Social and emotional development begins at birth. Infants form attachment bonds to caregivers and learn to depend on adults to meet their physical and emotional needs. Positive physical contact and secure, stable emotional relationships with caregivers in early childhood are associated with positive, satisfying emotional relationships in adulthood. The importance of healthy parental relationships continues into adolescence. A strong relationship with parents is predictive of higher self-worth, healthy emotional adjustment, and better academic outcomes (Wang & Sheikh-Kahil, 2014).

Adolescence is a time of identity exploration and development during which children strive to develop a coherent self-concept that incorporates their individual traits, values, and goals. On the way to identity achievement, adolescents may try on various roles and personas, take up and sometimes abandon extracurricular activities, and consider many different career paths. Through critical self-reflection, the individual claims some ideas, values, and beliefs and rejects others, thus coming to a consistent sense of self.

In adolescence, desire for peer interaction and approval becomes increasingly important. Children in adolescence spend more time with peers than parents due to school attendance and social activities. Peers can be an important influence on **identity development,** influencing behavior and values. Peer feedback is an important component to the development of an adolescent's self-image. As part of identity development, concerns about physical appearance and body image occur in both boys and girls during adolescence (Davidson & McCabe, 2006). Approval and acceptance from peers strengthen healthy identity development and improve self-esteem, whereas negative feedback and rejection can lower self-esteem and impede the development of a strong, positive identity (Ryan, 2000). Parents also affect identity development. Authoritative parents, who provide both security and a sense of autonomy, contribute to healthy identity development by allowing adolescents a supportive environment from which to engage in exploration.

**Sexual Behavior and Romantic Relationships.** Sexual behavior begins in early childhood, during which children exhibit curiosity about their own and others' bodies and may engage in exploratory and pleasure-seeking touching of their genitals. As children grow older, they may engage in sexual play (e.g., playing "doctor," truth or dare, or other games that involve kissing). Older children actively seek out information about sexual topics, including viewing pictures of naked bodies. Children receive information about sexuality from parents, siblings, peers, and other sources, including the internet. Shyness develops around their own bodies, and the need for privacy increases. Masturbation becomes more purposeful, with orgasm as a goal, particularly for boys, as youths enter puberty (National Child Traumatic Stress Network, 2009).

Adolescents typically experience their first romantic or sexual attraction during puberty. Sexual development in adolescence is influenced by peers, family members, and the media (Brandon-Friedman, 2019). Additionally, sexual orientation develops. It is important to note that among adolescents, sexual identification may be a fluid and evolving process during which individuals experiment with a variety of sexual attitudes and behaviors until a stable sexual identity emerges in late adolescence to early adulthood (Tolman & McClelland, 2011). *(See Chapter 4 of this volume for a detailed treatment of disability and sexual orientation.)*

Research shows that adolescents place high value on the social and emotional aspects of romantic relationships as well as physical gratification. By middle adolescence, most youth have been involved in at least one romantic relationship, and most young adults have or have had a serious romantic partner. In young adulthood, romantic and sexual relationships are correlated with emotional well-being (Brandon-Friedman, 2019). One study that examined the romantic and sexual experiences of youths showed that for adolescents in grades 7–12 across racial and ethnic categories, 94% of the participants reported holding hands with their partner, 63% reported sexual touching, and 45% reported engaging in **sexual intercourse.** Social behaviors such as hanging out together in a group and telling others about their status as a couple typically preceded sexual activity. Furthermore, there was a consistent progression among respondents from less intimate activities (i.e., hand-holding) to more intimate behaviors (i.e., sexual intercourse; O'Sullivan et al., 2007).

**Appropriate Management of Physical Pleasure.** Healthy sexual development in adolescence requires the appropriate management of physical pleasure as well as the development of emotional relationships. Arbeit (2014) defines healthy development in this area as the ability to communicate and negotiate effectively with a partner regarding consent, use of protection, and giving and receiving physical pleasure. Consent is defined as an agreement to participate in sexual activity (Planned Parenthood, 2020). Consent should be explicit and freely given, meaning that consent should be requested in such a way that makes clear that both an affirmative answer (yes) and a negative answer (no) are equally acceptable, and no sexual contact should be initiated without an explicitly affirmative expression of consent. **Protection** refers to actions taken to reduce possible negative consequences of engaging in sexual activity. This includes using various forms of birth control as well as condoms to prevent the transmission of disease, but it also includes the ability to engage in risk assessment with regard to which sexual behaviors a person chooses to engage in, where, when, and with whom, and to make choices accordingly (Arbeit, 2014). Healthy adolescent sexual expression also requires effective communication to negotiate mutually pleasurable physical acts. Masturbation and erotic fantasy are means for adolescents to learn about their own sexual desires and responses. Youth may then use this knowledge to communicate their preferences and desires to partners (Arbeit, 2014).

Masturbation is a common behavior in young children and adolescents. In middle childhood, masturbation appears to decrease, but it may be that children's increased desire for privacy and internalization of social norms regarding genital touching cause the behavior to become covert. In adolescence, masturbation, often accompanied by sexual fantasy, is common and considered to be a normal, healthy behavior for both boys and girls. In a recent study 80% of 17-year-old males reported having masturbated at least once, with 58% of 17-year-old females reporting at least one instance of masturbation (Robbins et al., 2011). Masturbation is more common than partnered sexual behaviors in both female and male adolescents. Masturbation in adolescence is associated with increased sexual satisfaction and positive self-image in adulthood, particularly for women (Robbins et al., 2011).

**Procreation and birth control.** The purpose of human sexual development from a biological standpoint is procreation. In general, adolescents are not considered to be in an ideal position to become parents due to a variety of factors: economic—teens do not have the financial means to provide for a child, social—teens are usually unmarried and may not have a strong social support network of family and friends, and developmental—teens are still growing into adulthood and may lack the emotional maturity and life experience to parent effectively (Mollborn, 2010; Crugnola et al., 2017).

Teens can and do become pregnant, however. The rate of teen pregnancy is higher in the United States than in other developed countries: one in eight adolescent girls in the United States will become pregnant before age 20. Birth control methods such as the pill or hormonal implants protect girls from unwanted pregnancy, whereas condoms help to prevent pregnancy and reduce the risk of sexually transmitted infections (STIs) for both partners. Both condom and hormonal contraceptive use have increased since the 1990s, but condom use is reportedly inconsistent: 40% of adolescents admitted to not having used a condom during their last sexual encounter (U.S. Department of Health and Human Services [HHS], Office of Adolescent Health [OAH], 2019).

**Sexually Transmitted Infections.** Adolescents and young adults ages 15–24 account for half of all new cases of STIs each year, for a total of 10 million new infections per year. Two in five sexually active adolescent girls will contract an STI. Rates of HIV exposure are very low among adolescents, with males making up 80% of all cases in youth aged 13–19 (HHS, OAH, 2019). The U.S. government's Centers for Disease Control and Prevention (CDC) recommends that all people ages 9–26 receive the human papilloma virus (HPV) vaccine to prevent the spread of the virus and to prevent later complications including some cancers (CDC, 2019).

**Dating Violence and Sexual Abuse.** According to the CDC (2019), violence between two adolescents in a close relationship can take several forms: physical violence (one partner uses physical force to injure, dominate, or control the other), sexual violence (forced sexual contact, through physical or other means of coercion), psychological aggression (verbal and nonverbal behavior that seeks to control or intimidate), and stalking (a pattern of surveillance, unwanted attention, and contact that causes fear or distress on the part of the recipient). Teen dating violence is common: 1 in 11 girls and 1 in 15 boys reported having experienced at least one form of dating violence (CDC, 2019).

Sexual violence in the United States is common among youth and young adults. One in three women and one in four men report having been the victim of sexual violence. One in three female rape victims reports that their attack occurred between the ages of 11 and 17. For male victims of rape, one in four were attacked between the ages of 11 and 17. Typically, the perpetrator is known to the victim. The negative effects of sexual violence impact more than victims' physical well-being; sexual violence survivors may experience mental and emotional problems, including posttraumatic stress disorder (PTSD), that significantly compromise the individual's ability to succeed in school and at work (CDC, 2019).

**Sexual abuse** in adolescence is defined as sexual activity in the absence of freely given consent (CDC, 2019). If the adolescent is a minor and the other party is a legal adult, the definition of sexual abuse includes all sexual acts; minors are not considered to be able to give legal consent. States may have different regulations as to the age at which a minor can give consent for sexual activity with an adult. Therefore, sexual abuse of minors by adults may occur without violence or coercion in the context of what both of the involved parties consider to be a mutually consenting relationship. Individuals with disabilities are more likely than their nondisabled peers to become victims of sexual abuse (Dryden et al., 2014).

## Impact of Disability on Sexual Development and Behavior

Puberty is a challenging time for most youth; numerous physical, cognitive, social, and emotional changes must be managed. For young people with disabilities, this period presents special challenges, particularly with respect to sexual development. Sexual maturation occurs at the same age for individuals with disabilities as without, except in the case of certain medical conditions such as Type 1 diabetes and cystic fibrosis, which may delay the onset of puberty in some individuals (Murphy & Young, 2005). Individuals with disabilities typically experience the same desire for knowledge about sexuality and for sexual experiences and romantic relationships as their peers without disabilities (Murphy & Young, 2005). However, the attitudes of others have significant effects on the sexual development of individuals with disabilities (Murphy & Elias, 2006; Sinclair et al., 2015).

Societal attitudes regarding individuals with disabilities as unattractive, asexual, or as potentially aggressive and unable to control sexual urges negatively impact the ability of youth with disabilities to attain positive sexual development (Murphy & Elias, 2006). Parents are often a child's primary resource for information about puberty and sexual development. Parents or caregivers of a child with a disability may neglect this aspect of their child's education due to lack of knowledge about sexuality in individuals with disabilities (Ballan, 2012). The increased level of care needed by some youth may cause parents to fail to notice and support the process of emotional maturation and separation that naturally occurs between parents and their adolescent children. Parents may be motivated by a desire to protect their child from rejection or exploitation, or they may simply not recognize their child's desire for romantic and sexual experiences. Dependence on others for physical assistance and transportation may cause some youth with disabilities to experience restricted access to age-appropriate social activities, further decreasing their opportunities to learn social skills, and limiting the pool of potential romantic partners they may encounter. Reliance on others for care may limit privacy and restrict opportunities for sexual encounters (Murphy & Young, 2005).

Other barriers to healthy sexual development for youth with disabilities include negative self-image and lack of confidence in relating to potential romantic partners. Youth with disabilities who perceive themselves to be physically different and therefore less desirable than their peers will be less confident about entering into romantic relationships. This in turn will limit their opportunities to gain knowledge about how to conduct themselves in relationships, further slowing their social and emotional development, and further impeding their ability to attract and maintain romantic partners (Brodwin & Frederick, 2010).

Negative societal perceptions about and treatment of people with disabilities can also impede healthy sexual development for adolescents with disabilities. Peers may socially reject youth with disabilities. School programs may segregate individuals with disabilities into separate classrooms or programs. In both cases, youth with disabilities miss out on opportunities to learn age-appropriate knowledge about sexual attitudes, language, and behaviors from their peers. This lack of knowledge persists into young adulthood, even when the individuals with disabilities are attending college (Oakes & Thorpe, 2019).

Barriers to age-appropriate knowledge about socially acceptable sexual behavior can cause significant problems for adolescents with disabilities. Kim (2010) identified five characteristics of individuals with disabilities that may make them more vulnerable to abuse: (a) dependence on others for personal care can provide opportunities for physical and sexual abuse, (b) lack of descriptive vocabulary to effectively report abuse can perpetuate abuse, (c) attendance at school programs that emphasize compliance increases vulnerability to exploitation, (d) social isolation and poor social skills decrease defenses against manipulation, and (e) lack of knowledge about sexual matters may contribute to youth not realizing that abuse is occurring. Girls with disabilities are two to four times as likely to be sexually abused than their neurotypical peers (Dryden et al., 2014). Both boys and girls with disabilities are more likely to be victims of sexual abuse, but boys with disabilities are 45–55% more likely to commit sexual assaults than nondisabled youth due to poor understanding of appropriate sexual behavior (Cambridge & Mellan, 2000).

## Effects of Specific Disabilities on Sexual Development and Behavior

### Intellectual and Developmental Disabilities

Adolescents with intellectual and developmental disabilities (IDD) experience the same physical development during puberty as their nondisabled peers. Youth with IDD exhibit similar levels of interest in emotional intimacy and sexuality as typically developing youth; however, they are often perceived as either childlike and asexual, or as sexually aggressive due to an inability to control sexual urges. Parents, teachers, and other caregivers often feel the need to protect individuals with IDD, leading to reduced social engagement and restricted opportunities to learn socially appropriate sexual behaviors from peers.

Individuals with IDD are often denied access to appropriate sexuality education. One study showed that while 50% of students with mild IDD received some form of sexuality education, typically by attending school-based sexuality education programs or classes with general education peers, only 16% of students with moderate to severe IDD attended such programs. Often, the communication abilities of the individual determined whether the student was provided with sex education: students with higher levels of communicative abilities were significantly more likely to receive sexuality instruction (Barnard-Brak et al., 2014). Additionally, much of the sexuality instruction provided to individuals with IDD is reactive; that is, it is provided only in response to some form of sexually inappropriate or problematic behavior on the part of the student (Tullis & Zangrillo, 2013).

Inadequate sex education for students with IDD means that these youth lack knowledge about reproductive physiology, contraception, and STIs, as well as having a poor understanding of appropriate social norms for sexual behavior and healthy relationships. Some individuals with IDD may not distinguish acceptable from unacceptable times and places for sexual behaviors, including masturbation. Some youth with IDD may experience difficulty interpreting interpersonal cues regarding whether romantic overtures or physical contact is wanted (Post et al., 2014). These youth may also lack awareness of the need to obtain and provide consent prior to engaging in **partnered sexual activities.** Language deficits may negatively impact their ability to effectively negotiate partnered sexual activities. The cognitive characteristics of individuals with IDD require that they receive explicit instruction with multiple opportunities to practice and receive feedback in order to ensure effective acquisition of appropriate sexual knowledge and behavior. Additionally, individuals with IDD may require additional instruction and rehearsal to promote generalization of skills across settings.

## Autism Spectrum Disorders

Individuals with autism spectrum disorders (ASD) desire romantic relationships and engage in sexual activity at rates similar to neurotypical adults. However, individuals with ASD report higher rates of difficulties with interpersonal relationships relative to people with other disability classifications, and they tend to exhibit higher rates of inappropriate sexual behavior than same-age peers without ASD. One factor that may contribute to interpersonal difficulty for individuals with autism is limited social communication skills. Since communication is an integral part of healthy romantic and sexual relationships, youth with ASD may struggle to make their own needs and preferences known, and they may have difficulty interpreting the verbal and nonverbal initiations and responses of their partner.

Although individuals with milder ASD symptomatology experience higher levels of success in romantic relationships relative to individuals with more severe ASD and ID (Hartmann et al., 2019), individuals with ASD are more likely to be victims of sexual victimization than other adolescents. Similar to their neurotypical peers, adolescents with ASD use web-based dating apps such as Tinder. Although the use of these apps has been linked to higher levels of risky sexual behavior (defined as multiple sexual partners, sexual activity without the use of a condom, and sexual activity with strangers [CDC, 2019]), living at home with parents is a protective factor for adolescents and young adults with ASD, as is greater parental supervision and limit-setting with respect to computer use (Hartmann et al., 2019).

In terms of sexuality education, individuals with ASD pursue and receive information about sexuality through many of the same sources as typically developing peers: parents, peers, sex education programs in school, and the internet. However, families of youth with ASD engage in less discussion of sexuality than neurotypical families. Additionally, communication and social difficulties may lead youth with ASD to rely more on impersonal and potentially problematic sources of information such as the internet and pornography (Hartmann et al., 2019). Due to difficulties with social perception, verbal and nonverbal communication, and interpersonal relationship skills characteristic of individuals with ASD, sexuality education for individuals with ASD should include explicit communication, social, and emotional regulation skills instruction as well as information regarding human biology, contraception, STIs, and healthy relationships. Furthermore, youth with ASD are five times more likely to identify as sexual minorities than neurotypical individuals (Hartmann et al., 2019); therefore sexual education for adolescents with ASD should make sure to specifically address issues regarding same-sex attraction and sexual identity.

## Physical Disabilities

There is a wide range of physically disabling conditions, some of which may seriously impede an individual's ability to engage in normative sexual activity. However, individuals with physical disabilities desire the same types of emotional and sexual connection as other youth. Adolescents with physical disabilities may experience issues with mobility, coordination, and physiological aspects of sexual response that may make sexual activity difficult to achieve. Additionally, negative perceptions about their own physical attractiveness on the part of the individual with a physical disability may significantly deter the individual from pursuing romantic relationships and sexual experiences. Like individuals with other disabilities, youth and young adults with physical disabilities may be overlooked as potential sexual and romantic partners by nondisabled peers.

Parents, teachers, and other caregivers may also neglect to address the sexual education needs of these youth out of concern for their physical and emotional well-being, erroneously believing that youth with physical disabilities are uninterested or unable to engage in romantic and sexual activities. Youth with physical disabilities require the same information about sexual and emotional health as other adolescents regarding human biology, pregnancy and contraception, prevention of STIs, and healthy relationship skills. In addition, they may also need specialized information pertinent to their unique physical circumstances.

## High-Incidence Disabilities

High-incidence disabilities (HID) include learning disabilities (LD), mild ID, emotional and behavioral disorders (EBD), and attention-deficit/hyperactivity disorder (ADHD). Adolescents with HID progress through the development of sexual maturity during puberty in the same manner as typical youth. Additionally, the relative differences in intellectual and behavioral performance between the various types of HID are only slightly significant: students with EBD tend to get suspended more frequently than those in other groups, and students with mild ID scored slightly lower than others on academic tests (Gage et al., 2012). Common areas of need across the population of students with HID related to sexual development are deficits in executive functioning related to impulse control, difficulty using and interpreting pragmatic language in social situations, trouble reading nonverbal interpersonal cues such as tone of voice and facial expressions, and the need for systematic, explicit instruction when learning new knowledge and skills.

Most youth with HID spend most of their school day in the general education setting and tend to have greater access to typical peers and social opportunities than students with other disabilities. However, students with HID experience peer rejection at higher rates than peers without disabilities and as a result may associate with negative peer groups in which risky or inappropriate behaviors are tolerated (Heward et al., 2017). This may limit the ability to engage in prosocial peer activities where they are able to learn appropriate social and sexual behaviors. Adolescents with HID attend school-based sexual education programs with typical peers when that kind of instruction is available; however, the teaching strategies and materials may not be suitable for their special learning needs. Youth with HID require the same information about sexual and emotional health as other adolescents regarding human biology, pregnancy and contraception, prevention of STIs, and healthy relationship skills, particularly in the area of communication and negotiation. This instruction should be systematic and explicit in order to ensure mastery.

# Summary

Youth with and without disabilities undergo a series of physical and cognitive changes during puberty. Their bodies become sexually mature, and they develop improved cognitive abilities. Additionally, they undertake the complex process of identity development, during which they experiment with a variety of behaviors, traits, and values until settling upon a coherent sense of self. Youth also begin thinking about and pursuing romantic relationships and sexual experiences during adolescence. Having a disability can affect a person's sexual development, both through characteristics related to the disability and through the perceptions, reactions, and treatment of others. Individuals with disabilities may experience limitations in opportunities to engage in romantic and sexual relationships with peers and are more vulnerable to sexual abuse than typical peers. Youth with disabilities are entitled to sexuality education that addresses their unique needs in order that they may have the information and skills necessary to become fully developed, sexually mature adults with the skills and knowledge they need to pursue meaningful and mutually satisfying romantic and sexual relationships.

# Resources

## Internet Resources

*The National Alliance to Advance Adolescent Health*: http://www.thenational alliance.org/

Advocacy organization providing resources and engaging in research and collaboration to promote integrated physical, behavioral, and sexual health care for adolescents, including transition to adult services.

*Scarleteen*: http://scarleteen.com

Founded in 1998, Scarleteen is an independent international sexuality education organization and website providing information and links to local services for young people ages 15–25.

*RespectAbility*: https://www.respectability.org/resources/sexual-education-resources/

Nonprofit organization led by individuals with disabilities working to fight stigma by promoting diverse and realistic portrayals of individuals with disabilities, advance opportunities for full community participation, and create leadership opportunities for individuals with disabilities. Website includes a section with links to videos, books, and other sexuality education materials.

*Your Child: Development and Behavioral Resources*: http://www.med.umich
.edu/1libr/yourchild/disabsex.htm

List of websites and other materials for sexuality education for youth with
disabilities, curated by the University of Michigan.

*Talking About Sex in Canadian Communities*: https://tasccalberta.com/sexuality
-and-disability/

Website with comprehensive information about sexuality for adolescents
with disabilities, including sexual development, personal hygiene, healthy
relationships, and safer sex practices.

## Books/Articles

*Sex and Relationships Education for Young People and Adults with Intellectual
Disabilities and Autism* by Jan Burns (Pavilion Publishing and Media Ltd.,
2019).

Practical guide to sexuality and relationship education for parents, caregivers, and teachers of students with ASD and co-occurring ID. https://www
.amazon.com/Relationships-Education-People-Intellectual-Disabilities/
dp/1912755521

*A Girl's Guide to Growing Up: Choices and Changes in the Tween Years* by
Terri Couwenhoven (Woodbine House, Inc., 2012).

Written at a third-grade reading level, describes physical and emotional
changes during puberty, appropriate for adolescents with disabilities. https://
www.amazon.com/Girls-Guide-Growing-Up-Choices/dp/1606130269

*A Boy's Guide to Growing Up: Choices and Changes in Puberty* by Terri Couwenhoven (Woodbine House, Inc., 2012).

Companion to the Girl's Guide above, written at a third-grade reading
level, describes physical and emotional changes during puberty, appropriate for adolescents with disabilities. https://www.amazon.com/Boys-Guide
-Growing-Up-Choices/dp/1606130897

*Boyfriends and Girlfriends: A Guide to Dating for People with Disabilities* by
Terri Couwenhoven, 2015.

Companion to the Boy's and Girl's Guides listed above. Covers topics
including determining who is an appropriate dating partner, how to read
others' behavior to assess mutual interest, how to ask someone out on a
date, and how to turn down a date, as well as how to handle rejection,
sexual feelings, and relationship difficulties. https://www.amazon.com/
Boyfriends-Girlfriends-Dating-People-Disabilities/dp/1606132555

## Videos

*Somebody to Love: Sex and Disability,* 2017

> Documentary
> Director: Anna Rodgers
> Examines love and sexuality in the lives of a variety of individuals across disability categories. https://www.amazon.com/Somebody-Love-Disability-Anna-Rodgers/dp/B01LWNIBP7

*Autism in Love,* 2015

> Documentary
> Director: Matt Fuller
> Depicts the romantic experiences of four individuals with ASD. https://www.youtube.com/watch?v=1eFa8Sk_SWo

Diverse City Press, Inc.

> DVDs with accompanying books designed to teach individuals with developmental disabilities about healthy and safe sexual practices. http://diverse-city.com/online-store-2/dvds/

Marsh Media

> Books and DVDs for adolescents with disabilities, as well as parents, nurses, and teachers, covering topics including development during puberty, personal hygiene, and personal safety. https://marshmedia.com/collections/puberty

# CHAPTER 7

# The Team
Jacquelyn Chovanes

*Alone we can do so little; together we can do so much.*

—Helen Keller

## Overview

This chapter provides a rationale and strategies for collaboration between parents and caregivers and professionals in the development and implementation of sexuality curricula for students with disabilities. Teaming enhances the quality of sexuality education for students with disabilities by integrating the varied expertise of stakeholders including teachers, parents and caregivers, therapists and related service providers, and medical professionals. Team members share knowledge, resources, and responsibilities, as well as accountability for outcomes. Through teaming, critical stakeholders are identified and recruited. Effective teaming practices include clear definition of roles, identifying goals and assigning tasks, setting a schedule and structure for meetings, developing a process for dealing with conflict, and monitoring and evaluating outcomes.

Readers will

- define teaming,
- state the reasons teaming is necessary when planning and implementing sexuality instruction for students with disabilities,
- describe how to build effective teams,
- list and describe the rationale for including various individuals as team members, and
- describe effective strategies for successful collaboration and teamwork.

# Case Study

*Mrs. Allen is a 6th-grade life skills teacher at Smallville Middle School. All 6th-grade students at Smallville Middle School receive sexuality education instruction in the general education setting. The teachers use a commercially available sexuality education curriculum chosen at the district level. Although Mrs. Allen's students are included in the health class in which the curriculum is taught, Mrs. Allen is concerned that the content may not address the specific needs of her students, many of whom have both cognitive and other disabilities. In addition, she worries that the instructional strategies and materials used in the curriculum may not be appropriate to the instructional level of her students. Mrs. Allen has some ideas about how the curriculum might be adapted to address her concerns. However, with a full teaching load and many other responsibilities, tackling the job of rewriting the adapted curriculum on her own seems daunting. Mrs. Allen decides to approach Mrs. Williams, the principal, to ask whether they might be able to create a team to work collaboratively on the curricular adaptations necessary to meet the needs of her students.*

# What Is a Team?

In education, a team is defined as "a set of interdependent individuals with unique skills and perspectives who interact directly to achieve their mutual goal of providing students with effective educational programs and services" (Friend & Cook, 2017, p. 134). In collaborative teaming, the group works together to achieve a set of common goals. Successful teams operate on principles of voluntary participation, parity between participants, and mutual goals (Knackendoffel, 2007). While one team member may assume the role of team leader, the contributions of all team members are valued equally. Team members share responsibilities, resources, and accountability for outcomes (King-Sears et al., 2015).

# Why Team for Comprehensive Sexuality Education for Students with Disabilities?

Aside from the fact that teaming and collaboration in the education of students with disabilities is required under the Individuals with Disabilities Education Improvement Act (IDEA) of 2004, **sexuality education** encompasses knowledge, skills, and behaviors that are relevant to stakeholders across school, home, and community environments. Sexuality is a fundamental part of human existence. Comprehensive sexuality education empowers adolescents to develop a positive image of themselves as sexual beings, to acquire the knowledge of how to engage in sexual behaviors safely and responsibly, and to learn the social and emotional skills they need to develop healthy relationships. Students with disabilities have unique individual needs and circumstances, and require specially tailored sexuality curriculum and instruction (McDaniels & Fleming, 2016). In order to provide comprehensive sexuality education to youth with disabilities, the information, perspectives, and strategies provided by parents, teachers, therapists, and other members of the multidisciplinary team, as well as community-based service providers, such as doctors, nurses, caregivers, and counselors, are critical to the quality, feasibility, and acceptability of the sex education curriculum.

Specific reasons to use a team approach to creating and implementing comprehensive sexuality education curricula include:

1. *Share knowledge and resources.* Each member of the team brings a specialized body of knowledge and set of experiences to the table (Knackendoffel, 2007). Teachers have expertise in instructional methods and content knowledge regarding adolescent development and human sexuality (Howard-Barr et al., 2005). Physical, occupational, speech/language, and orientation/mobility therapists can provide specialized knowledge related to motor, language, and adaptive behavior skills relevant to self-care and sexual functioning (Areskoug-Josefsson & Gard, 2015; Berman et al., 1999; Krantz et al., 2016; Murza, 2019). Counselors and psychologists may contribute input about social skills and emotional development in adolescence, with additional information pertinent to individuals with disabilities (Kuff et al., 2019). Medical professionals contribute critical information related to specific physiological needs as well as general sexual health care (Breuner & Mattson, 2016). Parents know their child's history, preferences, and important details about the child's functioning in home and community environments. Parents also share information about the family's beliefs and values, which helps to ensure the curriculum will be acceptable to families and community members (Barnard-Brak et al., 2014).

2. *Share responsibilities and maximize support to students, families, and educators.* Creating comprehensive sexuality education curricula and teaching it effectively to promote healthy sexual development and behavior in adolescents with disabilities is a multifaceted endeavor. Critical content needs to be selected, teaching methods chosen, and instructional materials created, edited, and published. Even when commercially available curricula are used, adaptations

will need to be made in order to make the program suitable for individuals with disabilities. Assessments must be designed to measure the effectiveness of the instruction. Instruction is then delivered, outcomes assessed, and the data used to determine whether modifications or supplemental teaching are needed. When stakeholders share their expertise, time, and talents to perform these steps, they are better able to create and deliver high-quality sexuality education to students with disabilities (Sinclair et al., 2017; Solone et al., 2020).

3. *Ensure appropriateness and acceptability of content.* Societal attitudes toward sex education for students with disabilities are compromised by misconceptions, including that students with disabilities are childlike and asexual and therefore do not need sex education, that youth with intellectual and developmental disabilities (IDD) are unable to comprehend and therefore will not benefit from sex education, and that providing sexual education to students with disabilities will encourage sexual activity (McDaniels & Fleming, 2016). Research shows that none of these is accurate, and that students with disabilities benefit from sex education by gaining increased knowledge about a range of sex-related topics, including dating and healthy relationship skills; physiological knowledge about menstruation, pregnancy, and sexually transmitted infections (STIs); how to recognize and report sexual abuse; and how to engage in masturbation and partnered sexual behaviors safely and responsibly (Saxe & Flanagan, 2014). However, it is important to consider the context in which sex education will be occurring. Certain topics, including masturbation, premarital sex, birth control, and abortion are likely to be viewed differently by team members (Ditchman et al., 2017). Familial and community beliefs, values, and attitudes toward sexuality deserve thoughtful consideration. Through mutually respectful dialogue and sharing of information and perspectives, team members can effectively advocate for the inclusion of sensitive content and ensure that the resulting curricula is both comprehensive and acceptable to all stakeholders.

4. *Enhance quality of instruction.* Teachers have expertise in the area of designing and delivering effective instruction. Special education teachers also have specialized knowledge and skills regarding teaching students with disabilities. However, other team members are likely to make valuable contributions to instructional quality as well (Solone et al., 2020). Doctors and nurses may provide critical information regarding effects of particular disability categories on physical and sexual development and function during puberty and young adulthood (Breuner & Mattson, 2016). Nurses, as well as physical

and occupational therapists, may have had experience teaching individuals with physical or cognitive disabilities how to perform personal hygiene tasks, and can help with task analysis and creating teaching routines for these and related skills (Krantz et al., 2016). Speech and language clinicians can review instructional language to ensure it is appropriate for the target population, and can suggest pre- or subskills to include in the curriculum to promote acquisition and comprehension of content (Ehren & Whitmire, 2009). Social workers and counselors can provide general information about adolescent social and emotional development and specific information regarding how peers and the media influence adolescent behavior, and can suggest effective strategies to use when discussing sensitive topics with adolescents (Romano & Kachgal, 2004). Parents are often experts in how their children learn and can provide critical feedback regarding the efficacy of specific instructional strategies, in addition to suggestions for individualization of instruction for particular students and strategies for ensuring generalization of knowledge and skills across home, school, and community environments (McDaniels & Fleming, 2016; Staples & Diliberto, 2010).

5. *Promote generalization of knowledge and skills.* Students with disabilities learn better when they are provided with opportunities to rehearse and practice new knowledge and skills across settings—that is, when what they learn in school is repeated and reinforced at home and in the community (Gage et al., 2012; Schaafsma et al., 2015). McDaniels and Fleming (2016) suggest that **ecological validity**—the extent to which students are able to use knowledge and skills gained in instructional settings outside of the classroom at home and in the community—is a critical factor in assessing the quality of comprehensive sexuality curricula. Teaming allows stakeholders in school, home, and community environments to share and communicate the same set of assumptions, principles, information, and strategies to students with disabilities. This type of reinforcement promotes purposeful learning and generalization of critical skills and content taught in the comprehensive sexuality education curriculum across all relevant settings.

## Building Effective Teams

The first step in building an effective team is to identify the critical stakeholders (Bambara & Kunsch, 2014). Often overlooked, but of central importance to the team, is the student or group of students to whom the curriculum is targeted. Detailed analysis of the needs and capabilities of the target population is necessary to ensure relevant content and skills, and feasible instructional methods (Sinclair et al., 2017). Individuals with disabilities can effectively communicate their own interests, needs, and preferences regarding sexuality education (Graff et al., 2018), and can make valuable contributions to the creation and implementation of comprehensive sexuality education curricula.

Parents and caregivers are important members of the team, particularly for students with IDD. Caregivers and parents have detailed knowledge of the youth's physical, cognitive, emotional, and behavioral strengths and needs (Sinclair et al., 2017). Additionally, they can contribute pertinent information regarding the physical and social environments students spend time in outside of school. Using this information, the team can plan for generalization by explicitly teaching students effective strategies to use at home and in the community to promote healthy sexual behavior and positive relationships. Furthermore, parents and caregivers can inform the rest of the team about the attitudes, beliefs, and values of the student's family and the surrounding community to ensure that the resulting sexuality education program meets the needs of the students and the expectations of the family and community (Ditchman et al., 2017; Solone et al., 2020). *(For a detailed treatment of family systems and how they contribute to sexuality education for students with disabilities, see Chapter 12.)*

The teacher's role is to synthesize the contributions of other team members into an effective instructional program (Sinclair et al., 2017). This includes overseeing the creation of instructional materials, designing assessments that are aligned with the course content and objectives, delivering instruction that meets the objectives, and conducting assessments to determine the effects of instruction on students' knowledge and behavior. Teachers of students with disabilities are often assisted by paraprofessionals, commonly referred to as teacher's aides. Paraprofessionals can be trained to effectively instruct students in many content and skill areas (Walker et al., 2020). Paraprofessionals should work under the direction and supervision of a licensed teacher or other certified clinician, such as an occupational therapist. The role of the paraprofessional is to assist the teacher in delivering instruction, typically through monitoring students' guided and independent practice, to support positive behavior, and to administer assessments (Brock & Carter, 2013). Paraprofessionals rarely have the training needed to effectively create curricula or plan instruction; however, their expertise in working directly with students can be invaluable in informing instructional planning and making curricular adaptations (Carter & Hughes, 2006; Walker et al., 2020).

The role of the administrator may be somewhat removed from instructional delivery, but it is critical nonetheless (Pugach & Winn, 2011). Administrators provide organizational structure that allows time for collaborative teaming and co-planning of instruction, and material support for curricular materials and space in which to meet and work. Administrators can also serve as liaisons between teachers and other team members, such as community-based professionals, particularly in the early stages of team formation. Finally, administrators can serve as mediators when conflicts arise between team members, and they can help to refocus attention on common goals (Rafoth & Foriska, 2006).

Psychologists, social workers, and other school or community-based counselors can provide insight into social and emotional aspects of adolescent development. They can explain the ways in which peers and the media influence adolescent behavior. They can use their clinical experience to highlight the concerns and day-to-day experiences of youth with disabilities to increase the relevance of the sexuality curricula to its target audience—adolescents with disabilities. These professionals can also provide guidance and offer specific strategies to lessen anxiety—on the part of the instructors as well as the students—regarding talking about sensitive topics. They can use their professional knowledge and expertise to establish effective communication, help resolve conflicts, and sustain working relationships between group members, thus improving the group dynamic as a whole (Romano & Kachgal, 2004).

Therapists from many disciplines may work with students with disabilities, including speech/language, occupational, physical, and behavior specialists. Depending upon the area of expertise, therapists and clinicians may offer insights into specific content and strategies worthy of inclusion in the curriculum, as well as ways in which to teach content and skills effectively. For example, a speech/language clinician can contribute knowledge about how to teach the use of pragmatic language skills to students with autism spectrum disorder during role-playing exercises where students practice giving and receiving explicit consent. An occupational therapist might provide valuable input into how to teach an individual with a cognitive disability to distinguish appropriate from inappropriate touches, as well as how to perform self-care skills related to personal hygiene and sexual activities. A physical therapist might recommend exercises or assistive devices to aid individuals with physical disabilities in achieving greater access to typical sexual activities. Behavior specialists can assist individuals in learning self-monitoring and emotional regulation skills to promote responsible behavior and healthy relationships (Ehren & Whitmire, 2009; Krantz et al., 2016).

Medical professionals, including doctors, nurses, physician assistants, and nurse practitioners, can contribute valuable information regarding the physiological effects of specific disabilities on human sexual development and behavior. They can also offer insight into the capability of students with physical disabilities or other health conditions to engage in typical sexual behaviors, and what medical treatments or therapies might aid in enhancing sexual function in individuals with disability-related sexual dysfunction. Furthermore, they possess expertise in the biological and physiological aspects of birth control, pregnancy, and abortion, and reducing the transmission of STIs through safer sexual practices (Berman et al., 1999; Greenwood & Wilkinson, 2013).

The individuals identified above as potential team members are likely to be busy professionals with many competing demands on their time. One element critical to successful teaming is voluntary participation (Friend & Cook, 2017). Unlike an individualized education program (IEP) team, in which participation is regulated by law (IDEA, 2004), teaming for instructional planning for sexuality education for students with disabilities is noncompulsory, unless the student has specific goals related to sexuality in their IEP. In most cases, the sexuality curriculum team will not plan individualized interventions for specific students but will instead work to prepare a sexuality curriculum that will be relevant and accessible to students with disabilities. In all cases with teaming, however, a successful and productive group must be made up of individuals who believe in and are willing to work cooperatively to achieve the group goals. In order to create interest and solicit participation on the part of prospective team members, a rationale for participation should be provided. The person serving as the initial team leader, typically the teacher or administrator, explains to each prospective member the goals of the process (Bambara & Chovanes, in press). The goals of creating and implementing effective sexuality curricula for students with disabilities are to improve overall life satisfaction for individuals with disabilities by giving them the knowledge and skills they need to engage in age-appropriate sexual behavior and to develop healthy relationships, to reduce negative consequences of risky sexual behavior, and to protect individuals with disabilities from sexual abuse and exploitation (Treacy et al., 2018). Finally, the team leader will explain why the individual's participation is critical to achieving the goals.

*Mrs. Williams listens to Mrs. Allen's concerns about the content and the instructional materials and methods used in the general sexuality education curriculum and agrees that adaptations would likely benefit the students in Mrs. Allen's life skills class.*

*She supports Mrs. Allen's suggestion of creating a team to work on the adaptations. Mrs. Williams suggests including at least one parent or caregiver of a student in Mrs. Allen's class on the team. Mrs. Allen mentions that Mr. Rios, the occupational therapist, Ms. Washington, the physical therapist, Mrs. Davenport, the school nurse, and Mr. Lewis, the paraprofessional in Mrs. Allen's life skills classroom, would all offer valuable contributions to the team. Mrs. Williams points out that the school social worker, Mr. Henry, and Mr. Booker, the speech therapist, should also be invited to participate. Mrs. Williams agrees to allow Mrs. Allen and the team to use school supplies and equipment to create adapted curricular materials and offers the faculty conference room as a meeting place.*

*Mrs. Allen sends an email invitation to each of the individuals she and Mrs. Williams identified as possible group members. Mrs. Allen is glad when all of the educators responded affirmatively to her invitation. Additionally, Mr. Johnson, the parent of one of her students, agreed to participate. Mrs. Allen visits Mrs. Wallace, the health teacher, to obtain a copy of the teacher's manual and students' materials, which she will review prior to the first team meeting.*

Once team members have been recruited, the team meets and decides upon role definitions for each member. The goal of role definition is to make the best use of the expertise and the most efficient use of the time of each team member. The definition of roles should be clear to avoid confusion and conflict. For example, who will chair the meetings and act as the general team leader? This is a critical role; the team leader is responsible for maintaining focus and following the agenda during meetings (Bambara & Chovanes, in press). The team leader should model the acceptance of differences, respectful communication, and collaborative problem solving that are expected of all team members (Bambara & Chovanes, in press). It is the responsibility of the team leader to step in when other members violate the expectations regarding respectful, productive collaboration. For example, if one team member dismisses another's suggestion by saying, "That will never work," the team leader should help to reframe the discussion by asking the respondent to clarify what about the idea seems unworkable, "You seem to have strong feelings about this, Bob; can you tell us more about why you think Maria's idea won't work?" In this way, the team leader shifts the focus from Bob's dismissal of Maria's contribution to a discussion of the pros and cons of the suggestion. The team can then use the problem-solving process to evaluate the pros and cons of each of the ideas to identify a workable solution.

Another aspect of teamwork that is related to role definition is the division of labor. How will critical tasks be divided? Which team members will be recognized as leaders in particular areas (e.g., topic and content selection, resource identification, lesson plan writing, material creation and publication)—or will these responsibilities be subdivided among individuals according to areas of expertise (e.g., the occupational therapist selects content, identifies resources, plans instruction, and creates materials for all topics related to self-care and personal hygiene)? It is important to remember that members without professional training in particular areas may still have valuable insights and practical contributions to make. Logistical duties are also important. Who will record the minutes of the meeting and ensure that housekeeping tasks, such as keeping records and sharing documents, are completed? Every team must work out an arrangement for assigning roles and duties that suits their own unique situation. Teams should be responsive to feedback from individual members and may renegotiate roles as needed.

*On the day of the meeting, Mrs. Allen welcomes the team members. She begins by explaining the purpose of the team: to create an adapted sexuality curriculum for the students in her life skills class. The team then discusses roles. It is agreed that Mrs. Allen will be the team leader, and that each of the other members will take responsibility for tasks that fall within their area of expertise. They agree that Ms. Washington, the physical therapist, will participate on a consultative basis, but will not need to attend every meeting because none of the students in Mrs. Allen's class has a physical disability. Mrs. Allen will assess the curriculum and plan instructional modifications, with consultation and input from the speech and occupational therapists and nurse, who will help by suggesting specific modifications and strategies and will create specialized lessons and materials as needed. Mrs. Allen will also design the assessments to measure how well the students learned the skills and content. Mr. Lewis will be the timekeeper and notetaker during meetings and will be responsible for creating copies of the instructional materials designed by Mrs. Allen and the therapists. Mr. Johnson will provide information about home and community settings to promote generalization of skills and to ensure acceptability of the curriculum by parents and the community.*

# Working Together: Strategies for Successful Collaboration and Teamwork

The first strategy used in creating a productive **team** is to establish trust among team members. Critical factors in establishing trust are effective communication, acceptance, and respect. Effective communication begins with listening and interacting effectively. Ground rules for participation in group meetings should be established to ensure that all group members have the opportunity to contribute their ideas and perspectives. Sexuality is a topic that is universal yet associated with a wide range of beliefs and values. In order to function effectively as a team, it is critical that members communicate authentically and unambiguously. As a means to create the atmosphere of safety and respect needed for authentic communication, all members of the group should listen attentively, taking care to keep their body language and facial expressions positive or neutral. Team members should make every effort to communicate succinctly when speaking and to avoid interrupting others. Professionals should avoid specialized jargon in order to ensure authentic understanding for all team members (Knackendoffel et al., 2018). Team members will disagree at times; this is to be expected. However, each individual should acknowledge the validity of other members' points of view. Questioning strategies can be used to promote mutual understanding in the event of a disagreement (Knackendoffel et al., 2018). ("Mr. Rios, I heard you say you're frustrated that you are the only person working on creating the materials for the lessons on personal hygiene, and that you understood that Mrs. Davenport would be helping with this task; is that what you meant? Or would you like to clarify so we better understand your position?"). Using open-ended questions can elicit important information about individual perspectives ("Mrs. Davenport, please tell us what you understood your assigned tasks to be."). Finally, checking for mutual understanding can ensure that all parties feel heard and respected: "So does everyone agree that Mr. Rios will finish creating the materials with Mr. Lewis's help, Mrs. Allen will design the assessments, and the team will meet next week to review the completed items?" (King-Sears et al., 2015).

Effective communication promotes the acceptance and respect among team members that is necessary for productive teaming. Team members should be sensitive to the diverse knowledge, experiences, and perspectives of others. **Prejudgment** (i.e., coming to conclusions before hearing what other team members have to say), and **stereotyping** (i.e., forming opinions about a person based upon general characteristics rather than observations of the individual's attitudes and behavior), are to be avoided (Knackendoffel et al., 2018). When there are significant differences in opinions and values between team members, steps to achieve bridge-building should be undertaken (adapted from King-Sears et al., 2015, pp. 82–83):

1. Identify the issues in disagreement (example: some group members do not want to include information about hormonal birth control in the curriculum).
2. Identify all parties' underlying values relative to the issues (example: members in favor believe students with disabilities have the right to know all of their options with respect to preventing pregnancy and want students with disabilities to have effective protection from pregnancy as a result of abuse or faulty decision making; members opposed have religious objections to the use of hormonal birth control and believe that providing the information will encourage irresponsible behavior, so they prefer abstinence-only instruction).
3. Discuss all sets of beliefs (calmly and with respect for different viewpoints).
4. Collaborate by focusing on shared values and goals (the shared goal is protection from negative consequences of unwanted pregnancy; compromise can be achieved by including information about hormonal birth control in the curriculum, along with explicit practice in refusal to consent to sexual activity, and by affirming parents' prerogative to supplement the school curriculum with home-based instruction in religious values regarding the use of birth control versus practicing abstinence [Guilamo-Ramos & Bouris, 2009]).

*Mrs. Allen presents the elements of the curriculum, which includes information about the physical and emotional changes of puberty, personal hygiene, healthy relationships, and safe, appropriate sexual practices. At first, Mr. Johnson is uncomfortable with the idea of including information about sexual intercourse and masturbation. "Kids with disabilities don't need to know about that," he says decisively. Mr. Rios, the occupational therapist, replies, "Of course they do, let's not be naive!" To redirect the conversation in a more productive direction, Mrs. Allen says, "Mr. Johnson, please tell us about your concerns with providing this information to our students." Mr. Johnson shares his thoughts that students with disabilities will not experience the same sexual feelings as other adolescents; therefore they only need to know how to care for their hygiene needs and how to protect themselves from unwanted advances. Mrs. Allen then asks the group to share their expertise regarding the sexual development of students with disabilities.*

*Mr. Johnson is surprised to learn that adolescents with disabilities experience the same sexual desires as other teens, and that many also engage in sexual activity similar to their nondisabled peers. He agrees that the curriculum should include instruction about sexual feelings and appropriate ways to express them. He shares that he is now worried about his son engaging in inappropriate or risky behaviors. Mrs. Allen reassures him, "I appreciate your concerns, Mr. Johnson. I will be sure to involve you when I work on the materials for the lessons having to do with how to manage sexual feelings appropriately. Does that alleviate some of your concerns?"*
*"Yes, it does somewhat. Thank you," Mr. Johnson affirms.*

The second strategy used in effective teaming is identifying common goals (Bambara & Kunsch, 2014). With respect to creating and implementing high-quality sexuality education curricula for students with disabilities, some general instructional goals are helping students with disabilities to:

1. understand the physiological changes they will experience during puberty;
2. understand the social and emotional changes they will experience during puberty;
3. develop a healthy self-image and sense of identity;
4. learn healthy relationship skills, including social skills, self-advocacy, and how to give and receive consent for sexual activity; and
5. understand safe and responsible sexual practices, including preventing pregnancy and the transmission of STIs. (Blanchett & Wolfe, 2002; Sullivan & Caterino, 2008; Wolfe et al., 2019)

*The team brainstorms ideas about what the purpose of their adapted sexuality curriculum should be. After some discussion, they decide that their shared goals will include teaching students:*

1. *the information and skills they need to successfully manage the physical and emotional changes of puberty, including the development of a positive sexual identity;*
2. *self-advocacy and healthy interpersonal relationship skills; and*
3. *safe sexual practices, including information related to preventing pregnancy and STIs, and appropriate management of sexual feelings and behavior.*

In order to achieve these goals, the third strategy in effective teaming is to divide various objectives into manageable tasks (Bambara & Kunsch,

2014). The team should decide who will be responsible for completing each task, when the tasks should be completed, and how the members will communicate with each other to receive feedback and support during the process. Technology can be very useful during the working stages. Quick questions or progress notes may be easily communicated through email or text. Video-conferencing platforms such as Zoom or Skype can be used for more substantive topics requiring back-and-forth dialogue. Communication preferences should be negotiated and may be individualized based upon members' specific needs (Knackendoffel et al., 2018). For example, an itinerant occupational therapist may prefer email, whereas a parent without reliable internet access may prefer printed notes sent home with their child.

> *Mr. Johnson advocates for the inclusion of explicit instruction in talking to parents before engaging in sexual activity, and Mrs. Allen agrees to create a lesson for that skill in addition to the other lessons she is preparing. Mr. Henry, the social worker, stresses the importance of self-advocacy training, and offers to work with Mr. Booker, the speech therapist, to create specific lessons to teach students to say no to unwanted advances, with practice in reporting these experiences to parents or teachers. Mr. Rios and Mrs. Davenport pair up to work on the personal hygiene lessons. Mr. Lewis will assist in creating materials as requested by other team members.*

The fourth strategy used in effective teaming is to set a schedule and structure for team meetings (Bambara & Kunsch, 2014). Team meetings serve the functions of promoting effective, detailed communication, allowing opportunities for feedback and support, and holding team members accountable for meeting deadlines. It is important to set both a schedule and a structure for team meetings (Bambara & Kunsch, 2014). Regular meeting times make it easier for members to plan to attend, and a structure for organizing the meeting promotes efficient use of members' time. For the most comprehensive collaborative work, in-person team meetings are optimal; however, whole-group meetings can also be conducted via Zoom or Skype. Using online meeting platforms can facilitate participation by eliminating travel time, allowing members to remotely attend an in-person meeting they otherwise would have missed. Meetings can also be video- and audio-recorded, allowing absent members to catch up on what they missed (Knackendoffel et al., 2018). One possibility for meeting structure would be to appoint a meeting chair, who solicits input from members prior to the meeting and sets the meeting agenda. The chair is responsible for directing the meeting and assuring that the agenda is followed, but also ensuring that all members have the opportunity to share information and voice concerns (Bambara & Kunsch, 2014). Old business is revisited as needed, progress on ongoing work is presented by each member, questions and feedback are discussed, and then new tasks are assigned, with specific expectations as to what, when, and by whom the work will be done. An additional consideration in scheduling is whether the team may split into smaller working groups (Bambara & Kunsch, 2014). These small groups may be assigned specific tasks and may meet between whole-group meetings to work together, to review and give feedback on completed tasks, and to provide support and encouragement to ensure the timely completion of assigned tasks that then may be presented during the whole-group meetings. Smaller groups may be well suited to initially identifying and discussing potential problems that may then be brought to the whole group (Bambara & Kunsch, 2014).

*The team decides that biweekly meetings will be held in person. The team agrees that email will be used primarily for between-meeting communications, but that individual team members working collaboratively on particular tasks may determine their own communication methods, including Zoom and texting. Mrs. Allen sets an agenda for the meeting where, after initial greetings, each team member will provide an update on their progress. The feedback from the team members is positive: Mr. Johnson approved of the lesson Mrs. Allen created to teach students to talk to their parents about their sexual feelings; Mr. Henry and Mr. Booker had created a series of four lessons teaching how to respond to sexual or romantic overtures and how to report troubling incidents to trusted adults; and Mr. Rios and Mrs. Davenport were halfway done with the personal hygiene lessons. Mr. Johnson thought that the lessons were thorough and detailed but is concerned that his son will have difficulty remembering all of the steps in the showering routine. The team agrees that this will likely be the case for many students. They begin the process of collaborative problem solving to find a solution.*

Collaborative problem solving is the fifth strategy used in effective teaming (Bambara & Kunsch, 2014; Knackendoffel, 2007). Conflict and disagreement are inevitable in any relationship, and working teams are no exception. Creating and implementing high-quality sexuality education curricula for students with disabilities is a complex process with many choices to be made. The team will need to make decisions about scheduling, resource allocation, and role and task assignment, not to mention prioritizing skills and content, instructional methods, and instructional materials used in the curriculum. Best-practice guidelines for teaming recommend that a problem-solving framework should be used to promote effective conflict resolution (King-Sears et al., 2015). This framework includes the following steps (King-Sears et al., 2015, pp. 94–103):

1. Identify the problem: The team determines and defines the critical issues of concern, and prioritizes them in order of importance, tackling the most pressing one first. Example: A consistent meeting time convenient for all team members cannot be identified.
2. Generate possible solutions: The team brainstorms as many solutions as possible, recording all ideas without judgment or criticism. Example: Meet after school, ask the administrator to reschedule faculty morning bus duty to allow meetings before school, but still within the working school day.
3. Note pros and cons of the solutions: The team respectfully discusses the merits and flaws of each of the proposed solutions, eliminating the ones that will not work, until only viable options remain. Example: Meeting after school violates the faculty contract, paraprofessionals do not receive hourly pay for after-school duties, parents need to be home to greet the school bus; all faculty and staff are scheduled for morning bus duty three mornings per week, but the administrator could schedule morning bus duty assignments to make sure team members have one common morning free to meet with the team.
4. Identify a solution: By consensus, the team selects the best of the viable options. Example: Ask the administrator to reschedule faculty morning bus duty to allow meetings before school.
5. Target an action plan: The team collaboratively designs a plan to implement the selected solution, designating who will implement the plan and including a timeline for implementation. Example: The team decides that the teacher will approach the principal this week to request the morning bus duty scheduling change; the teacher will send out a text and an email reporting the designated meeting time for the following week.
6. Evaluate the plan and make needed changes: The team also specifies a time, typically the next whole-group meeting, to review progress and determine whether the plan was successful in correcting the problem, or whether further modifications are needed. Example: At the next team meeting the following week, the team records which members are present, and notes whether any absences are due to

scheduling conflicts. All members are present, so the plan is not in need of further modification. (King-Sears et al., 2015)

*Mrs. Allen names the problem: some of the personal hygiene routines include many steps and might be difficult for students to remember. Mr. Rios suggests breaking the routines into smaller chunks. Mrs. Allen suggests that they keep the lessons as written but add visual cues in the form of photos and drawings to illustrate the steps in the personal hygiene routines. The team discusses the two options and decides that although it is true that students might learn abbreviated routines more easily, it would be more efficient to teach each routine as one whole process. Therefore they decide to use photos and drawings as visual supports to help students remember the steps. Mr. Lewis volunteers to take the photos, and questions whether he should laminate the cards with photos and drawings that will be used in the personal hygiene lessons. All agree that would be a good idea. They will use direct observation of the students performing the routines to assess the effectiveness of the lessons using visual supports once instruction begins, and based on student response, they could break the routines into smaller sub-skills later.*

The final strategy in effective teaming involves monitoring and evaluating outcomes (Bambara & Kunsch, 2014). As stated above, the goals of sexuality education curricula for students with disabilities are helping students with disabilities to:

1. understand the physiological changes they will experience during puberty;
2. understand the social and emotional changes they will experience during puberty;
3. develop a healthy self-image and sense of identity;
4. learn healthy relationship skills, including social skills, self-advocacy, and how to give and receive consent for sexual activity; and
5. understand safe and responsible sexual practices, including preventing pregnancy and the transmission of STIs. (Blanchett & Wolfe, 2002; Sullivan & Caterino, 2008; Wolfe et al., 2019)

The team designates sub-tasks for each goal, selects or designs criteria based upon the sub-tasks for each goal, and then applies the criteria to the progress reported by the members responsible for the sub-tasks. For example, sub-tasks for the goal of helping students with disabilities to understand the physiological changes they will experience during puberty might include:

a. making a list of physiological changes for boys and girls during puberty;
b. determining the critical content and skills (if applicable; one example would be personal hygiene skills for menstruation) associated with each of the listed items;
c. creating lessons designed to teach the critical content and skills for each item (may differentiate based on individual need; for example, boys would need to learn about menstruation as a physiological process but would not need to learn the personal hygiene skills of using pads or tampons, whereas girls would need both);
d. creating instructional materials to be used in the lessons, including visual aids, task analyses for specific skills, procedural facilitators, graphic organizers, etc.; and
e. creating assessments to evaluate the effectiveness of the instruction by measuring student acquisition of content and performance of skills (setting performance criteria to determine mastery of skills and content).

The team would decide which members would be responsible for each of the sub-tasks. The responsible parties would complete the tasks and report back to the team. It is critical to the morale of the team to celebrate successes and to publicly acknowledge the contributions of individual members (Bambara & Kunsch, 2014). When goals and criteria have not been met, or when scheduling and structure are not meeting the needs of all members, the team collaborates using the problem-solving steps to adapt and revise procedures as needed.

*After several weeks of working on the adaptations to the sexuality education curriculum, the team meets to review the completed lessons. Because the whole team has been meeting weekly to provide feedback to each sub-team on their work, the lessons and materials are approved as ready for implementation. Mrs. Allen thanks everyone for their contributions, saying, "I am looking forward to implementing the curriculum with our students. I will use the assessments and checklists I created to measure how the students respond to instruction. Let's meet again in two weeks and I will provide a progress report. At that time, we can decide if any modifications are needed. For now, though, let's take a moment to congratulate ourselves on a job well done, thanks to our effective teamwork!"*

# Summary

Teaming promotes collaboration between parents and professionals in the development and implementation of sexuality curricula for students with disabilities. Integrating the varied expertise of stakeholders including teachers, parents, therapists, and medical professionals enhances the quality of sexuality education for students with disabilities. Team members share knowledge, resources and responsibilities, and accountability for outcomes. Effective teaming practices include clear definition of roles, identifying goals and assigning tasks, setting a schedule and structure for meetings, developing a process for dealing with conflict, and monitoring and evaluating outcomes.

# Resources

## Internet Resources

*U.S. Department of Health and Human Services: Children with Disabilities: Teaming and Collaboration*: https://eclkc.ohs.acf.hhs.gov/children-disabilities/article/teaming-collaboration

Contains several articles and links designed to inform families of children with disabilities about the opportunities for and benefits of team-based services for children with disabilities. Includes learning modules to teach parents and professionals to use effective communication practices.

*High-Leverage Practices 1, 2 & 3: Collaboration with Professionals, Facilitating Effective Meetings, and Collaborating with Families*: https://highleveragepractices.org/collaboration/

Downloadable pdfs with instructions and guidance supporting effective teaming among professionals and families to promote achievement for students with disabilities.

*The New Sex Ed; from Teaching Tolerance*: https://www.tolerance.org/magazine/summer-2016/the-new-sex-ed

Article that explains why inclusive, comprehensive sexuality education is needed; includes resources for elementary-level sexuality education focusing on healthy relationships and pro-social behavior.

*Sexuality Education Program from Children's Hospital of Chicago*: https://www.luriechildrens.org/en/specialties-conditions/sexuality-education-program/

Age- and grade-level programs to teach personal safety, healthy relationships, gender issues, development in puberty, reproduction, sexual health, and specialized support for LGBTQ students.

*First Impressions*: https://stanfield.com/product/first-impressions/

Commercially available curriculum that incorporates video modeling (DVDs included) to teach hygiene and grooming skills.

## Books

Friend, M., & Cook, L. (2021). *Interactions: Collaboration skills for school professionals* (9th ed.). Pearson.

King-Sears, M. E., Janney, R., & Snell, M. E. (2015). *Collaborative Teaming* (3rd ed.). Paul H. Brookes.

Knackendoffel, A., Detmer, P., & Thurston, L. P. (2018). *Collaborating, consulting, and working in teams for students with special needs* (8th ed.). Pearson.

## Videos

*Teaching in the Inclusive Classroom: Collaboration and Team Teaching from QEP Video Courses for Teachers*

Illustrates concepts and methods of collaboration for including students with disabilities in general education settings; useful for the information on co-planning and implementing differentiated instruction. https://www.you tube.com/watch?v=E2eZwku-QyM

*Teacher Collaboration: Spreading Best Practices School-Wide*

Depicts the process of team building and how faculty learned to appreciate the benefits of teaming. https://www.youtube.com/watch?v=85HUM HBXJf4

*Time Matters: Teacher Collaboration for Learning and Leading*

Examples from four successful collaborative schools to show how to maximize teacher productivity and student achievement through effective time management. https://www.youtube.com/watch?v=Ex1zfl-MsDk

*Best Practices: Collaborative Teams*

Delineates the effective and intentional use of assessment in collaborative planning and instruction. https://www.youtube.com/watch?v=_-_Ep4z5 RkQ

*Key Elements for Effective Teacher Collaboration*

Overview of best practices in collaborative teaming for educators. https:// www.youtube.com/watch?v=leB13CFt8a8

# CHAPTER 8

# Individualized Education Program and Sexuality Education

Lisa Goran, David F. Bateman, Heather Hess, and Amy Finn

*Jerry is a 9th-grade student with autism spectrum disorder (ASD) attending Central High School. He readily initiates activities of interest but is easily distracted and requires redirection and prompts to remain on task. Jerry receives instruction in a special education classroom for content classes and receives support in a general education environment for electives. He is friendly with his classmates, particularly with girls, and has expressed a desire to learn more about dating and relationships. Jerry's parents indicate they would like him to receive instruction related to sexuality education, because he recently has had some inappropriate interactions with female friends.*

## Overview

This chapter will discuss the necessary elements to incorporate comprehensive sexuality education in the individualized education program (IEP). It will review the required components of the IEP and the importance of input from stakeholders, including teachers, service providers, and the student. Specific focus will be on the present level of performance, goals, and service delivery options, with attention to how these connect to transition planning.

Readers will

- cover the components of the IEP, focusing on how the present level statement directs the other components;

- cover annual goals and objectives and how they tie to needs identified in the present level statement, and write them to be observable, measurable, and challenging;
- provide examples of goals, tied to the present level statement;
- cover the necessary supports and services as a part of the implementation of the IEP; and
- conclude with resources on how to stay informed related to writing legally defensible IEP goals and objectives.

# Components of the IEP

There are many required components of an **individualized education program (IEP)**. At its core, the IEP focuses on the needs and strengths of the student as identified in the **present levels of academic achievement and functional performance (PLAAFP)**. This section of the IEP serves as the basis for the entire document, identifying the prioritized areas of need (Goran et al., 2020). For students of transition age, sexuality education may be an area of identified need and an important part of the plan for instruction. The PLAAFP is developed by the IEP team and must include adequate detail to lay the foundation for the rest of the individualized education program, including meaningful and ambitious goals and specially-designed instruction, services, and supports (Goran et al., 2020; Graves & Graves, 2013; Harmon et al., 2020).

## Present Levels of Academic Achievement and Functional Performance (PLAAFP)

The PLAAFP provides a descriptor of a student's present ability levels, skills, strengths, and limitations—academically, socially, and in terms of physical/motor ability. By regulation, the PLAAFP is defined as "a statement of the child's present levels of academic achievement and functional performance including—(i) How the child's disability affects the child's involvement and progress in the general education curriculum (i.e., the same curriculum as for nondisabled children)" (IDEA regulations, 2012). In plain language, it is intended to explain how the student's individual needs and differences affect their ability to learn from the general education curriculum. The PLAAFP creates a picture of a student at a particular time and place in their education. An effective and meaningful PLAAFP must include four parts:

1. individual factors to consider,
2. current performance/baseline data,

3. the impact of the exceptionality, and
4. the resulting needs of the student.

These components should range from very broad to very specific and should include information not only about a student's academic achievement, but also about their functional performance. Harmon and colleagues (2020) provide a worksheet to help organize the collection of this information to create the PLAAFP and guide the design of ambitious goals and effective instructional services and supports. For a more comprehensive review, please see the Harmon et al. (2020) article on present levels.

To further explain the four parts, *Factors to Consider* might include testing and evaluation data such as cognitive performance, functional academic achievement, motor ability assessment, speech and language assessments, and/or evaluation of adaptive behavioral skills. Intellectual limitations/disabilities, developmental delays, etc. pose special considerations when designing a meaningful and individualized PLAAFP statement; these factors will help to direct, as in the case of sexuality education, what is the most appropriate approach and level of instruction in this content area.

*Current Performance/Baseline Data* might include a student's learning strengths and needs, parent/caregiver concerns, learning rate, and instructional preferences. Progress monitoring data on student growth and performance should be provided from all involved teachers and service providers. Additionally, information from state and local testing can be considered, as well as information about a student's social/emotional well-being. Progress monitoring data and information related to transitional skills also would be included in this section.

The *Impact Statement/Information* and *Needs Information* cover how a student's exceptionality affects their involvement and progress within the general education curriculum. In other words, what is the correlation between a student's performance and the expectations of the curriculum's standards? How are this student's needs different from those of typically developing peers? How is the student's exceptionality impacting (or limiting) their progress within the given curriculum? References to progress monitoring data, testing performance, and specific areas impacted by their disability should all be noted.

It is vital for the present level statement to include information from all involved in the student's education to provide a clear picture of their strengths, needs, current levels of performance, and aspirations/goals for the next academic year and beyond. This information should be gathered from the student, parents/guardians, special education teacher(s), general education teacher(s), and any other service provider or involved professional staff member, such as the school nurse, school counselor, speech-language pathologist, occupational therapist, paraprofessional, etc. Depending on the needs of the student, it might be necessary to document medical and health-related concerns or attendance, supports and services related to executive functioning, or even self-care and self-awareness skills that may be assumed to be present for typical peers, but require instruction and/or modeling for some students with disabilities. For students of transition age, the PLAAFP should include the specific desires of the student related to post-secondary options (Harmon et al., 2020) and address any concerns/needs related to sexuality education.

Table 8.1 provides example statements of some of the various components of the PLAAFP. Each of these example statements relate to our case example, Jerry, and potential impact on sexuality education. It is important to note these examples do not represent a complete PLAAFP, but highlight areas that may be overlooked. Collectively, the PLAAFP should provide a clear picture of the student's strengths and needs, as well as direction for areas of continued need in academic and functional growth. This direction is what informs the IEP goals.

Table 8.1  **PLAAFP Example Statements**

| PLAAFP Examples | Jerry |
|---|---|
| Introductory Paragraph | Jerry is currently a 9th-grade student identified with autism spectrum disorder. He demonstrates behaviors that impede his learning and that of others. Given the severity of his behaviors, he receives instruction for his core classes, which include English Language Arts and Mathematics, in the special education classroom in order to better address behaviors of concern, while enabling him to increase his access to instruction in these areas. He is in the general education environment for homeroom, electives, lunch, and dismissal with his homeroom teacher. Jerry requires frequent prompting and cueing to engage with academic tasks and to remain on task. Jerry is a student who is very easily distracted and therefore needs redirection and prompting to stay motivated and on task. In addition, he gets frustrated easily and needs breaks throughout the day. Both Jerry and his parents have expressed a desire to receive instruction related to sexuality, because Jerry has had some inappropriate interactions with members of the opposite sex. |
| General Strengths and Needs | Jerry is a friendly student who is interested, as is developmentally appropriate, in establishing relationships with others. However, he has identified needs in the areas of self-awareness, self-expression, and recognizing the intentions of others. Jerry will require skill development and modeling of how to improve in these areas, specifically in the context of sexuality education. For example, Jerry might be vulnerable to unwanted or inappropriate advances from others or not making his needs and wants/dislikes known. |

| PLAAFP Examples | Jerry |
|---|---|
| Special Considerations | *Health: The school nurse reports Jerry regularly visits the nurse's office at lunchtime to take his medication, and he no longer needs a prompt or reminder to do so. He passed his vision and hearing tests. Jerry has reported to the nurse he is interested in the opposite sex and would like to have a girlfriend. He has asked multiple questions related to intimacy.* |
| Present Levels of Academic Achievement | *Jerry receives English Language Arts instruction in a special education setting. He is currently reading at the 4th-grade level. He is able to access content material provided at his reading level but requires texts to be broken down into smaller chunks, read aloud, and discussed to gain comprehension of the material. His reading limitations could not only hinder his progress in a given curriculum, but also negatively impact his understanding of information presented in functional or applied settings, such as personal hygiene, contraception usage, etc.* |
| Present Levels of Functional Performance | *Mr. Salinas, Jerry's homeroom teacher, reports Jerry comes to homeroom in the morning to drop off his backpack and coat and then goes to the computer lab. He does not use a locker because he needs a less crowded environment when he is unpacking and packing his things each day. There have been two incidents involving Jerry and other students. The first incident was on the bus. Jerry inappropriately touched another student multiple times. The student had asked Jerry to stop but Jerry did not cease the behavior. In the other incident, Jerry was removed from lunch for inappropriate touching and was taken to the office. Jerry does not seem to understand where and when it is appropriate to touch other individuals. Furthermore, he does not seem to understand or respect the personal space of others and their wishes when asked not to do something they are requesting.*<br>*Ms. Cho, Jerry's science teacher, reports, "I teach Jerry in a special education class called STEAM. At times, he has difficulty working with others in a group setting. He tends to invade their personal space. I have observed him trying to sit near certain females in the class. These females are individuals who have expressed their discomfort with sitting near Jerry." Jerry interacts appropriately with adults and tries his best to complete the activities that are assigned. He needs reminders to stay in his seat and to respect others' personal space.* |
| Student-Specific Factors (executive functioning, communication, transition, etc.) | *Attendance: According to the school records, Jerry has been absent four days this school year. Of these four days, he has been medically excused two days and the other two days he was suspended from the bus due to inappropriately touching another student. Due to bus suspension, he was unable to obtain a ride to school.*<br>*Transition: Jerry enjoys watching cooking shows and has expressed an interest in becoming a chef like the ones he watches online. He would like to take a cooking class next year. Jerry likes to experiment with recipes at home, but his parents report concerns with his ability to follow a recipe, handle knives safely, and work with hot surfaces/materials safely because he is distractible, impatient, and doesn't always think through actions/consequences. These executive functioning skills related to focus, following directions, and self-control would benefit him in all areas of academic and functional performance.* |

## Annual Goals and Objectives

As mentioned in the previous section, there must be a direct relationship between the annual goals and the needs identified in the PLAAFP. An annual IEP goal is defined as "a specific, time-limited goal aimed to take the student from their current level of performance to a realistic higher level during a preassigned time period, typically 1 year" (Goran et al., 2020, p. 335). Realistic goals address the student's unique needs, identify a targeted result, and provide a specific time frame for meeting the goal (Hedin & DeSpain, 2018). With the Supreme Court ruling in *Endrew F. v. Douglas County School District* (hereafter referred to as *Endrew F., 2017*), the obligation of schools was clarified to include offering "an IEP that is reasonably calculated to enable the child to make progress appropriate in light of the child's circumstances" (*Endrew F., 2017*, p. 11). The call is to create challenging, ambitious, yet reasonable IEP goals for the individual student. As such, it is imperative the goals are not based on a district curriculum or other external standards (Hedin & DeSpain, 2018), but are based on the student's individual needs and the IEP team's assessment of the student's potential for growth across the year (Goran et al., 2020).

Based on the extensive work related to developing IEP goals, coupled with the updated standards provided by the *Endrew F.* ruling, Mitchell Yell and colleagues developed five rules for writing good goals (Goran

**Table 8.2  Five Rules for Writing Good Goals**

| | |
|---|---|
| Rule 1 | Write clearly: make the goal brief, succinct, jargon-free, and objective. Choose wording that communicates the intent, leaving little room for interpretation. |
| Rule 2 | Write about the student and expected skill/behavior that is targeted. The goal is *not* about the process of instruction or what a teacher will do. |
| Rule 3 | Write goals connected to the PLAAFP, not a curriculum. IEP goals must address only the areas of identified need in the PLAAFP. |
| Rule 4 | Write goals that include these five characteristics:<br>Audience—the student<br>Behavior—the target behavior/skill, what the student is expected to do<br>Conditions—the context in which the target behavior/skill should occur<br>Degree—criterion or standard required for mastery of the target behavior/skill<br>Timeline—the expected date (time) by when the goal will be met |
| Rule 5 | Write goals that are "challenging" and "appropriately ambitious." This is the updated standard provided by the *Endrew F.* ruling. Goals should be meaningful and based on the student's unique educational needs. |

*Note:* Adapted with permission from Goran et al., 2020.

et al., 2020). These rules, which expand upon the ABCD-T framework developed by Winegarden (2005), are summarized in Table 8.2.

The five rules and ABCD-T framework offer guidance for writing IEP goals, for both academic and functional skills/behaviors. For students with intellectual disabilities, these skills include sexuality education individualized and based on the current needs and considerations of the student. For example, a student of a given age and/or developmental level is likely to experience puberty, sexual desires, and feelings whether or not they understand why. Similarly, a student could be confronted with sexual stimuli, advances, and/or persuasions even if they have not been schooled or informed about what those look like or from whom they might originate.

Self-awareness (including body awareness and awareness of one's feelings) as well as safety awareness and understanding are essential areas to address in sexuality education for students with disabilities. While these areas of sexual education are important to include and should not be withheld, the way this information is presented and disseminated should be in accordance with a student's individual needs.

Based on the example provided for Jerry, the IEP team could readily identify areas of need related to social skills that connect to sexuality education. One example is the need to address skills related to identifying appropriate physical contact. Following the ABCD-T framework, a realistic goal for Jerry might be:

> *When given scenarios of physical contact (Conditions), Jerry (Audience) will improve his ability to identify appropriate physical contact (Behavior) from 30% correct to 90% correct (Degree) on three data days in the quarter (Time).*

Notice that the goal does not specifically address sexuality education as the curricular topic, nor does it specify the instructional method used by the teacher.

Another example identified in the PLAAFP is the need to interpret and respond to social cues. A realistic ABCD-T goal for Jerry regarding this skill could include specific mention of both social and sexual cues, such as:

> *When given scenarios of social settings (Conditions), Jerry (Audience) will improve his ability to identify appropriate social/sexual cues of those around him in order to determine appropriate reactions (Behavior) from 10% correct to 70% correct (Degree) on three consecutive data points in one month (Time).*

A third area of need identified in the PLAAFP is the academic area of reading. Jerry struggles with reading and is currently reading significantly below his grade level. Using the ABCD-T framework, a realistic reading goal for Jerry is:

> *After teacher read-aloud of a course text (Conditions), Jerry (Audience) will answer comprehension questions—for example, verbally, pointing to a picture, or selecting a multiple-choice option (Behavior) with 80% accuracy (Degree) on four consecutive texts based on one year's data collection records (Time). Baseline: 20%.*

IEP goals are written to address the targeted behavior/skill of the student. This behavior will have a positive impact on Jerry both in the educational setting and as he works toward his transition goals.

## Services and Supports

Once the IEP goals are written, the team can focus on the special education services and supports needed to help the student address the goals. These services include specialized instruction, related services, supplementary services, and program modifications. For students who need sexuality education, the IEP team should ensure considerations of what supports are necessary to address the academic and functional goals across all needed contexts. As mentioned above, goals are written to address student growth and development of the behavior/skill in areas of needs identified in the PLAAFP. Each identified need will require at least one of the services listed.

When considering services and supports, the IEP team must consider what is being offered in the classroom to the individual child, not the entire classroom of students. If there is some instruction the student needs to be successful that all students in the classroom do not receive, this is a specially-designed instruction (SDI). Each of these SDIs must be included in the IEP and then implemented by those individuals who teach and work with the child. For example, there are many times students may have questions related to human anatomy, self-care, or even hygiene but are uncomfortable speaking in front of a group of people. In this case, the child may need to have an SDI to speak to someone like the nurse to answer their questions.

A great deal of the literature advocating for the awareness and respect of the rights of students with disabilities as they are instructed in the area of sexuality education stresses the importance of recognizing individuals can be sexualized, sensitive beings with unique needs and feelings, particularly when it pertains to one's sexual health and desires (Harkins Monaco et al., 2018). Being cognizant of this can help promote sensitivity and individualization when outlining a student's PLAAFP statement. An additional consideration is that many students with disabilities, such as IDD and ASD for example, are highly susceptible to sexual abuse and exploitation. Information and skills about recognizing and establishing healthy relationships with others, as well as recognizing when to report and seek help when faced with inappropriate or unwanted sexual advances, are critical to all populations of young adults, but must include specific approaches and interventions for individuals with disabilities due to their unique needs.

Understanding a student's background, family culture, and social comfort levels can be critical when outlining an approach regarding sexuality education. Role playing and boundary awareness should be part of this approach as well and can provide interactive examples of the understanding and skills being developed.

Real-life examples should be included in the sexuality education curriculum whenever possible, even if only as a point of reference. Social media, pop culture, and what adolescents perceive as social norms and expectations must not be ignored. *(See Chapter 13 for more information about social media and pop culture.)* The experiences, abilities, and limitations of the individual student play a critical role when considering these factors. Within the PLAAFP statements, how actively a student is engaged in the world of social media, the student's level of exposure to pop culture, and the impact their intellectual and developmental abilities and limitations have on their perspective are important to note when outlining background information, baseline data, and statements regarding needs, abilities, and progress—particularly as those components relate to the implementation of a sexuality education curriculum.

In the case of Jerry, based on the present levels, he is a student who struggles with both academic (reading) and functional (social/behavioral) skills and he needs to learn concepts regarding sexuality. It is important to note he needs the content presented to him at his instructional level, which is lower than that of his same-age and grade-level peers. This requires both specialized instruction and modified/adapted materials. It may be very difficult to find materials presented at his level and also appropriate for him. Many students, like Jerry, are intellectually at an elementary level of learning, which makes it difficult to educate them in regard to a subject generally presented to an audience of much greater maturity and ability to comprehend the content.

The IEP team may consider direct related services from a speech-language pathologist (SLP) to support Jerry in learning the foundational skills related to reading comprehension, as well as the social/pragmatic skills identified as goal targets. The team might also determine the SLP should provide consultation support to Jerry's teachers to help facilitate instruction at an appropriate level as well as generalization of social skills to a variety of settings. If the professionals are working together, using the same supports/prompts/reminders, Jerry will have more consistent expectations and be able to transfer skills across environments.

The services and supports identified by the IEP team tie directly to the present levels of performance, annual goals, and transition goals/needs. This process is truly individualized to the student and requires information from all involved stakeholders.

## Summary

This chapter discussed the necessary elements to incorporate comprehensive sexuality education in the IEP. It reviewed the required components of the individualized education program and the importance of input from stakeholders, including teachers, service providers, and the student. Specific focus was on the present level of performance, goals, and service delivery options, with attention to how these connect to sexuality education.

## Resources

### Internet Resources

Virtual IEP Meeting Tips: https://www.parentcenterhub.org/wp-content/uploads/repo_items/virtual-iep-meeting-tipsheets.pdf

Special Factors in IEP Development: https://www.parentcenterhub.org/special-factors/

IRIS Module: Developing High Quality IEPs: https://iris.peabody.vanderbilt.edu/module/iep01/

IRIS Module: How administrators can support the development of high-quality IEPs: https://iris.peabody.vanderbilt.edu/module/iep01/

Strategies for Setting Data-Driven Behavioral Individualized Education Program Goals: https://intensiveintervention.org/resource/high-quality-behavior-IEP-goals

### Books

Bateman, B. D. (2007). *From gobbledygook to clearly written annual IEP goals*. Attainment Company.

Bateman, B. D., & Herr, C. M. (2010). *Writing measurable IEP goals and objectives*. Attainment Company.

Lake, S. E. (2002). *The top 10 IEP errors: How to avoid them, how to fix them*. LRP.

Mager, R. F. (1997). *Preparing instructional objectives: A critical tool in the development of effective instruction* (3rd ed.). Center for Effective Performance.

Marzano, R. J., & Kendall, J. S. (Eds.). (2006). *The new taxonomy of educational objectives*. Corwin Press.

## Journal Articles

Complete issue of *TEACHING Exceptional Children*:
*TEACHING Exceptional Children*, 52(5), May/June 2020

## How to Stay Up to Date

1. Info on IDEA 2004: http://idea.ed.gov/
2. Wrights Law: http://www.wrightslaw.com/
3. LD Online: http://www.ldonline.org/
4. CEC: http://www.cec.sped.org/
5. NCLD: http://www.ncld.org/
6. Education Week: http://www.edweek.org/topics/specialeducation/

# CHAPTER 9

# Comprehensive Sexuality and Relationship Education Curriculum and Teaching Strategies

Victoria Slocum, Ruth M. Eyres, and Pamela S. Wolfe

*Quality sex education goes beyond delivering information. It provides young people with opportunities to explore their own identities and values along with the values and beliefs of their families and communities. It also allows young people to practice the communication, negotiation, decision-making, and assertiveness skills they need to create healthy relationships—both sexual and nonsexual—throughout their lives.*

(Future of Sex Education Initiative, 2020)

*Why didn't anyone tell me about this? I feel like you let me down (self-advocate).*

It is important for persons with disabilities to have access to sexuality education. Access alone does not guarantee comprehension of skills taught. This chapter provides an overview of important components of comprehensive sexuality and relationship education and provides specific descriptions and examples of utilizing effective instructional strategies for teaching.

Readers will

- understand that persons with disabilities have the right to sexuality education;
- identify how sexuality and relationship education should be comprehensive in nature;

- analyze how specialized instruction increases access to sexuality education concepts for persons with disabilities; and
- evaluate sexuality and relationship education curricula to guide family members, caregivers, and school staff.

## Importance of Sexuality and Relationship Education

All individuals, including adolescents with disabilities, have a right to developmentally appropriate sexuality and relationship education including information about sexual health care and opportunities for socializing and sexual expression (Future of Sex Education Initiative, 2020; SIECUS, 2004). For individuals with disabilities, often access to sexuality and relationship education has not been provided (Barnard-Brak et al., 2014; Sinclair et al., 2015; Swango-Wilson, 2009). Access is often limited by multiple barriers, including practitioner or parental personal beliefs and stereotypes (Healy et al., 2009; Lafferty et al., 2012; McConkey & Ryan, 2001; Sinclair et al., 2015; Wilkenfeld & Ballan, 2011). Sexuality and relationship education is important when considering self-determination for people with disabilities (Travers et al., 2014). Aligning with the self-advocacy component of self-determination and approaching sexuality and relationship education using a rights-based lens helps practitioners understand that like all people, persons with disabilities benefit from comprehensive sexuality education because it teaches youth skills to

- understand medically accurate information,
- communicate and make decisions about their sexual health,
- understand consent and healthy relationships,
- respect their own and others' body autonomy,
- stay healthy and remain in school, which increases likelihood of academic success (Bridges & Alford, 2010), and
- respect people of all sexual orientations and gender identities. (Bridges & Hauser, 2014; Future of Sex Education Initiative, 2020)

Without meaningful sexuality and relationship education, people with intellectual and developmental disabilities (IDD) and autism spectrum disorder (ASD) are more likely to be the victim of sexual abuse (Swango-Wilson, 2008) and are more likely to commit sexual abuse (Davis, 2009). According to Swango-Wilson (2008), 39–60% of females and 16–30% of males with IDD experience sexual abuse by age 18. A National Public Radio series on sexual abuse of people with IDD (NPR, 1/8/18–1/20/18) found that the rate of rape and sexual assault against people with IDD is more than seven times the rate against people without disabilities. Women with IDD are 12 times more likely to experience sexual assault than those without disabilities.

# Evidence-Based Best Practice in Sexuality and Relationship Education

There are important components necessary for a curriculum to meet the needs of people with high- and low-incidence disabilities, particularly those with DD. Educators/families should consider the following when selecting curricula/resources (Blanchett & Wolfe, 2002):

1. consider chronological age and developmental level,
2. utilize lessons from a variety of programs as needed per student,
3. use curricula as a guide and use evidenced-based instructional strategies to deliver content, and
4. build in opportunities for generalization of content skills learned.

Additionally, the Future of Sex Education Initiative (2020) offers a statement on comprehensive sexuality and relationship education (see Textbox 9.1).

Sexuality education should not be a single stand-alone event, nor should it emphasize teen pregnancy prevention while ignoring all other health and social benefits. It should be a developmentally appropriate, sequential K–12 curriculum focusing on providing information and strategies to help young people develop bodily autonomy, self-advocacy, consent, and healthy relationships, as well as awareness of the diversity of the human experience. Comprehensive sexuality and relationship

## ■■■■■ TEXTBOX 9.1 ■■■■■

### Description of Effective Sexuality Education

#### Goals of Comprehensive Sexuality Education

The goal of sex education is to help young people navigate sexual development and grow into sexually healthy adults. To be effective, sex education must include medically accurate information about a broad range of topics such as consent and healthy relationships; puberty and adolescent development; sexual and reproductive anatomy and physiology; gender identity and expression; sexual identity and orientation; interpersonal and sexual violence; contraception, pregnancy, and reproduction; and HIV and other STDs/STIs.

*Source:* Future of Sex Education, 2020, p. 6.

education should give students the opportunity to explore their own identities and values, as well as practicing relationship skills, and to make appropriate decisions for themselves (SIECUS, 2004).

There are two types of curricula: comprehensive and specialized. **Comprehensive sexuality education** (CSE) goes far beyond the topic of sexual behavior and encompasses key components as outlined by the Sexuality Information and Education Council of the United States (SIECUS, 2004) and the American Academy of Pediatrics (Breuner & Mattson, 2016). CSE uses ongoing developmentally appropriate, age-respective, and evidence-based education about sexuality, sexual reproduction, relationships, and sexual health provided by pediatricians, educators, other professionals, and parents (Breuner & Mattson, 2016).

Table 9.1  **Curricula Designed for People with IDD**

| Curriculum | Contents | Price | Target age |
|---|---|---|---|
| Attainment Company: Learn About Life | • Your body-my body<br>• Being a woman/man<br>• Having a baby<br>• Be safe<br>• Relationships | $99 | Adolescents and adults |
| Elevatus: Sexuality Education for People with Developmental Disabilities | • Relationships<br>• Healthy sexual activities<br>• Physical aspects of sexuality<br>• Internet, social media & communication<br>• Gender identity and expression | $299<br>$150 (PDF) | Adolescents and adults |
| King County, Washington: FLASH | • Puberty<br>• Abstinence<br>• Safe sex<br>• Consent<br>• Reproductive health | $68–$375<br>Free download in King County, Washington | Elementary through high school |
| Stanfield: Circles | • Social and relationship boundaries<br>• Interpersonal skills<br>• Relationship-specific social skills | $499–$1399 | Elementary through adult |
| University of Wisconsin Waisman Center: Safety Awareness for Empowerment (SAFE) | • Relationships<br>• Social rules<br>• Safety and sexuality<br>• First aid<br>• Self-defense | Free download (PDF) | Adolescents and adults |

Specialized curricula for people with ID and ASD should be individualized (AAIDD, 2008), be theory or evidence based, include proper needs assessment, and have measurable outcomes to conduct proper evaluations (Schaafsma et al., 2013). Schaafsma and colleagues (2013) described several sexuality and relationship education curricula and found that none were theory or evidence based. The curricula had no specific outcomes, theoretical basis, or systematic evaluation. There are, however, curricula available that attempt to meet the needs of people with IDD. Table 9.1 lists several curricula designed for people with disabilities.

# Content of Sexuality and Relationship Education

## Comprehensive Sexuality Education Components

The key topics recommended by the *National Sex Education Standards* (*NSES*), 2nd Edition (Future of Sex Education Initiative, 2020) and the American Academy of Pediatrics (Breuner & Mattson, 2016) are listed in Table 9.2.

## National Sexuality Education Standards

The goal of the *National Sex Education Standards: Core Content and Skills, K–12* (2nd ed., 2020) is "to provide clear, consistent, and straightforward guidance on the essential, minimum, core content and skills needed for sex education that is age-appropriate for students in grades K–12 to be effective" (p. 7).

**Table 9.2  Key Topics of Comprehensive Sexuality Education**

| NSES | AAP |
| --- | --- |
| Consent and healthy relationships | Healthy sexual development |
| Anatomy and physiology | Gender identity |
| Puberty and adolescent sexual development | Interpersonal relationships |
| Gender identity and expression | Affection |
| Sexual orientation and identity | Intimacy |
| Sexual health | Body Image |
| Interpersonal violence | |

The Future of Sex Education Initiative (FoSE, 2020) promotes CSE in all U.S. K–12 schools with a vision of healthy sexual development for all students. The first-ever *National Sexuality Education Standards* for school-age children was made available in 2012 to support educators in working toward this vision. The standards were updated in 2020 to include

- a trauma-informed lens;
- principles of reproductive justice, racial justice, social justice, and equity;
- social determinants of health and how these can lead to inequitable health outcomes; and
- an intersectional approach. (FoSE, 2020, p. 7)

The sequential K-12 curriculum standards (Figure 9.2) outline for educators what to teach and how to teach. For example, Advocates for Youth's Rights, Respect, Responsibility: A K–12 Sexuality Education Curriculum (http://3rs.org/3rs-curriculum) is a free curriculum aligned

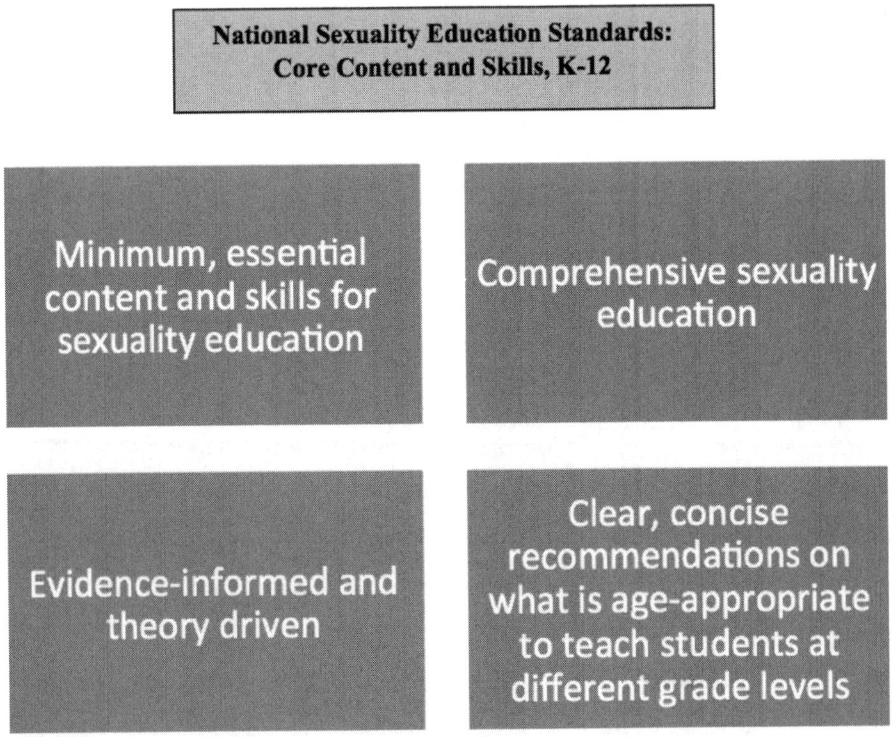

**National Sexuality Education Standards: Core Content and Skills, K-12**

Minimum, essential content and skills for sexuality education

Comprehensive sexuality education

Evidence-informed and theory driven

Clear, concise recommendations on what is age-appropriate to teach students at different grade levels

**Figure 9.1** National Sexuality Education Standards: Core Content and Skills, K–12

to the NSES. It is flexible and can either be downloaded or used in a Google Classroom format. This comprehensive sexuality education curriculum, along with suggested instructional strategies, differentiation, and adaptations from this chapter, can be used to teach students with IDD.

## Instruction of Sexuality and Relationship Education

A variety of methods are appropriate to teach sexuality education. Often it is assumed that some type of special instructional strategy is needed to teach sexuality education topics. This is not the case. In practice, the same instructional strategies that are effective in teaching students with disabilities in other curricular areas are also effective in teaching sexuality education concepts. Often, sexuality education is not provided due to attitudinal barriers, including fear and lack of understanding and comfort level in the content specific to comprehensive sexuality education. Some effective strategies for teaching students with learning differences include pacing of instruction, materials on reading level and comprehension level, providing visual and environmental supports specific to student needs, structured instruction delivered in short periods of time,

**Table 9.3  Examples of High-Leverage Practices & Teaching Sexuality Education Topics**

| High-Leverage Practice Area | High-Leverage Practice | Sexuality Education Concept | Individualization to Student |
|---|---|---|---|
| Collaboration | Collaborate with families to support student learning and secure needed services. | Identify different kinds of family structures. | Get to know student's family and include family member pictures during instruction. |
| Assessment | Use multiple sources of information to develop a comprehensive understanding of a student's strengths and needs. | Identify parents and other trusted adults they can talk to about relationships. | Utilize informal and formal assessments to determine student understanding of trusted adults in their lives. |
| Social/emotional | Teach social behaviors. | Explain that all people, including children, have the right to tell others not to touch their body when they do not want to be touched. | Teach, model, and create opportunities for student to practice telling others they do not want to be touched. |

| Instruction | | | |
|---|---|---|---|
| | Adapt curriculum tasks and materials for specific learning goals. | Use proper names for body parts, including male and female anatomy. | Use anatomically correct dolls to teach correct body part names. |
| | Provide intensive instruction. | Demonstrate refusal skills (e.g., clear "no" statement, walk away, repeat refusal). | Teach self-advocacy by teaching student they can choose to say "no"—practice using role play. |
| | Teach students to maintain and generalize new learning across time and settings. | Identify sources of support such as parents or other trusted adults that they can go to if they are or someone they know is being bullied, harassed, abused, or assaulted. | Help student identify various support persons, including trusted adults in the community and school. |

utilizing simple and concrete terms and materials, and ensuring repetition and generalization of skills learned (National Research Council, 2001; Snell & Brown, 2011). The High-Leverage Practices in Special Education (Council for Exceptional Children & CEEDAR Center, 2019) can also guide educators in designing instruction to teach sexuality education concepts. Table 9.3 provides examples of **high-leverage practices.**

## Differentiation of Instruction

As mandated in the Individuals with Disabilities Education Act (IDEA), instruction for students with disabilities should be individualized (IDEA, 2004). Just like other curricular subject matter, sexuality education curricula may need to be adapted to meet the needs of students with special needs. Typically, adapting curricula centers on questions of what, how, and where to teach content (Thompson et al., 2018).

### What to Teach

Related to what to teach, it may be beneficial to consider the importance of the skill to the individual student. Questions that may aid in identifying important content can include:

- Is the skill needed now or in the immediate future?
- Does the student need the skill to be more fully integrated into inclusive environments?

* Is the skill necessary for safety or well-being?
* Is the skill designated by the family or student as important?

## How to Teach

When determining how to teach the content, the individual's unique strengths and challenges should also be considered (Anderson et al., 2012). Characteristics that may affect what is taught in sexuality education can include:

* Social
* Emotional
* Cognitive
* Communication
* Motor
* Sensory
* Behavior

A variety of instructional strategies should be used to teach sexuality education content. Table 9.4 provides a listing of possible instructional strategies and their definitions. Table 9.5 offers some suggestions on how curricula can be adapted. Janney et al. (2000) provide a model of modifying assessment and instruction that can be applied to sexuality education.

**Table 9.4  Definitions and Examples of Instructional Strategies**

| Instructional Strategy | Definition | Example |
| --- | --- | --- |
| **Task analysis** (Franzone, 2009) | Task analysis is the process of breaking a skill into smaller, more manageable steps in order to teach the skill. | Wiping after toileting |
| **Visual supports** (Hume et al., 2014) | Visual supports are concrete cues paired with, or used in place of, verbal cues to provide information about a routine, activity, behavioral expectation, or skill demonstration. Visual supports can include pictures, written words, objects, etc. | Identifying body parts |
| **Social narratives** (Gray, 2010) | Social narratives describe social situations for learners with ASD by providing relevant cues, explanation of the feelings and thoughts of others in the social situation, and descriptions of appropriate behavior expectations. Typically, social narratives are individualized based upon the needs of the learner, short, and written from the perspective of the learner. | Consent: personal space, saying "no" |

| Instructional Strategy | Definition | Example |
|---|---|---|
| **Modeling** (McDowell et al., 2015) | Modeling allows the learner to observe someone performing a target behavior. Modeling can provide a primer to task completion or serve as a prompt. Modeling works best when used along with prompting and reinforcement. | Asking someone out |

**Table 9.5  Ways to Adapt Curricula**

- Teach fewer steps or limit context/environment.
  Conduct an ecological inventory to highlight sub-environments to identify where to begin instruction.
  - Shorten a task analysis or limit the steps to be targeted.
  - Identify the "big" idea and select one or two components to teach.
  - Scaffold instruction to build on critical skills.
- Teach with different instructional strategies.
  - Use explicit teaching methods rather than lecture or discussion.
  - Employ systematic prompting such as least to most or most to least.
  - Use "model, prompt, check" prompting.
  - Use visuals, video modeling, task analyses.
- Reteach frequently.
  - Repeat guided practice of skills.
  - Teach the skills in a variety of environments, with different people and different prompting to promote generalization.

*Note.* Adapted from Wolfe, P. S. (2020).

## Where to Teach

Where to teach takes on more significance when related to sexuality education. Although some content could be taught in general education classrooms with typical peers, there may be some content/skills that are best taught outside of the general education classroom. For example, a student who is learning how to dispose of a sanitary napkin would not undertake the skill in the classroom, but rather, in a bathroom. Equally, a student who is learning how to shave also would undertake the task in the bathroom. The setting used to learn the skill is important in terms of social validity as well as the likelihood of generalization of the skill to the actual environments in which the student will function (Janney et al., 2000).

## Self-Determination

Self-determination as a component of comprehensive sexuality education is important because having greater independence and control of one's life through decision making (Travers et al., 2014) is a crucial part of learning the skills necessary to make personal sexual decisions. Including sexuality education concepts into self-determination instruction often presents barriers for families and educators. Personal beliefs, stereotypes, and fear often prevent access to sexuality education for individuals with developmental disabilities (Wilkenfeld & Ballan, 2011). Table 9.6 offers sexuality education topics related to self-determination and strategies/materials to use for instruction.

**Table 9.6   Sexuality Education Topics, Strategies, and Materials Related to Self-Determination**

| In order to help students learn . . . | Teach this: | Use this: |
|---|---|---|
| Self-awareness | • Personal care/hygiene<br>• Autonomy<br>• Relationships (friendship, dating, marriage)<br>• Healthy choices<br>(Eyres et al., 2016) | • Hygiene kits<br>• Preference assessments<br>• Pictures of family, friends, teachers, etc.<br>• Visual sequences of personal care steps |
| Safety and personal rights | • Public vs. private<br>• How to say no<br>• Consent<br>(Healthy Bodies Toolkit, 2013) | • Public behavior pictures<br>• Private behavior pictures<br>• Role play |
| Self-advocacy | • Personal space<br>• Communicating preferences, desires, and opinions<br>• Interpersonal communication skills<br>(Cabeza et al., 2013) | • Hula hoop to visualize personal space<br>• Participation in IEP conferences |

Eyres, R. M., & Harkins Monaco, E. A. (2018). The birds and the bees: Specific skills and teaching strategies. In E. A. Harkins Monaco, T. Gibbon, & D. Bateman (Eds.), *Talking about sex: Sexuality education for learners with disabilities*. Rowman & Littlefield.

# Evaluating Quality Sexuality and Relationship Education Curricula

**Sexuality education curricula** must be effective for both the teacher or implementer and the students for whom instruction is targeted. As noted in the sections above, curricular content is of paramount importance. The content in comprehensive curricula is wide-ranging and can vary in depth and breadth (Curtiss, 2018; Schaafsma et al., 2017; Wolfe, Wertalik, Domire Monaco, & Gardner, 2019). In addition to content, other variables can contribute to a quality curriculum. Wolfe et al. (2019) conducted a review of nine commercially available curricula for individuals with developmental disabilities. The authors examined the curricula for quality features based on reviews of literature and SIECUS (2004) guidelines. Table 9.7 displays the features that were examined in the review. Features that were most frequently absent from the reviewed curricula

**Table 9.7  Features of Quality Sexuality Education Curricula**

| Curricular Feature | Description of Feature |
| --- | --- |
| Assessment | Methods to determine student learning of the material |
| Staff development | Strategies, training material, forms to prepare staff to teach the curriculum |
| User friendliness | Layout of materials, objectives, lesson components, materials for teachers and student |
| Reference aids | Suggestions for further information |
| Theoretical support | Theory supporting curricular strategies (e.g., Applied Behavior Analysis [ABA], Treatment and Education of Autistic and Related Communications Handicapped Children [TEACCH] cognitive/social relationship model) |
| Medical accuracy | Content reflects physiologic and biologic bases of current science |
| Age appropriateness | Information, depictions match the stated age for which the curriculum was designed |
| Cultural diversity | Information, depictions demonstrate the spectrum of racial, ethnic, gender identities |
| Current representation | Information, depictions match the time frame in which the curriculum was used |
| Parental involvement | Text, resources, materials, forms demonstrate/provide ways to include parents in the socio-sexuality education process |

*Note.* From Wolfe, Wertalik, Domire Monaco, & Gardner (2019).

included assessment, staff development, theoretical/empirical support, and parental involvement.

## Assessment

Assessment is a critical component of quality curricula to identify current levels of learning and document whether learning has occurred (Witmer et al., 2017). Assessment measures will vary based on the skills/concepts being targeted and the abilities of the student with disabilities (Finnerty et al., 2019). In order to assess with reliability, it is critical to begin with a well-defined and precise content goal and then match the assessment to the goals (Schaafsma et al., 2015). Wolfe, Wertalik, Domire Monaco, Gardner, and Ruiz (2019) found that most assessments in the reviewed curricula consisted of knowledge assessment (pre/post-tests) with relatively fewer associated with actual performance and skills. As the authors acknowledge, not all skills related to socio-sexuality education can be ethically evaluated by skill demonstration but there are some performance-based skill assessments that are feasible, such as a task analysis of how to perform a hygiene task or discrete skills such as charting the timing of menstrual periods. In addition to skill assessment, assessment of concept formation may be necessary for topics such as "assertiveness," "respect," "trust," and other more conceptual ideas. Assessment for concepts should include both examples and nonexamples to assist the student in the formation of the concept (Archer & Hughes, 2011).

## Staff Development

Research consistently has shown that support personnel feel unprepared to teach sexuality education to students with disabilities (Saxe & Flanagan, 2014; Saxe & Flanagan, 2016). Curricula that include components of staff development are critical to successful implementation. Aside from instructional strategies and resources, staff may need training related to assessment of their own values and on how to communicate about sexuality without sending negative messages (Curtiss, 2018; Saxe & Flanagan, 2014).

## Theoretical Support

Wolfe, Wertalik, Domire Monaco, Gardner, and Ruiz (2019) found that curricula often do not have a theoretical basis for either content or instructional strategies. The need for a theoretical basis is critical in order to assure that the curriculum is cohesive and can be empirically assessed (Travers et al., 2014). One theoretical approach that has a strong empirical basis for individuals with developmental disabilities, particularly autism, is applied behavior analysis (National Professional Development Center on Autism Spectrum Disorders, 2014). Applied behavior analysis strategies can be applied to sexuality education for students with disabilities (Wolfe et al., 2009).

## Input from Persons with IDD

Schaafsma, Stoffelen, Kok, and Curfs (2013) state that all sexuality and relationship education programs for people with IDD should include proper needs assessment, focus on people with IDD, involve people with IDD in designing programs, and have measurable outcomes to conduct proper evaluations. They conducted a study of five programs and determined that none of the programs were theory or evidence based. None of the programs had specific program outcomes, a theoretical basis, or systematic evaluation. Members of relevant groups (i.e., people with IDD) were not included in the development process. They determined that none of the programs they reviewed would be effective.

In comparison, the Multnomah County Health Department (2018), in conjunction with the University Center for Excellence in Developmental Disabilities at the Oregon Health and Science University (OHSU), developed a set of sexual health guidelines for people with IDD. These guidelines, *In Their Own Words* (https://multco.us/file/73965/down load), were created with input from youth with IDD regarding what help they felt they needed, as well as with input from people in their lives regarding what support they felt they needed in providing sexuality education.

## Parental Involvement

The need to involve parents in sexuality education for students with disabilities is critical. Of utmost importance is the need to secure parental permission to teach the curriculum (Travers & Tincani, 2010). Equally important, parental involvement aids in assuring that the curriculum will not be compromised, and that generalization of the skills/information will occur (Travers & Tincani, 2010). SIECUS (2004) has provided suggestions to further the involvement of parents in sexuality education including providing parallel curriculum for parents, and/or homework assignments that include home instruction. Because of the nature of the topics, it also may be beneficial if parental involvement included communication strategies.

## Evaluation Instruments

There are several evaluation instruments and guidelines to assist in evaluating sexuality education curriculum. SIECUS has identified 10 characteristics of quality sexuality education programs, adapted from Kirby (2007). These characteristics are presented in Table 9.8. The National Sexuality Education Initiative's characteristics of comprehensive sexuality education are presented in Table 9.9. Table 9.10 provides an overview of the Health Education Curriculum Analysis Tool (HECAT) developed by the Centers for Disease Control (CDC). The HECAT is an extremely detailed evaluation instrument that is tied to National Health Standards, including sexuality education.

#### Table 9.8   Elements of Quality Sexuality Education Programs

Focus on reducing one or more sexual behaviors that lead to unintended pregnancy or HIV/STD infection.

Are based on theoretical approaches that have been demonstrated to influence other health-related behavior and identify specific important sexual antecedents to be targeted.

Deliver and consistently reinforce a clear message about abstaining from sexual activity and/or using condoms or other forms of contraception.

Provide basic, accurate information about the risks of teen sexual activity and about ways to avoid intercourse or use methods of protection against pregnancy and STDs including activities that address social pressures that influence sexual behavior.

Include activities that address social pressures that influence sexual behavior.

Provide examples of and practice with communication, negotiation, and refusal skills.

Employ teaching methods designed to involve participants and have them personalize the information.

Incorporate behavioral goals, teaching methods, and materials that are appropriate to the age, sexual experience, and culture of the students.

Last a sufficient length of time (i.e., more than a few hours).

Select teachers or peer leaders who believe in the program, and provide them with adequate training.

*Note.* From Sexuality Information Education Center of the United States (SIECUS): *Guidelines for comprehensive sexuality education* (3rd ed), (2004).

**Table 9.9 Characteristics of Comprehensive Sexuality Education**

Is research based and theory driven.

Focuses on clear health goals and specific behavioral outcomes.

Provides functional knowledge that is basic, accurate, and directly contributes to health-promoting decisions and behaviors.

Provides opportunities to reinforce essential skills that are necessary to adopt, practice, and maintain positive health behaviors.

Addresses individual values, attitudes, and beliefs and group norms that support health-enhancing behaviors.

Focuses on increasing personal perceptions of risk and harmfulness of engaging in specific unhealthy practices and behaviors, as well as reinforcing protective factors.

Addresses social pressures and influences.

Builds personal competence, social competence, and self-efficacy by addressing skills.

Uses strategies designed to personalize information and engage students.

Provides age-appropriate and developmentally appropriate information, learning strategies, teaching methods, and materials.

Engages in cooperative and active learning strategies.

Incorporates learning strategies, teaching methods, and materials that are trauma informed, culturally inclusive, sex positive, and grounded in social justice and equity.

Provides adequate time for instruction and learning and for students to practice skills relating to sex education.

Provides opportunities to make connections with other influential persons.

Encourages the use of technology to access multiple valid sources of information, recognizing the significant role that technology plays in young people's lives.

Includes teacher information and a plan for professional development and training to enhance effectiveness of instruction and student learning.

*Note.* Future of Sex Education Initiative National Sexuality Education Standards (2020).

**Table 9.10  Health Education Curriculum Analysis Tool (HECAT)**

Focuses on clear health goals and related behavioral outcomes.

Is research based and theory driven.

Addresses individual values, attitudes, and beliefs.

Addresses individual and group norms that support health-enhancing behaviors.

Focuses on reinforcing protective factors and increasing perceptions of personal risk and harmfulness of engaging in specific unhealthy practices and behaviors.

Addresses social pressures and influences.

Builds personal competence, social competence, and self-efficacy by addressing skills.

Provides functional health knowledge that is basic, accurate, and directly contributes to health-promoting decisions and behaviors.

Uses strategies designed to personalize information and engage students.

Provides age-appropriate and developmentally appropriate information, learning strategies, teaching methods, and materials.

Incorporates learning strategies, teaching methods, and materials that are culturally inclusive.

Provides adequate time for instruction and learning.

Provides opportunities to reinforce skills and positive health behaviors.

Provides opportunities to make positive connections with influential others.

Includes teacher information and plans for professional development and training that enhance effectiveness of instruction and student learning.

*Note.* From Centers for Disease Control and Prevention (CDC). *What works: Sexual health education from 3/4/2020.* https://www.cdc.gov/healthyyouth/whatworks/what-works-sexual-health-education.htm

# Summary

In this chapter, we provided an overview of the importance of sexuality and relationship education for people with low- and high-incidence disabilities. We discussed evidence-based best practices, including comprehensive and specialized curricula, as well as a variety of methods to evaluate, teach, and differentiate sexuality education. Finally, we provided a list of resources for educators, caregivers, and parents.

# Resources

Cabeza, B., Magill, L., Jenkins, A., Carter, E. W., Greiner, S., Bell, L., & Lane, K. L. (2013). *Promoting self-determination among students with disabilities: A guide for Tennessee educators.* Project Support and Include, Vanderbilt University, Nashville, Tennessee.

Couwenhoven, T. (2012). *The boy's guide to growing up: Choices and changes during puberty*. Woodbine.

Couwenhoven, T. (2012). *The girl's guide to growing up: Choices and changes in the tween years*. Woodbine.

Couwenhoven, T. (2015). *Boyfriends + girlfriends: A guide to dating for people with disabilities*. Woodbine.

Goodall, E. (2016). *The autism spectrum guide to sexuality and relationships*. Jessica Kingsley.

Grossberg, B. (2019). *Autism and your teen: Tips and strategies for the journey to adulthood*. American Psychological Association.

Hartman, D. (2014). *Sexuality and relationship education for children and adolescents with autism spectrum disorder*. Jessica Kingsley.

Hartman, D. (2015). *The growing up book for boys: What boys on the autism spectrum need to know*. Jessica Kingsley.

Hartman, D. (2015). *The growing up guide for girls: What girls on the autism spectrum should know*. Jessica Kingsley.

*The healthy bodies toolkit*. (2013). Vanderbilt Kennedy Center.

Pacer Center. *Family advocacy and support training (FAST) project training materials*.

Reynolds, K. E. (2014). *Sexuality and severe autism: A practical guide for parents, caregivers, and health educators*. Jessica Kingsley.

Walker-Hirsch, L. (2007). *The facts of life . . . and more*. Paul H. Brookes.

# CHAPTER 10

# Transitional Considerations
## Anne O. Papalia and Willa Papalia-Beatty

*IDEA, 2004, mandates FAPE [free appropriate public education] and planning for transition aged youth in areas of employment, post-secondary education and when applicable, independent living. Therefore, these broad federal requirements for special education should also support sexuality education in preparing students with disabilities for full quality of life.*

(Sinclair et al., 2015)

## Overview

Chapter 10 will discuss comprehensive sexuality's importance to post-secondary outcomes, including considerations like guardianship, post-secondary opportunities such as college and careers, and community involvement. The transition plan will address the necessary connections to community partners around sexuality development.

Readers will

- explain the importance of including comprehensive sexuality as a domain in transition planning;
- identify barriers that prevent comprehensive sexuality from being addressed in transition planning and means for addressing them;
- understand how addressing comprehensive sexuality education during transition addresses foundational transition goals of self-determination and quality of life;
- outline specific domains related to comprehensive sexuality education to be addressed during transition planning;
- explain the importance of social, financial, and community access skills as foundational components of comprehensive sexuality education within transition;

- state the importance of providing information on sexual health and sexual knowledge for adolescents with disabilities during transition; and
- describe the importance of proactively addressing marriage and parenting goals during transition.

"Toto, I've a feeling we're not in Kansas anymore." These words were uttered by Dorothy in *The Wizard of Oz* when she and Toto are suddenly transported to the Land of Oz when a cyclone unexpectedly hits. This sudden transition from familiar, known surroundings to new, exciting, yet challenging environments potentially represented the abrupt transition that youth with disability face when leaving high school and entering the adult world prior to mandated **transition services.** In an extension of the Wizard of Oz simile, Dorothy successfully makes the transition with the support of friends and by unmasking the mysterious powers of Oz. To youth with disabilities and their families, the exploration of sexual maturity, activity, and relationships has the same mysterious connotations. Transition planning works best when done collaboratively with stakeholders and youth with disabilities are supported in understanding factors contributing to their sexuality. The purpose of this chapter is to explore transition issues related to sexuality development. The importance of including comprehensive sexuality as a domain in transition planning is outlined. Typical barriers that prevent comprehensive sexuality are identified and means for addressing these barriers are presented. In addition, content and issues to be considered in comprehensive sexuality transition planning is presented (e.g., relationships, privacy, living conditions, marriage, parenting, income, community involvement).

## Overview of Transition Planning

Transition planning involves the development and implementation of individualized and actionable services across academic, vocational, and community living domains. Transition services are defined by the Individuals with Disabilities Education Act (IDEA) of 2004 as a coordinated set of actions for youth with disabilities within a results-oriented process focused on improving academic and functional achievement of youth with a disability to facilitate their movement from school to postsecondary activities including postsecondary education, vocational education, integrated employment (including supported employment), continuing and adult education, adult services, independent living, or community participation. Transition service planning is individualized through considering each student's strengths, preferences, and interests. Transition services are comprised of specifically designed instruction, related services, community experiences, the development of employment and other post-school adult living objectives, and when appropriate, the acquisition of daily living skills and functional vocational evaluation.

The transition planning process should begin early. According to IDEA 2004 transition goals and services should be incorporated into the individualized education program (IEP) during the year in which the student turns 16. Some states are more proactive, requiring transition planning to begin at age 14. Despite the legally mandated timelines, transition planning essentially begins when the students enter special education. The multidisciplinary teams should consider adult outcomes when planning a child's IEP throughout the time in special education. This proactive planning should be used when considering issues of comprehensive sexuality for an individual with disabilities as well. *(Content regarding comprehensive sexuality during school years is addressed in Chapter 9 of this book.)*

Although not directly identified as a domain in transition planning, comprehensive sexuality education should be addressed when considering adult living, independent living, and community participation. The inclusion of comprehensive sexuality in transition is important for a variety of reasons. Youth with disabilities, like all individuals, are sexual beings. Adolescents with and without disabilities tend to experience similar age of onset and rates of sexual activity (Tice & Harnek Hall, 2008). Sexuality also impacts quality of life. It encompasses the basic human needs of being liked and accepted, displaying and receiving affection, and sharing thoughts and feelings (Murphy & Elias, 2006). In the following section, the importance of including sexuality education within the transition planning and preparation for adult life is discussed.

## *Importance of Addressing Comprehensive Sexuality Education in Transition*

Including sexuality education content and goals within the transition planning directly reflects key principles of transition. These principles include self-determination, **natural supports,** and quality of life. Self-determination is broadly defined by having the skills and opportunities to steer one's life in ways that contribute to personally meaningful outcomes, such as dating, intimate relationships, marriage, and parenting (Westling et al., 2015). Natural supports involve using typical activities within the individual's everyday environment to provide support. In terms of sexuality education, identification of key relationships (i.e., friendships and romantic partners), opportunities to practice social skills and build relationships within the community, gain sexual knowledge from existing medical providers and support systems (i.e., information on hygiene, conception, and sexual function), and foster privacy and identify appropriate opportunities for intimacy within residential or support living environments are examples of natural supports.

Quality of life indicators include components such as allowing for choice and decision making and environmental control, an emphasis on wellness, and health-related information. Supporting quality of life issues regarding sexuality during transition is consistent with the concept of intimate citizenship. Intimate citizenship is defined as "the control (or not) over one's body, feelings, relationship: access (or not) to representations, relationships, public spaces, etc.; and socially grounded choices (or not) about identities, and gender experiences" (Siebers, 2012, p. 38). Otherwise stated, intimate citizenship is control over one's body, and choices made in context of that body. From an intimate citizenship perspective, individuals with disabilities must have full access and participation in decisions regarding all aspects of sexuality (e.g., relationships, identity development, and sexual orientation; Sinclair et al., 2015).

Although addressing comprehensive sexuality in transition planning appears consistent with its key principles, it tends to be neglected. Blanchett (2001) found sexuality education was regarded as being a less important transition competency by almost 30% of special educators. Likewise, competencies related to sexuality education, such as providing medical care, building relationships, and student participation in recreational activity were rated equally as low. Additionally, Blanchett noted the students who lacked sexual knowledge were more at risk of unwanted pregnancies, and sexually transmitted diseases such as HIV/AIDS. Educator, parent, and caregiver ideological barriers to this topic lead to less sexuality education in the transition process.

## Barriers to Sexuality Education in Transition

Multiple barriers exist that block sexuality education from being addressed during transition. These barriers vary based on the extent of the disability, attitudes toward sexuality of individuals with disabilities, and values and awareness of the stakeholders. For adolescents with high-incidence disabilities (HID; i.e., learning disabilities, mild intellectual disabilities, etc.) parents and teachers may not recognize sexuality education as a domain that would require intervention because students may receive sexuality education within the general education curriculum. This view underestimates the difficulty students with high-incidence disabilities have understanding the sexuality education content if it is not adapted to their instructional needs (Rowe et al., 2018) and the impact of social pragmatic skills of associates with these disabilities in navigating dating and romantic relationships. Parents and special education teachers also may feel uncomfortable or lack skills needed to approach the topic with youth and young adults with disabilities or believe that sexuality education may lead to unwanted sexual behavior and avoid the topic (Sinclair et al., 2015; Treacy et al., 2018).

These same issues apply to adolescents with low-incidence disabilities; however, the more significant impact of their disability creates additional barriers. For example, these individuals may be perceived as asexual and not recognized as needing sexuality education. Parents, teachers, and caregivers may erroneously believe that adolescents with low-incidence disabilities are not interested in sexual relations or do not have the capability of understanding their own sexuality or sexual information (Sinclair et al., 2015). Likewise, it may be assumed that individuals with low-incidence disabilities do not have the capability to engage in intimate relationships or sexual acts, and/or be desirable as partners. As a result, aspects of adult life such as dating, engaging in romantic relationships, acquiring medical information about sexuality, safe sex practices, and birth control are considered unnecessary. Likewise, parents, educators, and other stakeholders may avoid the topic of sexuality as a means of protecting individuals with low-incidence disabilities because they are perceived as vulnerable to abuse from engaging in sexual activity (Sinclair et al., 2015).

The consequence of these barriers results in adolescents and young adults who are vulnerable, underestimated, and uninformed. Therefore, despite these barriers, comprehensive sexuality education is a necessary component of transition planning. Sexuality education is essential for protection. The notion of appropriate touch and boundaries is necessary in safe adult relationships. Access to sexual information is vital to health and productivity, which is especially important during the transition process. Adolescents and young adults with disabilities should receive information regarding sexual health, birth control, and prevention of sexually transmitted disease. An unexpected pregnancy can derail career or postsecondary education options for adolescents with high-incidence disabilities and result in **custody** and child-rearing issues for families of adolescents with low-incidence disabilities. Sexuality education focuses on building meaningful relationships. A lack of understanding of this domain can result in loneliness, social isolation, and the lack of a support system, which can contribute to depression, substance abuse, and increased suicide risk (Joiner, 2005). Additionally, a lack of sexuality education may diminish quality of life. Sexuality is a fundamental aspect of the human condition. It is a source of pleasure, personal fulfillment, and a source of love and connection to another human being. Therefore, sexuality education must be considered during transition to permit individuals with disabilities to fully realize their human potential as sexual beings throughout their lifespan.

Given the importance of sexuality education in transition, various components of sexuality education must be directly addressed during transition. Family involvement is essential to effective transition in general. The involvement of families in addressing sexuality education content in particular is vital (Morningside et al., 1995; Sinclair et al., 2017). Sexuality education is a moral-driven process. It is influenced by ethical, spiritual, cultural, and moral concerns (Sexuality Information and Education Council of the United States [SIECUS], n.d.). Families provide the voice and insight into these elements during transition and will be particularly important when addressing sexuality education–related goals.

The content to be included in transition planning should be guided by the components of comprehensive sexuality education and focus on the specific needs of the particular individual with a disability and their families. These components include social, financial, and community access skills needed to build relations, social pragmatic skills required to understand personal boundaries and consent, and self-care and self-advocacy skills needed to obtain medical and functional sexual information. In addition, legal aspects of sexuality education should be addressed. These aspects include marriage requirements, age of consent, and child custody requirements for individuals who may not have the ability to be the primary caretaker of a child. *(This is discussed in more depth in Chapter 3.)*

## Social and Relationship Skills

Social skills, involvement with peers, and community interactions form a foundation for healthy and meaningful sexual interactions and are important components of transition planning. Inherent in sexual development is interaction and connection with other people, and social skills are the foundation for these connections (McDaniels & Fleming, 2018). In order to build relationships that lead to dating and romantic relationships, adolescents and young adults with disabilities must have the ability to interact socially and establish friendships that could lead to more significant relationships. Additionally, access to the environment, a degree of independence, and the financial resources to participate in leisure activities are required. The degree to which these components are addressed within transition planning is based on the extent of the person's disability and the willingness of families to support independent activities.

**Social Skills.** The ability to navigate the social pragmatics of friendships and dating relationships can be a daunting task for adolescents in general. It can prove to be even more challenging to adolescents with disabilities. Sinclair et al. (2015) found that adolescents with disabilities desired information on how to start romantic relationships. Adolescents with high-incidence disabilities that impact language processing (e.g., learning disabilities, emotional and behavior disorders, and mild autism) may benefit from transition goals that focus on how to build peer relations and friendships. Examples of these skills include introducing yourself, expressing your feelings, apologizing, negotiation skills, starting conversations, and interpreting the hidden meaning in peer interactions (Kavale & Mostert, 2004; McDaniels & Fleming, 2018). Direct instruction can be provided using a social skills curriculum such as *Skillstreaming the Adolescent: A Structured Learning Approach to Teaching Prosocial Skills Elements of Understanding*, and *ASSET: A Social Skills Program for Adolescents*. Individuals with low-incidence disabilities such as intellectual disabilities and autism may benefit from training on how to interpret facial expressions, emotions, and nonverbal behaviors, all of which, if inappropriately decoded and deemed sexual in nature, may result in relational challenges (Travers & Tincani, 2010). Opportunities for role play, guided practice of social skills, and debriefing of attempts to implement these skills in authentic environments are important components as well.

**Social and leisure activities.** In addition to learning discrete relationship skills, adolescents with disabilities require opportunities to practice them in authentic situations within the community. This structured practice is important because social skills become a gateway for community interactions. Greater independence and participation in community activities is often determined by an individual's level of social skills (McDaniels & Fleming, 2018). Providing this practice requires the development of social access skills, leisure skills, and opportunities for independence and choice. Therefore, the transition process should include identifying social and leisure activities that an adolescent or young adult enjoys that promote social engagement with peers to provide a foundation for developing relationships. This process involves preference assessments to identify potential interests, and community knowledge to identify opportunities.

Once preferred activities are identified the individual needs to acquire specific skills required to perform the activity. These skills may involve specific rules or procedures for a structured activity (e.g., how to hold a bowling ball and read the electronic score) or social expectations for more informal interactions (e.g., how to order a drink at a coffee shop and where to sit in a snack bar). In addition to learning the skills, transition plans should also include to actually participate in the event. These skills include obtaining event information, meeting participation requirements, and securing any required materials or equipment. Transportation issues, such as the ability to use public transportation or working with families to provide it, also must be considered. Additionally, a degree of independence to engage in social interactions is required. Adolescents with disabilities may require time away from direct supervision by parents to interact with peers. Skills and expectations to obtain an appropriate degree of social independence should be addressed collaboratively with family members and support staff as part of the transition process.

**Dating.** Social skills specific to dating need to be addressed during transition. The concepts of love and intimacy should be explored based on the individual's context. Social skills involved in the dating process, such as evaluating social situations to determine if mutual attraction exists, risk taking in asking someone for a date, and emotionally handling rejection or acceptance should be explored. Additional skills for maintaining a relationship, such as sharing mutual interests, frequent and appropriate social contact, control in relationships, jealousy issues, and negotiation skills should be considered (Travers & Tincani, 2010). Education on when and how to end a relationship may be required as well. The ability to communicate effectively using appropriate means is a common thread underlying all these skills. Covert skills such as when to address someone face-to-face rather than through text or social media may need to be addressed.

The economic aspect of socialization and dating also must be addressed during transition. Many social events require admission fees, transportation costs, or incidental expenditures such as food or specialized equipment. Budgeting skills are required. The financial aspects of dating are often covert and fluctuate with situations and cultural expectations. Social and financial expectations of who should pay for a date need to be addressed in transition. These expectations will vary based on family norms, community norms, and gender role perceptions.

In addition to social skills, adolescents with disabilities may require support in making choices about their appearance that involve their sense of fitting into a peer group. Families and educators may provide opportunities for self-determination by allowing adolescents with disabilities to provide ideas and choices on age-appropriate haircuts and clothing. The topic of the appropriate age and use of makeup can also be discussed. Adolescents who require adaptive clothing can explore stylish ways to dress. For example, teens may choose to wear an untucked button-down shirt to cover pull-up pants if they are unable to wear pants with a fly (Weitlauf et al., 2013). Recently, retailers are including adaptive clothing on their online platforms to provide stylish options. The issue of **body image** may also need to be explored. The presence of a disability may impact how adolescents perceive their body and its desirability to others. An article in *Teen Vogue* addressed the issue of body image, sexuality, and disability and stressed the importance of exploring and promoting positive body images for all bodies (Henley, 2017). *(Please see Chapter 13 for more information on this topic.)*

Personal boundaries pertaining to involvement in sexual activity must be addressed. Issues involving boundaries, privacy, and consent should be addressed in the context of dating and later in the context of consensual committed relationships. Adolescents with disabilities, like their peers, may require training in the implications of giving and receiving consent for sexual activity, how to thwart unwanted advances, and identifying times and places for specific activities. Content such as good and bad touch, decision making and personal rights, and avoiding risky behavior can be incorporated into the transition goals (Wolfe & Blanchett, 2003). The issue of consent is particularly complicated for adolescents with intellectual disabilities. Legally, it is inaccurate to conclude that anyone with an intellectual disability is incapable of consenting to sexual activity; rather, each case must be analyzed individually based on specific facts. Evidence used to determine consent essentially mirrors the content of effective sexuality education transition planning and can include (a) all school evaluations and assessments of the adolescent's disability during his or her life; (b) the IEP from the school; (c) evidence of the individual's tendency to acquiesce (or not) in similar social situations; and (d) evidence of the individual's knowledge, or lack of knowledge, about sex (Rainville, 2013). Thus, in addition to fostering social skills related to sexuality, sexual knowledge is an essential transition planning component for adolescents with intellectual disabilities in particular and for all adolescents with disabilities in general.

## Sexual Knowledge

Daily living skills, such as self-care, and the ability to manage medical tasks are important transition components that are relevant to comprehensive sexual education. Sexual knowledge is foundational when addressing these tasks. For example, adolescents with disabilities, like other teenagers, need to master gender-specific hygiene and self-care skills; however, they may need additional support in order to perform these skills as independently as possible. Medical aspects such as birth control and gender-specific physical examination procedures must be considered. Likewise, adolescents with disabilities in general may not understand the mechanics of sexual acts. They may turn to peers or the internet for information, resulting in erroneous learning, misinformation, or victimization. Adolescents with physical or neurological disabilities may need to explore how and to what extent their particular body functions sexually given the presence of an impairment or disease. In the following section, transition skills related to sexual knowledge are presented. Daily living and hygiene skills, medical aspects of sexuality, and sexual functioning are addressed.

**Daily living and hygiene skills.** Many fundamental daily living and hygiene skills addressed in transition have direct implication to social skills, peer acceptance, and dating. As their bodies develop, adolescents with disabilities, like their peers, may need reminders or instruction in basic hygiene such as routine bathing, using deodorant, and wearing clean clothes. Individuals with low-incidence disabilities may require instruction when and where to touch or adjust their genitalia (i.e., privately in the restroom stall or bedroom). Grooming skills such as shaving for both men and women require instruction. Information regarding the mechanics and equipment for shaving must be reviewed. Some adolescents with disabilities may require a direct model for safely shaving areas such as the face, legs, or underarms. They also must learn to select the correct razor and know when to replace it. Instruction for using adaptive equipment for shaving may be required as well (Murphy & Elias, 2006).

Gender-specific daily living skills and knowledge are also required. Young women with disabilities must understand their menstrual cycle, be prepared for the onset of the period, and have the necessary supplies on hand. They may also require instruction on how to use various forms of feminine hygiene products such as pads and tampons, and when to change them. Navigating the social aspects of menstruation such as leaks or discreetly carrying pads and tampons should be considered. Young men may require training in keeping their penis and testicles clean, particularly if they are uncircumcised. They also may experience spontaneous erections and require coaching on how to handle this situation in a public setting (e.g., placing a book or jacket across their laps). The appropriate use of adult undergarments must be considered as well. Adolescent boys with disabilities may need support in selecting underwear (i.e., boxers, briefs, etc.) to accommodate their developing bodies.

Adolescent girls may require the same support with bras and panties. *The Healthy Body Tool Kit for Boys* and *The Healthy Body Tool Kit for Girls* are a useful resource for teaching gender-specific life skills (https://vkc.mc.vanderbilt.edu/healthybodies/). Developed by Vanderbilt Leadership Education in Neurodevelopmental Disabilities (LEND), the *Healthy Body Tool Kits* are designed to assist parents or guardians when teaching boys and girls with disabilities about puberty. The lessons and materials can be adapted for use by teachers as well. Gender-specific daily living skills can become more complex for individuals who do not identify with the gender binary. *(Please see Chapter 4 for more information about this topic.)*

**Sexual health.** In addition to understanding hygiene skills, adolescents with disabilities require knowledge about sexual health as they transition to adulthood. Sexual health is a key component of transition planning. Despite its importance, sexual information is often not provided during medical examinations. Medical examinations in general, but especially for adolescents with disabilities, typically focus on disease-specific issues such as adherence to medical regimens or medical stability, as opposed to sexual and reproductive health issues (Louis-Jacques & Samples, 2011). Likewise, primary care physicians indicated that they do not feel equipped to educate adolescent patients with disabilities about sexual health, and few adolescents with disabilities directly request information (Gleit et al., 2014). Consequently, adolescents with disabilities lack knowledge of general sexuality issues such as puberty, menstruation, masturbation, and homosexuality, as well as sexual health issues including pregnancy, childbirth, contraception, abortion, and prevention of sexually transmitted diseases (Galea et al., 2004; Sinclair et al., 2015).

Several resources exist for assessing sexual health and knowledge among adolescents with disabilities. They include (a) the Human Relations and Sexuality Knowledge and Awareness Assessment for People with ID (HRSKAAP-ID); (b) the Assessment of Sexual Knowledge (ASK); (c) the Sexual Knowledge, Experience, and Needs Scale for People with an Intellectual Disability (SexKen-ID); (d) the Socio-Sexual Knowledge and Attitudes Assessment Test-Revised (SSKAAT-R); (e) the General Sexual Knowledge Questionnaire (GSKQ); and (f) the Sexual Knowledge and Behaviour Assessment Tool (SKABAT). The majority of instruments include topics relative to relationships and what is appropriate for public versus private areas, legal issues associated with sexual relationships, physical aspects of development and sexuality (e.g., puberty, body parts, pregnancy), masturbation and intercourse, diseases, contraception, and orgasm. Drawings and photographs were provided as examples for some questions. The psychometric properties of the tools are largely unavailable, and limited reliability and validity information is provided (Thompson et al., 2016).

Wolfe and Blanchett (2003) recommend specific sexual knowledge content to include within transition. These domains include biology and reproduction (e.g., anatomy and physiology, gender differences, pregnancy, and birth control); health and hygiene (e.g., wellness, hygiene, sexually transmitted disease prevention); relationships (e.g., friendships and social skills, responsibilities to a sex partner, feelings and expression, and dating and marriage); self-protection and self-advocacy (e.g., protection from abuse); sexuality as a positive aspect of self; sexual behavior other than intercourse; and appropriate and inappropriate touching. These authors also address alcohol and drug use within these various domains because it can impact judgment and increase the likelihood of abuse.

In conjunction with sexual health in general, adolescents with disabilities should be informed about procedures for sexuality-specific medical exams prior to appointments and should have the opportunity to have a trusted caregiver present during the examination. Females with disabilities should be informed about the procedures for pelvic examinations and instruments used in advance. Positions for pelvic exams should also be considered and can be modified if needed depending on the physical or cognitive impact of the disability. This is especially important for young women with orthopedic or neuromuscular disorders. For example, rather than using the stirrups and frog-leg position, a V position, or elevation of the legs without hip abduction may increase comfort and decrease anxiety when examinations are indicated. Alternative procedures such as rectoabdominal examinations may offer an acceptable alternative to pelvic examinations (Murphy & Elias, 2006).

In addition to general knowledge of sexual health and function, adolescents with physical, neurological, or sensory disabilities may require individualized knowledge due to the impact of their disability on sexual functioning, pregnancy, and childbirth. This information typically is not addressed directly. For example, Thompson et al. (2016) found specific information about sexual acts, including libido, arousal, sexual aides or assistants, dysfunction, pleasure, and pain are not included within sexual information assessments. This information is important because sexual encounters may differ for individuals with disabilities. Areas of arousal may differ. For instance, an individual with spinal cord injury blocking feeling below the waist reported transferred feeling of arousal to other parts of the body such as his shoulder or chest. Fine and gross motor physical limitations, and visual or hearing impairments, may require individuals with disabilities to alter positions they use, the type of sexual activities they engage in, means of contraception used, and the nature of communication surrounding sexual activities (Kroll & Klein, 2001; Murphy & Elias, 2006).

Specific disabilities have implications on birth control, fertility, and pregnancy. Adolescents with disabilities and their families and support staff should address these issues during transition. The type of contraceptive method should be considered. Barrier devices, including condoms, cervical caps, and diaphragms require preplanning, cognitive understanding, and physical dexterity. Certain antiepileptic medication may decrease the effectiveness of oral or implanted contraceptives, and women with spinal cord injuries may be more susceptible to blood clots when using estrogen-based contraceptives such as birth control pills or patches. Fertility issues should be addressed as well. For example, fertility in females with spina bifida and spinal cord injury is generally preserved but reduced in males (Murphy & Elias, 2006). Health issues during pregnancy should be discussed. For instance, women with decreased bone density caused by a disabling condition are at increased risk of greater loss of density during pregnancy (Murphy & Elias, 2006).

## Marriage and Parenting

Along with addressing issues regarding fertility and pregnancy, the long-term topics of marriage, parenting, and custody must be considered. Adolescents with disabilities, like other teens and young adults, express an interest in marriage and family. These topics should be included in transition planning. However, for some adolescents with low-incidence disabilities, these particular issues require long-term planning, collaboration with families and community agencies, and residential support. In the following section, means for preparing for marriage, parenting, and custody during transition are presented.

Marriage is a potential outcome for adolescents with disabilities. Newman et al. (2011) found that 13% of young adults with disabilities reported being married within eight years of leaving high school as compared to 19% of their peers in the general population. An additional 11% of young adults with disabilities reported being engaged to be married, and 4% were divorced, separated, or widowed. Additionally, the 2018 Annual Report of People with Disabilities in America (Institute on Disability, 2019) reported approximately 40% of people with disabilities (ages 18–64) had never been married, inferring that 60% were at some point. As a result, aspects related to marriage should be addressed during transition.

The extent that marriage is directly addressed most likely depends on the impact of disabilities. Newman et al. (2011) indicated a greater percentage of young adults with high-incidence disabilities (i.e., learning disabilities, intellectual disabilities, and emotional behavior disorders) are married within eight years of leaving high school as opposed to those with low-incidence disabilities. Students with low-incidence disabilities are likely to require greater support with relationships, social skills, and independent living skills that are fundamental to marriage. Additionally, parents and service providers may perceive an adolescent with a low-incidence disability as more vulnerable to abuse in intimate relationships, or asexual and uninterested in marriage. As a result, parents and service providers are more restrictive regarding relationships and personal encounters for these individuals (Sinclair et al., 2015).

Although the initial thoughts on marriage may revolve around the sexual relationship, marriage is a complex legal agreement that impacts a variety of resources and has implications across various domains in transition. Individuals with a low-incidence disability who hope to marry must consider residential living situations that allow for dating, intimacy, and privacy as well as allowing married couples to live together. In addition, financial and legal considerations must be considered. For example, marriage may change an individual's eligibility for Social Security Disability funds and allow a spouse to make medical decisions. Parents and service providers may need to consider if their adolescent with a disability could marry and proactively address the residential, financial, and legal issues involved.

**Parenting.** Much of the comprehensive sexuality research pertaining to transition focuses on contraception and preventing pregnancy. However, given that a goal of transition is to focus on self-determination and the quality of life, the option of parenthood at some point in life should be addressed. Newman et al. (2011) noted the rate of parenthood for young adults with disabilities was consistent with the general population. The authors found that 29% of young adults with disabilities fathered a child during the first eight years after leaving high school as compared to 28% similar-age young adults in the general population. Of young adults with disabilities who had children, 49% had one child, 27% had two, and 25% had three or more children. Eighty-three percent reported that their children currently lived with them.

Given this rate of parenthood, several aspects regarding parenting can be proactively addressed during transition. The present and future needs of the adolescent with a disability should help guide this process.

Current strengths, resources, and support systems should be identified. These supports include physical, cognitive, financial, community, and family resources. Areas of need regarding parenting should be proactively identified as well, including the need to have trusted others in their lives to help with parenting issues. In addition, physical aspects of parenting should be assessed including the ability to hold and transport an infant, feeding skills, diaper changes, and dressing. The transition team can identify community agencies and financial resources that are available for prospective parents with disabilities.

Legal aspects of parenting or caregiving should be addressed. The potential competency of an adolescent with a disability to make decisions for a future child should also be considered. If competency is in question, custody agreements or legal guardianship arrangements should be anticipated. Custody is a court-ordered arrangement providing for the care of a minor child. A third-party custodian may be appointed by the court if necessary to fulfill the obligations that would normally be handled by the parents; however, the parent must be found unfit before a third party may be awarded custody of the child. Several types of custody exist: **physical custody** is the right to exercise physical control over a child for a defined period of time; **legal custody** grants exceptional authority to make decisions regarding a child's medical care, education, and legal rights. Custody is decided based on what is in the best interest of the child. In contrast, guardianship is a court-ordered relationship where an adult is appointed by the court to care for a minor child whose circumstances require it, and to make decisions about the child's education, support, and maintenance. Guardianship, unlike custody, limits the action one is permitted to take on behalf of a child. The extent of a guardian's power is decided by the courts based on the specific situation. If necessary, the court may appoint a guardian to take care and control of the child even though custody has been awarded to the parents (Justia, 2020). Requirements for custody and guardianships vary across states. Parents should be informed of the local requirements. Overall, pursuing custody or guardianship of a child whose parents are disabled should be addressed with care after a judicious examination of the facts that support it. It can create the assumption someone with a disability will automatically make a poor decision without understanding the consequence. According to Anderson (2019), sometimes what gets lost in translation is the fact that the same human rights exist for a person with a disability whether or not he or she has the capacity to understand those rights or assert them.

# Summary

This chapter explores transition issues related to sexuality development and highlights the importance of including comprehensive sexuality as a domain in transition planning. Typical barriers preventing comprehensive sexuality were identified and means for addressing these barriers were presented. In addition, content and issues regarding comprehensive sexuality transition planning were presented.

Transition planning in general involves developing and implementing individualized and actionable services across academic, vocational, and community living domains. Comprehensive sexuality education is a necessary component of transition planning because it is essential for protection, vital to health and productivity, and focuses on building meaningful relationships. It also directly reflects key principles of transition: self-determination, natural supports, and quality of life.

Despite its importance, comprehensive sexuality tends to be neglected in transition planning. Multiple barriers exist. Parents and teachers may underestimate the difficulty students with high-incidence disabilities have with navigating social pragmatics and understanding sexuality education content if it is not adapted to their instructional needs (Rowe et al., 2018). Parents and teachers may believe erroneously that sexuality education leads to unwanted sexual behavior or view individuals with low-incidence disabilities as asexual.

Transition planning should be guided by the components of comprehensive sexuality education and focus on the specific needs of the individual with a disability and their family. These components include social, financial, and community access skills needed to build relations, social pragmatic skills required to understand personal boundaries and consent, and self-care and self-advocacy skills needed to obtain medical and functional sexual information. Last, legal aspects of sexuality education should be addressed. These aspects include marriage requirements, age of consent, and child custody requirements for individuals who may not have the ability to be the primary caretaker of a child.

# Resources

## Internet Resources

National League for Nursing: Pregnancy in Women with Disabilities: http://www.nln.org/professional-development-programs/teaching-resources/ace-d/additional-resources/pregnancy-in-women-with-disabilities

*Social and Sexual Issues during Transition.* National Association of Special Education Teachers: https://www.naset.org/index.php?id=socsexualissues2

*The Healthy Body Tool Kit for Boys* and *The Healthy Body Tool Kit for Girls:* https://vkc.mc.vanderbilt.edu/healthybodies/

*Through the Looking Glass* (https://www.lookingglass.org/home) is a nationally recognized center that pioneered research, training, and services for families in which a child, parent, or grandparent has a disability or medical issue.

## Books/Articles and Other Resources

*ASSET: A Social Skills Program for Adolescents*

Kroll, K., & Klein, E. K. (2001). *Enabling romance: A guide to love, sex, and relationships for people with disabilities.* No Limits Communications.

*Skillstreaming the adolescent: A structured learning approach to teaching prosocial skills elements of understanding.* https://www.respectability.org/resources/sexual-education-resources/

## Sex Education Resources

https://www.respectability.org/resources/sexual-education-resources/

Sexual Health Resources: University Center for Excellence in Developmental Disabilities, Oregon Health and Science University. https://www.ohsu.edu/university-center-excellence-development-disability/sexual-health-resources

# CHAPTER 11

# Sexuality Education Policy

Lisa Goran and David F. Bateman

*As Chris grew up, he acquired an adult body and needs. He had sexual feelings. He developed emotional needs for friendship. He wanted to have fun. But as an individual with a developmental disability, he was permanently relegated to child status, without the freedom to determine where, with whom, and how he would like to do things. His family didn't receive much guidance on how to provide supports for him, nor did the schools focus on this; federal and state policies either restricted or did not provide supports or incentives for offering sexuality education to individuals like Chris.*

## Overview

This chapter discusses the relationship between policies related to students with disabilities and the descriptions of federal laws on comprehensive sexuality education, including accurate curriculum, contraceptives and abortion, abstinence policies, and mandated heterosexuality-focused instruction. The discussion involves federal laws; individual state laws are not addressed because there are too many variations across states to cover adequately. It is important to note that most state laws are based on not only the specifics of the federal laws but also the principles. The chapter also provides recommendations for school-aged transition practices related to students with disabilities.

The major focus of this book is on education related to students with disabilities, especially as it is associated with sexuality education. This chapter will discuss policies as they relate for the following reasons:

1. The Individuals with Disabilities Education Act authorizes state education agencies and local school districts to provide services to

students with disabilities between the ages of birth to 21, with 18 being the legal age for adulthood in most states.

2. Some individuals under 18 also qualify for services that are typically available only for adults, and therefore we need to address the role of state (non-education) agencies and how they work with these students. The most common, for our purpose, is vocational rehabilitation services, which some individuals may quality for at age 16.

3. The services provided by the various agencies are designed to help the students function independently (as much as possible) and the laws and policies guide this level of independence.

4. There needs to be consistent policies to help families understand the supports necessary to provide appropriate training for students eligible for special education.

5. There are skills that can be taught at all age levels. It is not a set of skills that should wait until the student is of transition age.

6. There are important resources that educators should review when looking at policies related to sexual education for students with disabilities.

## Federal Law: A Brief History of Sterilization

Historically, and as noted in several other chapters, the policy related to sexuality education for individuals with disabilities was based on preventing individuals with disabilities from procreating *(see the section on eugenics in Chapter 1)*. This was enumerated into the law with the Supreme Court decision in *Buck v. Bell.*

In *Buck v. Bell*, the U.S. Supreme Court in 1927 upheld a Virginia law providing for sterilization of people considered genetically unfit. The most famous line from the decision was "three generations of imbeciles are enough." When the court upheld the sterilization statute in Virginia, similar laws in other states were also approved. As a way of not having to spend money institutionalizing these individuals, over the next 30 years, an estimated 65,000 Americans were sterilized without their own consent or that of a family member (Cohen, 2016).

In 1942, the Supreme Court struck down a law allowing the involuntary sterilization of criminals. However, it never reversed or overturned *Buck v. Bell*, and therefore what is referred to as eugenic sterilization is still legal. In 2001, Virginia acknowledged the sterilization law was based on faulty science and expressed its "profound regret over the Commonwealth's role in the eugenics movement in this country and over the damage done in the name of eugenics" (Cohen, 2016).

The purpose of this chapter is to discuss policies and procedures related to sexuality education for students with disabilities and we would be remiss if we did not discuss some examples from state policies that allow for the sterilization of individuals with disabilities. Although not a direct bearing on our topic, it does relate to the mindset and attitudes regarding sex for individuals with disabilities. For example, North Carolina allows procedures to permit the sterilization of an individual who is deemed mentally ill or has intellectual disabilities and the procedure is deemed necessary. There must be doctor's or psychiatrist's approval, and the purpose for sterilization is for hygiene or convenience (Kaelber, 2014).

Laws like this must be considered on several levels. How much evidence of intellectual disability is necessary? What qualifies as a mental illness? What is medically necessary? Is this being done just for convenience? Is there an appeal process? Does the individual provide consent? Granted, these questions are outside the typical scope of education's parameters, but they need to be considered when we discuss society's attitudes toward sexuality for individuals with disabilities.

## Federal and State Policy: A Current View

A review of federal policy related to sexuality education for students with disabilities revealed little. After extensive research there was no evidence of specific policies related to sexuality education for students with disabilities in the many state rules and regulations. Discussed below, there are policies affecting the provision of educational services for students with disabilities that could include sexuality education, most notably the **Individuals with Disabilities Education Act (IDEA),** the Vocational Rehabilitation Act of 1973, and the **Carl Perkins Act of 1984.**

The principles of federal policy related to students with disabilities on sexuality education can be summarized in the following five statements:

1. Individuals with disabilities should be integrated into society as much as possible. Therefore, they should have the less-restrictive alternative whenever possible. This is exemplified in K–12 services by providing the student an education in the least restrictive setting (Yell, 2019).

2. All individuals with disabilities are entitled to due process protections as a means of holding the government accountable for the services provided. This important check on the education system is afforded to ensure students with disabilities receive an appropriate education (Yell, 2019).

3. Individuals with disabilities need advocates, not only for education, but to ensure the services provided are the ones necessary for their well-being. This ensures their rights and works to guarantee what is expected. The rights of individuals with disabilities would have little value without the due process protections mentioned in #2 above or without individuals advocating for appropriate services.

4. Individuals with disabilities have the right to express themselves. The concept of self-determination is very important in working with students with disabilities and, as these students transition to adults, it becomes an increasingly important part of the expectations of services. The ability to express wants, desires, and needs is an important part of anyone's life, and nowhere more so than as it relates to sexuality education.

5. The services provided to students with disabilities need to be individualized. This, in addition to the rights of self-determination, makes the program for each student unique, often very different from other students, even if they have the same disability. This may make the job of teachers or administrators more difficult; however, the rights of the student come first.

## Individuals with Disabilities Education Act (IDEA)

Individuals with disabilities were historically excluded from schools until the passage of PL 94-142 in 1975. The then-titled Education for All Handicapped Children's Act provided the first right to education for students with disabilities in the United States. This law has been amended several times based on the needs and changes that have arisen over time. For example, the original law provided services for students ages 5–18. It was later amended to include ages 0–21, and also amended to include the requirement that students should have plans that will help them **transition** from school to post-school life (Brady et al., 2020). In the federal requirements related to transition, there is nothing specific related to sexuality education for students with disabilities. However, the transition of students to post-school life needs to include more than just work; it should also include transition to social activities.

## Vocational Rehabilitation Act of 1973

**Section 504** is a brief but powerful nondiscrimination law included in the Rehabilitation Act of 1973. It extended to individuals with disabilities the same kinds of protections Congress extended to people discriminated against because of race and sex.

All students have the right to a free public education, and Section 504 ensures students with a disability that affects a major life function will continue to have access to an education despite their disability. Common disabilities covered by Section 504 plans in schools include ADHD/DD, nut allergies, and diabetes. The following are additional important points related to Section 504 (Bateman & Bateman, 2014):

- Section 504 is an anti-discrimination law. School districts receive no federal funds to implement this law.
- The responsibility not to discriminate against individuals with disabilities applies to all school personnel.
- In addition to students with disabilities, parents and employees also cannot be discriminated against.
- General education programs and teachers have the primary responsibility for the implementation of Section 504. Staff from special education may be consulted, but they do not have responsibility for implementation of the accommodations for the student.
- The accommodations required by Section 504 apply to the entire school and extend to parents and visitors to events.

## A Section 504 Plan

Similar to an IEP, a Section 504 plan lists the accommodations an eligible student would receive. It is individualized and based on the specific needs of the student's disability.

According to the U.S. Department of Education, "to be protected under Section 504, a student must be determined to: (1) have a physical or mental impairment that substantially limits one or more major life activities [learning is considered a major life activity]; or (2) have a record of such an impairment; or (3) be regarded as having such an impairment" (U.S. Department of Education, 2020).

An important consideration in determining eligibility is clarifying the specific problem students might have that would qualify them for a 504 plan. Examples of substantial life functions that, if impaired, would trigger an individual's eligibility include breathing, walking, talking, seeing, hearing, learning, and taking care of oneself.

All students eligible for special education are also eligible under Section 504. Even if a school decided not to implement special education under IDEA, they could still not discriminate under Section 504. Section 504 provides for accommodations for students with disabilities. It does not contain guidance related to sexuality education for students with disabilities. However, it is important that students with disabilities should not be discriminated against and should receive an appropriate education just like other nondisabled students.

## Carl Perkins Act of 1984

The other federal law often discussed relating to the transition of students with disabilities from high school to postsecondary is the Carl D. Perkins Vocational and Technical Education Act. First passed in 1984 and recently reauthorized in 2018, this law has as its sole purpose to increase the quality of technical education in the United States to help the economy. The big change brought about in the recent reauthorization was changing the term *vocational education* to *career and technical education*. However, as important as this law is for the transition of students with disabilities, there is no part of the law discussing sexuality education for students with disabilities (U.S. Department of Education, 2018).

## State Policies

As noted above, the purpose of this chapter is to discuss policies related to sexuality education for students with disabilities. Responsibility for education has historically been reserved to the states and there are a few recent state policies that need to be addressed. Though they do not specifically discuss students with disabilities, they do provide information related to the efforts of states to provide guidance regarding sexuality education.

In 2016, according to the National Conference of State Legislatures, all states were somehow involved in sexuality education for public school children (NCSL, 2016). Examples include:

- Twenty-four states and the District of Columbia require public schools teach sexuality education (21 of which mandate sexuality education and HIV education).
- Thirty-three states and the District of Columbia require students to receive instruction about HIV/AIDS.
- Twenty states require that if provided, sexuality and/or HIV education must be medically, factually, or technically accurate.
- Many states define parents' rights concerning sexuality education:
  - Thirty-eight states and the District of Columbia require school districts to allow parental involvement in sexuality education programs. Four states require parental consent before a child can receive instruction.

○ Thirty-five states and the District of Columbia allow parents to opt out on behalf of their children.

# Transition Policies

This section covers the requirements related to transition in great depth, providing suggestions not only for the formal requirements but also how to work with parents, and for social skills instruction, an often-forgotten component of sexuality education.

## Important Points

- Teachers should not wait until students are 16 or older to discuss post-school matters, especially as related to sexuality education.
- Transition includes making parents aware of resources and activities that can help as their student goes through various stages in post-school life.
- Schools have a responsibility to help a student prepare for post-school life, and all the student's teachers should work together in this effort.

## Transition: Purpose and Definition

The purpose of postsecondary transition is to help students and their families prepare for life after high school, which can be a major concern for students receiving special education. Transition is intended to be a coordinated set of activities provided by the school and outside agencies, and it is designed to promote a successful shift to independent living. These activities are outlined in the student's IEP and should focus on the ability and interests of the students, and not on what they cannot do (Prince et al., 2019).

The federal regulations in IDEA that relate to secondary transition include the following formal definition of "transition services":

Transition services means a coordinated set of activities for a child with a disability that—

- Is designed to be within a results-oriented process, that is focused on improving the academic and functional achievement of the child with a disability to facilitate the child's movement from school to post-school activities, including postsecondary education, vocational education, integrated employment (including supported employment), continuing and adult education, adult services, independent living, or community participation;

- Is based on the individual child's needs, taking into account the child's strengths, preferences, and interests; and
- Includes instruction, related services, community experiences, the development of employment and other post-school adult living objectives, and, if appropriate, acquisition of daily living skills and provision of a functional vocational evaluation. [34 CFR 300.43 (a)] [20 U.S.C. 1401(34)]

In its reauthorization of IDEA in 2004, Congress recognized that students with disabilities needed more assistance to help them get ready for post-school life (Prince et al., 2019). Congress expressly stated they would like schools to require more and better transition planning (Prince et al., 2019). As the definition indicates, the goal of transition is to promote successful outcomes for students with disabilities to either post-school education or employment. In turn, measuring students' success in moving to postsecondary institutions or employment would become an important component of accountability for schools (Prince et al., 2019).

## Transition Planning Policies

Although transition planning is an individualized process, there are some commonalities. Specifically, the federal regulations state the following:

Beginning not later than the first IEP to be in effect when the child turns 16, or younger if determined appropriate by the IEP Team, and updated annually thereafter, the IEP must include—

(1) Appropriate measurable postsecondary goals based upon age appropriate transition assessments related to training, education, employment and, where appropriate, independent living skills; and

(2) The transition services (including courses of study) needed to assist the child in reaching those goals. [§300.320(b)]

Post-school transition planning is required to begin at age 16 (or age 14, in some states), but for most students, age 16 is too late. Because developing a plan for a student's transition is part of the IEP team's responsibilities, the process can begin before age 16. Depending on the severity of the disability and the student's and family's goals for the future, specific issues need to be discussed and addressed well before the student turns 16. Many of the skills necessary for independent living and functioning need to be taught early on—and repeatedly.

Transition plans vary based on the student's individual needs, interests, strengths, and preferences. The IEP team should meet to talk about these aspects of the student's life and future goals to ensure that all team members are working toward the same end *(for more on IEP development, please see Chapter 8)*. The team should make sure the specific goals and objectives of the IEP relate to helping the student prepare for post-school life. Courses and experiences during the transition period should ensure the student leaves school with the skills needed for success in the next step after high school. The courses should contain information related to sexuality education. As you read the rest of this book, pay close attention to the history of sexuality education, the terms that are to be used, and the strategies for development of IEPs. It is all related.

Obvious sources for information related to sexuality education are conversations with the student and the parents as well as the student's teachers. One thing to keep in mind is the need to help students be realistic in their goals. The purpose is not to quash students' dreams, but to guide them through a decision-making process that results in achievable, measurable goals.

## Participants in Planning

Transition planning for students with disabilities is an integral responsibility of the IEP team, and all team members should participate in developing the plan, especially the student. Students often are not included in developing their IEPs in elementary school, but as transition planning begins, they should be involved as much as possible. Person-centered planning, which centers the student as the focus of the program, should be an important part of transition planning as it relates to sexuality education. Team members need to ask students to share their preferences and pay close attention to their answers, realizing these responses may change over time.

Parents should also be heavily involved. The IDEA amendments related to transition originated from the realization many students were graduating from high school without having been taught independent-living and work-related skills. As noted in the introduction of this book, sexuality education is often not discussed as a part of transition for students with disabilities. It is very important to remember parents and family members may be the only source of support for many of these students after high school, and their viewpoints are a key element in any decision that is made regarding the education of the student, especially as it relates to sexuality education.

Schools also should invite representatives from other agencies and vocational rehabilitation counselors to be part of the transition planning process, as needed. Parents are often lost as to what services are available for students after they leave high school. Providing these linkages in high school will help the parents understand a little more about what is necessary when the student leaves school. Additionally, such agencies also could be the ones responsible for the delivery of services needed by the student.

## Skills to Teach

In addition to the information related to sexuality education, there are many important social skills necessary for students with disabilities. Some of these skills will develop with experience, while others require explicit and repeated instruction. Some of these will need to be retaught many times over a student's career. Although they are not concepts specific to sexuality education, they tie in with fostering independence—an important part of transition.

### Seeking Assistance

All students need to know who they can go to for help if they have issues, concerns, or questions, and to realize that it is OK to stop what they are doing to ask for help. It is important to foster independence, but we also want students to know there will be times when they should seek assistance. They will need to understand not only when it is appropriate to do so, but also how to appropriately ask and who to ask—all of which depend on the specific tasks and activities at hand. You can use a variety of activities to start their thinking about the process of when to ask for help. As a future work skill, this is invaluable.

### Listening

Being able to listen to directions will have a dramatic effect on a student's independence and success both in school and in adult life.

### Attention to Others

Although it is important to teach students to work independently, teachers should also underscore the value of being aware of what is going on around them and seeing if what they are doing is the same as or different from what their peers are doing. This skill can help rectify a problem before it becomes severe.

## Frustration

We need to make sure we help students understand that frustration is a very real human emotion, that we all have to deal with it, and that there are appropriate ways of doing so. Students need to learn and understand that everything will not always go their way, and sometimes they will get frustrated by the course of events and the problems presented.

## Social Situations

Some of the social skills that students typically struggle with are those related to personal space, greetings, reciprocal play, conversation, perspective taking, and negotiating. As educators, we are continually addressing social skills with students, and instruction in these skills will probably need to be repeated multiple times. It is important to teach students how to recognize and deal with problems or issues related to interacting with others. Sometimes the rules are not clear and will vary depending on the situation.

## Empathy

We need to make sure students learn skills related to showing compassion, including understanding the difference between appropriate and inappropriate comments. Some of the individuals with whom students interact will have issues affecting their feelings and performance.

## Self-Determination

Students with disabilities have feelings, attitudes, and preferences about their future, and about their daily activities. We need to give them an opportunity to voice their interests and concerns, but they also need to understand that just because they make a choice, that does not mean it will automatically occur; other issues and concerns also come into play. For instance, a student's feelings regarding a specific student and companionship may not be fulfilled, for either logistical or health reasons. It is important to honor requests when possible and provide students an opportunity to make choices—and then, in turn, to learn from the choices they have made.

Transition is a normal part of every person's life, and the goal for school-related transitions is to make the process as smooth as possible for the student and the family. Schools are responsible to help ease this path for students, especially those with disabilities. Pay attention to the desires of the student and to those of the family. Parents will also need to familiarize themselves with the rights of their student and the school's particular procedures. Schools should provide clear information. Schools should also make it easy for parents to contact the relevant staff with questions. Starting this process before the start of school and with the goal of ongoing home-school collaboration is important for successful transitions.

## Resources on Policies Regarding Sexuality Education

There are several places to go for resources related to policies regarding sexuality education. Given the still-pervasive need for clarity regarding students with disabilities and sexuality education, one might have expected more central databases or clearinghouses with information related to policies and procedures. There are curricula, but there is surprisingly little information related to specific rules, practices, policies, or even recommendations. We realize all decisions regarding the education of students with disabilities who are eligible for special education and related services need to be made on an individual basis. However, that has not stopped Congress from adding the transition amendments to IDEA in 1990, which mandated activities and development of programs that lead to post-school activities for students. There had been some teachers and schools who were already implementing programs related to transition. However, there was no mandate from the federal government as a part of the education of students prior to 1990.

We believe there should be the development of a central database that would clarify procedures related to sexuality education for students with disabilities. This database would then assist in the development of policies and recommendations related to sexuality education practices for students with disabilities. Readers of this book will note the lack of guidance historically provided, other than simply not discussing it at all—a proverbial out of sight, out of mind. Not dealing with the need for sexuality education is one approach for dealing with it. However, it does not provide access to education and does not provide information for the student (soon to be adult) about how to make appropriate decisions.

There are a few resources that have some information regarding sexuality education, but it should be noted there is painfully little information related to students with disabilities. The existing resources listed below, at least, provide a starting point.

## Policy Information Related to Sexuality Education

- *American Sexual Health Association:* This association provides a wealth of resources on sexual health for both men and women, and specific resources directed at teens and young adults.
- *Center for Young Women's Health and Young Men's Health:* These websites provide information targeted at adolescents, including guides on a variety of sexual health topics.
- *Coalition for Positive Sexuality:* This website offers resources and tools for teens to take care of themselves and affirm their decision about sex, sexuality, and reproductive control.
- *Girlshealth.gov:* Offering guidance to teenage girls, this website provides facts on sex and STDs.
- *Planned Parenthood Federation of America:* Providing up-to-date, clear, and medically accurate information, Planned Parenthood helps both young men and women.

## Advocacy

- *Advocates for Youth:* This organization advocates for policies and programs that help youth make informed and responsible decisions about reproductive and sexual health.

# Summary

We've discussed the relationship between policies and laws related to students with intellectual disabilities and autism and comprehensive sexuality education, with a focus on the importance of accurate curriculum and of transition planning that includes specific skill instruction. The discussion focused on federal laws, but acknowledged that individual state laws must be considered because they vary widely. We provide recommendations for school-aged transition practices related to students with disabilities, with a recognition that each IEP team is charged with knowing what supports are needed by—and available to—the individual student.

# Resources

## Internet Resources

National Conference of State Legislatures: https://www.ncsl.org/research/health/state-policies-on-sex-education-in-schools.aspx
Sex Education Laws and Policies: https://www.plannedparenthoodaction.org/issues/sex-education/sex-education-laws-and-state-attacks
Sex Education and State Laws: https://www.guttmacher.org/state-policy/explore/sex-and-hiv-education
Sexual Education Policies by State: http://answer.rutgers.edu/page/state_policy/

## Books

*Education for life: Preparing children to meet today's challenges* by Donald Walters, published in 2004. This book does not have as its focus students with developmental disabilities and has a significant spiritual focus.

*Skills for families, skills for life: How to help parents and caregivers meet the challenges of everyday living*, 2nd ed., by multiple authors, published in 2010. It has one chapter focusing on sexual education, but the main focus is independent living aspects.

*The everything parent's guide to special education: A complete step-by-step guide to advocating for your child with special needs* by Amanda Morin, published in 2014, covers the basics of special education and how to advocate for your child who has a disability.

*Sexuality and relationship education for children and adolescents with autism spectrum disorders: A professional's guide to understanding, preventing . . . and responding to inappropriate behaviours*, published in 2014, focuses solely on individuals with autism. It has good information.

*Sexuality and relationships in the lives of people with intellectual disabilities*, by multiple authors in 2014. This book has a wealth of stories about individuals, by individuals with intellectual disabilities. It has great stories.

*Supporting disabled people with their sexual lives* by Tuppy Owens and Claire de Than, published in 2014. This book is a guide for people with disabilities.

*When young people with intellectual disabilities and autism hit puberty: A parents' Q&A guide to health, sexuality, and relationships*, by Freddy Jackson Brown and Sarah Brown, published in 2016. This book has a wealth of resources for parents in a question-and-answer format.

## Organizations

TASH: https://tash.org
Council for Exceptional Children: https://exceptionalchildren.org/

American Association on Intellectual and Developmental Disabilities: https://
www.aaidd.org/
National Autism Association: https://nationalautismassociation.org/

# CHAPTER 12

# Family Interactions and Culture

Christine Scholma and Sara Baillie Gorman

## Meet the Martinez Family

*Luis is an 18-year-old student with autism who attends the local public high school in a **self-contained classroom** with opportunities for **inclusion courses** in areas of interest and ability. Ms. Schultz, Luis's teacher, contacted the parents regarding a new behavior she was noticing at school, wondering if it was happening in the home setting as well and hoping to work with the parents to support the student. Mrs. Martinez answered the phone and Ms. Schultz asked if she would like to have the conversation in English or Spanish, knowing that Spanish is the language most frequently spoken in the home. Mrs. Martinez indicated that she preferred to speak in English and was not surprised to hear that Luis was engaging in inappropriate sexualized behavior within the school setting because it was happening at home too. Ms. Schultz asked Mrs. Martinez if she had any information that would help her understand the situation and Mrs. Martinez shared some information about her family.*

*The Martinez family is a Mexican American family comprised of a mother, father, 16-year-old daughter, and 18-year-old son, Luis. In addition, Mrs. Martinez's mother lives with the family. Mr. Martinez works two jobs and is rarely home while Mrs. Martinez assumes the role of homemaker and raising the children. The Martinez family is devout to the Catholic religion and their Hispanic heritage. As such, Mrs. Martinez explained to the teacher that in their culture, the father is the authority figure in the home. When Mr. Martinez is away from home, the authority goes to the first-born son, Luis. Lately, Luis has been engaging in self-stimulation in the living room in front of his 16-year-old sister. Unfortunately, Mrs. Martinez does not feel comfortable correcting his behavior.*

*Mrs. Martinez asked her husband and mother how to address the self-stimulation and received differing views. Mr. Martinez advised that she just ignore it; however, her mother approached it from a religious perspective. Based on the Christian Catholic religion, Mrs. Martinez's mother considers self-stimulation a sin. As such, she told Mrs. Martinez that she can't ignore the sexualized behavior or her son could be in danger of hell. This has left Mrs. Martinez confused and unsure of how to proceed. She is grateful for Ms. Schultz's call and is hopeful that the teacher can help her determine the best course of action.*

# Overview

This chapter will focus on the familial and cultural perspective of sexuality education for children and adolescents with disabilities. Families can experience a variety of perceptions related to sexuality development and education, leading to limited opportunities for sexual growth for children and adolescents with disabilities. In this chapter, cultural implications related to religion and ethnicity are considered, highlighting the importance of a collaborative, comprehensive approach to sexuality education for children and adolescents with disabilities. At the end of the chapter, suggestions for proactive advocacy are provided along with resources to support families in the process of partnering with school professionals to support the sexuality development of their children with disabilities.

Readers will

- develop an understanding of the complexity of the family role in sexuality education for children and adolescents with disabilities;
- be exposed to a variety of parental perceptions and barriers related to sexuality development of children and adolescents with disabilities;
- examine cultural implications including religion and ethnicity as it relates to sexuality development and education of children and adolescents with disabilities;
- identify the benefits of parental collaboration in sexuality education for children and adolescents with disabilities; and
- be equipped with strategies for proactive, collaborative sexuality education between the school and families.

# Family Role in Sexuality Education

Parents of children and young adults with and without disabilities have the same opportunities to positively influence their child's exposure to and education around the topic of sexuality; unfortunately, parents of children with disabilities are often fearful of approaching this topic with their child (Frank & Sandman, 2019). Parents taking a proactive role in supporting their child's sexual development should begin in early years of development and continue through adolescence. Unfortunately, for students with disabilities, parents indicate that if their child has received any instruction on sexuality at all, it has been delayed until late adolescence (Dupras & Dionne, 2014). One of the reasons for this delay or omission of education relates to a question of who should take the primary role in instructing the child about their physical development, sexuality, and relationships (Dupras & Dionne, 2014).

Parents, often feeling intimidated and ill-equipped to teach their child about sexuality (Dupras & Dionne, 2014), defer responsibility to the school professionals such as the general education teacher, the special education teacher, or the health instructor. Sexuality instruction provided exclusively within the school environment is often experienced by students through lecture-style lessons with little opportunities for review or repetition (Frank & Sandman, 2019). These sexuality lessons, typically taking place within the general education or health education classroom, are less likely to be adapted to meet the varied needs of learners with disabilities. Parents may perceive general education teachers and health educators as having the expertise to educate all students about sexuality, but often these professionals do not have the knowledge of how to effectively teach this topic to students with disabilities. Due to these challenges, it is common for parents of children with disabilities to fail to provide consent for their child to participate in these lessons (Frank & Sandman, 2019), thus delaying sexuality education until adolescence.

Special education teachers have the expertise to teach students with disabilities effectively but are often not prepared in their teacher preparation programs with the skills to teach sexuality education. The lack of focus on sexuality education in special education preservice teacher programs leads to a later onset of instruction within the transition years of schooling. Additionally, depending on state regulations, sexuality education may not be presented in the comprehensive approach but focus instead on abstinence and puberty. Knowing that students are receiving limited instruction within the school system, school professionals often perceive the role of sexuality educator to be the primary responsibility of the parents (Frank & Sandman, 2019). Role-related confusion can prevent students from receiving the integral support that they need within the formative years of physical and emotional growth.

To remediate this confusion and resulting delay or absence of instruction related to sexuality, it is recommended that parents and school professionals take a collaborative approach to educating children and adolescents with disabilities *(see Chapter 7: The Team)*. Parents can begin the introduction of topics related to sexuality at an early age and support their child alongside educators in a combined effort during school years. Approaching sexuality instruction in a comprehensive and collaborative way will support the student's development in a proactive rather than reactive way (Dupras & Dionne, 2014), contributing to holistic child development.

> *Let's return to the Martinez family. The phone conversation about Luis's sexualized behavior was between the teacher, Ms. Schultz, and Luis's mother, Mrs. Martinez. Based on what you just learned about role confusion with sexuality education, who do you think is taking the primary role in educating Luis? Is more instruction taking place in the home or the school? Is the approach collaborative in nature? Does it appear that the sexuality instruction that Luis received was proactive or reactive in nature?*

## Parental Perceptions Related to Sexuality Development

Fears about sexual abuse are prevalent in today's society. From Dr. Larry Nassar's abuse of gymnastics athletes becoming public to the "me too" movement, sexual abuse conversations are prevalent in our society *(see Chapter 3: Ethics)*. While media attention of abuses of sexuality may be enlightening to members of society, it adds another level of fear for parents and can be even scarier for parents of children with disabilities. A study in Turkey about sexuality and disability found that more than 72% of parent participants had concerns regarding the future of their children with a disability (Isler et al., 2009). One concern families have is that individuals with disabilities might be vulnerable to abuse and not be able to refuse inappropriate sexual activity.

Unfortunately, many of these fears related to sexual abuse are founded, as in the case of Anna Stubblefield. "Anna Stubblefield, an ex-Rutgers University Professor of Philosophy, was convicted in 2015 of the rape of an intellectually and physically disabled man after falsely obtaining his consent for sex via a technique known as Facilitated Communication (FC)" (Hemsley et al., 2018, p. 1). Stubblefield had been in the victim's life as a support, and yet rather than receiving support, the relationship ended in a rape conviction. When parents hear stories of abuse such as the one above, it can lead to responses of fear-based protection, limiting opportunities for sexuality education for their child with a disability.

In addition to abuse, parental fears related to health concerns are also at the forefront. Some families view sexual behavior related to its role in procreation. Research indicates that individuals with lower intellectual abilities have limited knowledge of health concerns related to sexuality, including knowledge of sex, sexual interactions, pregnancy, contraception, sexually transmitted diseases, marriage, and homosexuality (Isler et al., 2009). Sexual behavior can result in pregnancy, sexually transmitted diseases, and inability to access health care into the daily life of these individuals with disabilities. Significant health complications such as these can lead to increased parental fear for their child's well-being.

With these fears of abuse and health concerns, parents often wonder if sexuality instruction is appropriate for their child with a disability. Parents have feelings of confusion, anxiety, ambivalence, and inadequacy in relation to sexuality instruction (Frank & Sandman, 2019), leading some families to assume that the child is not emotionally ready to talk about sexual behavior. Specifically, parents fear that engaging in conversation about sex will promote sexual experimentation (Corona et al., 2016). Parents also wonder if their children already know too much, or on the contrary too little about sexuality. Since some families see a perpetuation of interest in children's television shows or toys beyond childhood for children with disabilities, there can be an assumption that adolescents with disabilities are not interested and/or are not ready to manage the emotions related to sexual behavior or impulses.

Finally, the overall perception of the general public also affects the parents' view of sexuality related to their child with a disability. Some parents have concerns regarding their children's behavior being misinterpreted in public (Corona et al., 2016). The concern of the public misinterpretation of sexual behavior includes the concern that the child might not understand privacy and engage in sexualized behavior at inappropriate times and places. All of these fears affect the sexuality education of the child with a disability and the family response to their child's sexual development.

*Think about the Martinez family again. What fears do you think Mrs. Martinez is holding as she has a conversation with the teacher?*

*How do her fears and the fears of other family members differ? How can teaching about sexuality address these fears?*

In addition to parental fears associated with sexuality education, it is common for families to make assumptions related to the terminology. First, parents may hear the term *sexuality* and associate it with sexual intercourse (Nichols & Blakely-Smith, 2009). Schools referring to their instruction on sexuality as **"sex ed"** perpetuate this limited view of sexuality education. Concerns relating to educating children with disabilities about sexual intercourse and the possibility that their child may have misunderstandings about the topic (Corona et al., 2016), paired with the knowledge of higher incidence of sexual abuse for children and adolescents with disabilities, leads some parents to respond by assuming the role of protector (Nichols & Blakely-Smith, 2009).

In response to fear for their child with a disability, parents taking the protector role can limit their child's opportunities for typical sexual development, including romantic relationships (Corona et al., 2016). Although parents may perceive their protective actions as positively impacting development in a safe environment, restricting opportunities for socialization can have the opposite effect. As adolescents enter adulthood with limited experiences and a lack of comprehensive knowledge of social skills, cognitive skills, and communication related to sexuality, adolescents are at a higher risk for negative sexual experiences and victimization (Corona et al., 2016). Additionally, restriction of sexual development and social opportunities perpetuates the historical stigma that individuals with disabilities are asexual beings without a basic need to be supported in this area in the same way as their peers (Dupras & Dionne, 2014).

Many of the fears and assumptions of parents related to sexuality education can be traced back to a lack of training and education for the parents. While curricula do exist, parents may not be aware of the resources available (Frank & Sandman, 2019). Similarly, while a sexuality education manual can be helpful, parents wanting face-to-face instruction with other parents may not find this offered locally. In lieu of resources and workshops, parents tend to revert to teaching their children with and without disabilities in the way that they were once taught. In these cases, parents are more likely to engage their children in talking about their developing bodies rather than sexual intercourse and sexually transmitted diseases (Klein et al., 2005). While this may be a problem with all children taught about sexuality narrowly in scope, it poses a greater challenge for children with disabilities, often gaining less sexual knowledge from their peers due to underdeveloped social skills (Nichols & Blakely-Smith, 2009).

*Why don't we think about Luis and his parents again? What sorts of assumptions do you think Luis's parents hold? What do you think their perception of sexuality instruction is? How do you think they might have been taught about sexuality in their school years? How does this influence how they are supporting Luis's sexual development?*

## Cultural Implications

Religious affiliations and beliefs can also affect sexuality development for all children, including children with disabilities. Most religions have assumptions and expectations around the topic of sexuality, with some religious institutions connecting sexuality directly with morality with a strong emphasis on sexual boundaries. For instance, in terms of sexual relationships, Judaism, Christianity, and Islam commonly assert that sexual intercourse be exclusive to lifelong marital partnerships (Mathewes, 2010). These religions historically hold a strong condemnation to LGBTQ+ relationships, believing that homosexual behavior is rebellious and a violation of God's order (Mathewes, 2010). However, it should be noted that modern religious institutions are reexamining historical views of sexuality, leading to evolving perceptions of sexuality.

Additionally, the religions of Judaism and Christianity tend to have particular views about one's own personal sexuality, believing that humans were not intended to engage in acts of self-pleasure (Mathewes, 2010). This view, stemming from a perception that sexual behavior is inexplicably linked to procreation, has implications that span from proper attire, particularly for females, to acts of self-pleasure, such as masturbation (Mathewes, 2010). Because these religious boundaries are often in opposition to cultural norms, the need for parental involvement in sexuality instruction is enhanced. When parents assume the responsibility of providing sexuality education to their children, including children with disabilities, they benefit from the opportunity to frame their instruction based on their religious beliefs and culture (Frank & Sandman, 2019).

Family structure and home life are a large aspect in the cultural perceptions that a family holds, each of which have value and must be considered. Let's consider one aspect of culture—authority. Some families are **matriarchal** (mother is the authority figure), others are **patriarchal** (father is the authority figure), some families are **gerontocracies** (authority is in elders), and yet other families are **egalitarian** (decentralized power). The social system under which the family operates might change perceptions regarding sexuality in the home. Another component to be considered is the size of the home and the physical space that is accessible to the child; it can affect where and when a person has access to private spaces to engage in sexual activities. As such, one cannot assume that every individual has access to a space that would be private in their home. The student might share a bedroom, or they might live in an arrangement in which they have roommates and use a public bathroom. These and other aspects of home life must be considered when planning for sexuality instruction for the student (Frank & Sandman, 2019).

Not only personal family beliefs, but the cultural context surrounding sexuality for the individual with a disability needs to be considered as well. The **sociopolitical** situations affect the instruction needed in a given place and given time (Rowe & Wright, 2017). For instance, a study examining the involvement of parents in sexuality education with their children with disabilities in Turkey indicated that more than 75% of the parents have had no formal sexuality education themselves (Isler et al., 2009). On the other hand, Dawood and colleagues examined how the epidemic of AIDS/HIV in South Africa led to including instruction about contracting this disease in sexuality education for individuals with disabilities in that country (Rowe & Wright, 2017). Sociopolitical contingencies affect the type of instruction needed.

*If we return to the Martinez family again, consider what parts of the family structure and home life affect the perceptions the family holds about sexuality and appropriate interventions for Luis's current behavior. How could you give value to these family's convictions as you ponder an appropriate intervention for Luis's increased sexualized behavior both in school and in the living room at home? How would this knowledge about the family change your intervention strategy in the school?*

## Benefits to Family Involvement

Although much of this chapter has discussed barriers and reasons why families are not engaged in sexuality instruction, the benefits of having the family as a part of the team cannot go without being emphasized. While there are curriculums available for students with intellectual and developmental disabilities, many of these lack training for families (Frank & Sandman, 2019). Yet, with the right approaches, the barriers can be overcome by developing a team approach with the family and educational team working together. With family involved in the instruction, family values can be at the forefront of the sexuality education process. Family structure and cultural considerations can be weighed when determining the appropriate way, and time, to teach sexuality instruction.

Besides the inclusion of family values, research indicates that another major benefit of having the family involved in sexuality instruction is the increase of communication between the parent and adolescent child. Frank and Sandman (2019) indicate that the "increased communication between parents and their adolescent children with ID about sexuality improves the parent-child relationship" (p. 332). In addition to improved relationship, these benefits also help to minimize some of the risks associated with sex as parents become a credible source of information to the teen about sexuality. When the parents become a credible source of information and the relationship strengthens between the parent and child, there is a decreased risk of adolescent pregnancy (Klein et al., 2005).

*Let's return to the Martinez family. If the family were invited to co-teach sexuality with the school, what possible benefits would you anticipate? How do you see the family engaging differently with the school if they could help with determining the content and learning strategies for Luis?*

## Instructional Approaches

Much of the research exploring the family role in sexuality instruction for people with disabilities includes information gathering. Most of the studies used surveys, interviews, or focus groups to gather information from the parents about the status of engagement with sexuality instruction as well as parental hopes and fears (Dupras & Dionne, 2014; Isler et al., 2009; Nichols & Blakeley-Smith, 2009; Pownall et al., 2011). Although much of the research is in the information-gathering stage, several interventions including parent involvement in sexuality instruction for children with disabilities have been evaluated. The most common intervention evaluated for effectiveness is parent training.

Overall, research has found that the parent training allowed participants to be more comfortable with the topic of sexuality, in particular talking about sexuality with their teen child (Corona et al., 2016; Klein et al., 2005; Nichols & Blakeley-Smith, 2009; Schuster et al., 2008). Even with the increase in comfort with the topics of sexuality, parents indicated that they needed more support (Nichols & Blakeley-Smith, 2009). Parent training for sexuality education for children with disabilities was often conducted over the course of one to two months (Corona et al., 2016; Klein et al., 2005; Nichols & Blakeley-Smith, 2009; Schuster et al., 2008). Feedback related to these training sessions included parents wanting the sessions to be longer than an hour and for a duration of longer than eight weeks (Nichols & Blakeley-Smith, 2009). It is recommended based upon these findings that training be provided to parents over multiple months.

Frank and Sandman (2019) created the Home-Based Adolescent Sexuality Education for Intellectual Disabilities (Home B.A.S.E.) curriculum. Using this curriculum, parents are educated on their role as the primary educator regarding sexuality for their adolescent children with intellectual disabilities. This curriculum was designed with the belief that sexuality is a human right for all. It is designed with an interactive small group format over multiple sessions. While this curriculum considers the barriers, benefits, and perspectives of this chapter, effectiveness data are not yet available. *(See Chapter 9 for more information.)*

With the limited number of researched methods for instructing sexuality alongside family, future educators are encouraged to be attentive to ensuring their sexuality education approach is effective for the students with disabilities they are supporting. Educators should frequently collect data during the intervention and review it regularly with the entire team. Analysis of the data will help the team make informed decisions about continuation of the intervention or revisions that are necessary to support the sexual development of the student.

> *Let's go back to Luis again. What do you think would be important to consider when determining an approach to teaching sexuality? What do you think are the priorities for him? How would you walk alongside the family in supporting the priorities you just identified?*

## Moving Forward

Sexuality education for all children and adolescents, not only individuals with disabilities, can be a sensitive topic and includes not only the aspects of sexuality and puberty but family dynamics and culture as well. When addressing topics of sexuality with people with disabilities, we recommend to first, BREATHE. When you use the mnemonic below before beginning sexuality instruction, you will ensure family involvement is encouraged.

■■■■■■■ **TEXTBOX 12.1** ■■■■■■■

## BREATHE Acronym

### Before Beginning Sexuality Instruction

**Beliefs**—Consider the family beliefs, culture, religion, and perceptions. How will those be taken into consideration? Has the family been invited into the conversation to share their thoughts and beliefs?

**Roles**—What type of role does the family want to take when it comes to this education? Define the roles of everyone involved in sexuality education. Has the family been specifically invited into this conversation?

**Explore**—Once you consider the family's beliefs, explore options of the existing curriculum and teaching methods alongside the family.

**Adopt**—Adopt a teaching method and/or curriculum that meets the needs of the individual.

**Train**—Ensure that all people assisting with the instruction, including family, are trained on the method and protocol that will be used.

**Help**—Work as a team. During the teaching process, come alongside the family to help them engage in the instruction together.

**Effectiveness**—Review the data with all parties and consider the effectiveness of the instruction. Change instruction as needed.

*For the last time, let's go back to the Martinez family. After learning about the family dynamics and cultural aspects of sexuality, the school team found it important to ensure the family felt their values were respected. Since the parents were not on the same page originally, the school team found a local agency that provided face-to-face instruction in both English and Spanish to parents. The parents decided they wanted to attend this instruction first, so they could come to a cohesive decision between the parents as to how they wanted sexuality instruction to be handled with Luis. After the face-to-face instruction, they promised to come back to the school team for a group planning session in four weeks.*

*With this information, go through the steps of the BREATHE considerations for this family. What would your recommendations be for this family moving forward?*

# Resources

## Internet Resources

Sex Ed Guide for Self-Advocates: https://researchautism.org/sex-ed-guide/
Sexuality and Down Syndrome: https://www.ndss.org/resources/sexuality/
Parent Center Hub: https://www.parentcenterhub.org/sexed/
Facilitated Communication and Sex Abuse: http://theconversation.com/its-time
-to-stop-exposing-people-to-the-dangers-of-facilitated-communication
-95942

## Suggestions for Extending Learning

- Conduct interviews with two teachers from any grade level to gain information about school expectations for sexuality education, their role as a sexuality educator, and interactions with parents related to their child's sexuality. Compare the two teachers' answers, looking for differences in philosophy. Were they taking a collaborative approach that was culturally sensitive?
- Watch NBC's show *New Amsterdam*, Season 2, Episode 6, "Righteous Right Hand." Consider how the individual with Down syndrome is treated regarding her sexual choices. Do you think that the hospital staff were looking out for her best interests?
- Think about how you would support a family's needs related to their child's sexualized behavior in both home and school settings. Practice this by creating a resource that you could provide the family to use at home in support of your instruction at school. This resource may be used at both home and school or exclusively at home. Some examples are a task analysis of a self-care skill such as changing a pad, a social story for what to do when you get an erection at school, or a choice board indicating public and private behaviors.
- Have a conversation with your own parent and/or guardian. Ask them about how they approached sexuality instruction for you. Was your family involved in the sexuality instruction for you? If so, how? If you have siblings, ask your parents if this was the same for each child or if it was different for other children. Explain how this might, or might not, be appropriate for a person with a disability.

  Search the internet for services in your area relating to sexual education. Create an annotated bibliography of these resources.

# CHAPTER 13

# Entertainment and Social Media

MaryAnn Shaw and Elizabeth A. Harkins Monaco

*There are a whole lot of misconceptions about disabilities. They range from thinking we need a miracle cure to live a full life to assuming we can't have sex.*

—Mike Kiel, from his autobiography, *Challenge the Moment*

## Overview

This chapter will examine minority rhetoric as it relates to comprehensive sexuality, including the influences of pop culture and the media on public perception. Readers will explore how entertainment media is an avenue for promoting accurate information for and about people with disabilities, but that stereotypes and misleading, inaccurate portrayals are common. This chapter will also discuss digital media and how it offers the opportunity for social interaction and intimate relationships, but for those with certain disabilities, its use can also result in misinterpretations and negative social and emotional consequences.

Readers will

- analyze the negative effects of pejorative language used to describe individuals with disabilities and the use of respectful, humanistic language;
- identify the principles of **person-first philosophy** and **identity-first language**;
- compare the positive and negative ways people with disabilities are portrayed in popular culture and ways to dispel stereotypes;
- identify possible consequences, both positive and negative, for people with disabilities when accessing the internet and using social media; and

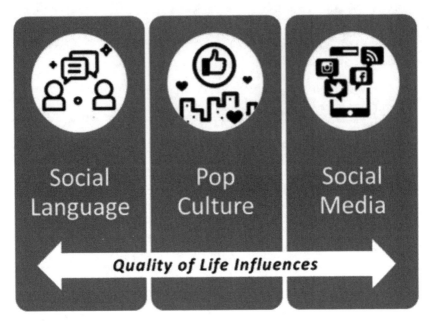

**Figure 13.1.** Quality of Life Influences

*Source:* Shaw, M., & Harkins Monaco, E. A. (2018). We can't hide: Pop culture and digital media. In E. A. Harkins Monaco, T. Gibbon, & D. Bateman (Eds.), *Talking about sex: Sexuality education for learners with disabilities.* Rowman & Littlefield.

- critique teaching tools and interventions for educators, parents, and counselors to improve understanding of the benefits and risks of using digital media for individuals with disabilities.

## Minority Rhetoric

Historically, individuals with disabilities were considered visually con-spicuous, as polarizing prodigies or monsters, deserved to be stared at, or politically and socially erased by society. By the early 20th cen-tury, they were considered deserving of torture or death. While this has improved over time, today there are three main **rhetorics** that portray people with disabilities with "unhealthy norms for inclusion" (Harkins Monaco, 2020). *(See Chapter 4.)*

1. The **wondrous rhetoric** shows people with disabilities as heroes when they complete everyday tasks. This, also known as "inspira-tion porn," promotes disability as the sum of the differences between people (Young, 2012). For example, "the media's focus on 'human interest' stories of so-called supercrips—including disabled athletes as well as supercrip 'celebrities' like Helen Keller, Stevie Wonder, and Stephen Hawking—those individuals whose inspirational stories of

courage, dedication, and hard work prove that it can be done, that one can defy the odds and accomplish the impossible" (Berger, 2013, p. 29–30.

2. The **sentimental rhetoric** presents people with disabilities as charitable cases who need money, time, and help from others (Garland-Thomson, 2002). This rhetoric portrays people with disabilities as "abnormal, inferior, or dependent people who at best should be pitied, treated as objects of charitable goodwill, or offered ameliorative medical treatment" (Berger, 2013, p. 29). Many times, charities or organizations advertise using this kind of rhetoric.

3. The **exotic rhetoric** presents people with disabilities as easy entertainment or promotional. For example, when advertisers use pictures of able-bodied models or celebrities in wheelchairs, or when wheelchairs are used as props. (Garland-Thomson, 2002; Harkins Monaco, 2020)

These rhetorics are deeply connected to current societal perspectives regarding disability, but they actually suggest unhealthy norms for inclusion (Harkins Monaco, 2020). "Rather, disability can be embraced, even celebrated, as a matter of group identity, as social minorities have done, as part of the broader fabric of human diversity, and as a site of cultural resistance to socially constructed conceptions of normality" (Berger, 2013, p. 29). The **realistic rhetoric** does just that by normalizing the disability experience. It presents people with disabilities as "normal" people who are capable of "normal" feelings, thoughts, and actions (Garland-Thomson, 2002), ultimately promoting equality.

## Rhetoric in Entertainment Media

When we examine the portrayal of characters with disabilities in literature, movies, television, and news, they typically fall into predictable categories associated with the wondrous, sentimental, and exotic rhetoric: tragic heroes with superhuman-like qualities who overcome obstacles in spite of their disabilities; appealing yet pitiful victims who often possess childlike qualities; or evil villains who turn to crime due to resentment over their disabilities (Lester & Ross, 2003). These stereotypes may seem like harmless entertainment, but when people do not have direct contact with individuals with disabilities, they are likely to form opinions based on what they read, see, or hear in popular media. While progress is being made to improve these portrayals, a segment of entertainment media continues to perpetuate stereotypes and stigmatize people with disabilities. This is documented as early as the 1930s with the horror film genre. See Table 13.1.

Table 13.1   **Historical Media Stereotypes**

| Stereotype | Characteristics | Barriers created | Examples |
|---|---|---|---|
| Grotesque villains | • Monsters<br>• Ugly<br>• To be feared | • Even when the person with the disability was not the villain, they are still presented as people to fear. | • *Frankenstein*<br>• *Moby-Dick*<br>• In *The Hunchback of Notre Dame* (1939) the main character, Quasimodo, was made to be as "grotesque as possible" (Berger, 2013, p. 185).<br>• *Sling Blade* (1993) promoted the idea that people with mental illness are dangerous to others. |
| Saintly sages (Norden, 1994; Berger, 2013) | • Wise<br>• "Secret" powers<br>• Exaggerated skills | • This implies that people with disabilities must have at least one specialized skill or strength to contribute to society. | • In *The Bride of Frankenstein* (1935) "we are introduced to . . . a blind hermit" who is the only character to understand Frankenstein's true character (Berger, 2013, p. 189).<br>• *Rain Man* (1988) portrayed a man on the autism spectrum as a savant but also not capable of living on his own as an adult. |
| Charitable cases (sentimental) | • Poor beginnings<br>• Humble lifestyle | • This reinforces that people with disabilities are dependent on help from others for survival. | • *A Christmas Carol*'s Tiny Tim is a boy with physical disabilities who is poor (Norden, 1994; Berger, 2013). |

To make matters worse, people with disabilities are historically under-represented in entertainment media, and when they do appear, the characters are based on negative stereotypes that are stigmatizing and present inaccurate messages. Actors frequently give exaggerated performances displaying every possible symptom from the diagnostic criteria of a given disability, or characters are portrayed as one-dimensional and uncomplicated, often to support the storyline of a major character. Rarely do storylines involve sexual or romantic relationships. Storylines

Table 13.2   **Current Media Stereotypes**

| Stereotype | Characteristics | Barriers Created | Examples |
|---|---|---|---|
| Hero (wonderous rhetoric) | • Possession of a rare talent<br>• Superhuman power<br>• Ability to "overcome" disability | • Creates unrealistic expectations<br>• Minimizes the real struggles that people with disabilities face daily<br>• Implies that a person with disability must overcome the disability or perform extraordinary acts | • Daredevil is a superhero who overcomes his blindness to become a superhero.<br>• Silhouette is a superhero who fights villains using martial arts despite having paralysis.<br>• Professor X from the Avengers. |
| Victim (sentimental rhetoric) | • Helpless<br>• Vulnerable<br>• Pitiful<br>• Asexual<br>• Childlike innocence<br>• "A child trapped in an adult's body"<br>• Depict disability as an insurmountable challenge | • Disempowers and objectifies people with disabilities by implying that they must be cared for and protected<br>• Restricts age-appropriate activities<br>• Influences caregivers to deny or remain unaware of sexual development, interests, and needs<br>• Influences caregivers to become overprotective and to prevent access to outlets for sexual behaviors or conversation (Attwood et al., 2014) | • Will Traynor in *Me Before You* and Maggie Fitzgerald in *Million Dollar Baby* both present suicide as a better option than living with a disability.<br>• Forrest Gump<br>• Lenny in *Of Mice and Men* |
| Villain (exotic rhetoric) | Less frequently used to depict individuals with intellectual or developmental disabilities<br>More often used to depict physical disabilities (Lester & Ross, 2003) | Dehumanizes individuals with disabilities<br>Implies that they turn to revenge out of resentment of their condition<br>Implies a tendency toward criminal behavior<br>Creates fear of people with disabilities | The villains in most James Bond movies, including *You Only Live Twice*, *GoldenEye*, *Casino Royale*, *Die Another Day*, and *Skyfall*<br>Darth Vader in *Star Wars*<br>Joaquin Phoenix's titular portrayal in *Joker* |

Shaw, M., & Harkins Monaco, E. A. (2018). We can't hide: Pop culture and digital media. In E. A. Harkins Monaco, T. Gibbon, & D. Bateman (Eds.), *Talking about sex: Sexuality education for learners with disabilities*. Rowman & Littlefield.

tend to focus on the disability, rather than the individual (Barnes, 1992). Not only does this create an unrealistic picture of people with disabilities; it dehumanizes by failing to portray individuals with unique feelings, thoughts, and personalities. When negative, inaccurate stereotypes of people with disabilities are perpetuated in popular culture, much damage is done to the quality of life of the individuals who are targeted. See Table 13.2.

# Combating Stereotypes

## Language

Labels are powerful; they can be valuable tools that open doors to services and funding, or weapons that create stigma and pain. Throughout history, people with disabilities have been known by many labels. When viewed through today's lens, some sound appalling. Words like moron and imbecile were originally used by medical professionals to describe people with intellectual disabilities but took on different connotations as they entered the popular culture of the time. When they became derogatory, they were replaced by non-offensive terms, which, in turn, took on new meanings as they filtered into society. The term **mental retardation** was adopted in the late 19th century and eventually developed a negative connotation, particularly as the derivative *retard* became part of the vernacular in the mid-20th century. In 2009, a movement was created called Spread the Word to End the Word in an attempt to eradicate the use of the term *retarded*, which became known in some circles as "the R-word" (Reynolds et al., 2013). In 2010, Congress passed **Rosa's Law,** which changed the term *mental retardation* to *intellectual disability*, and references to *a mentally retarded individual* to *an individual with an intellectual disability* in federal health, education, and labor laws and policy. Changes were also made in the *DSM-5* and public education terminology (American Psychiatric Association, 2015; Reynolds et al., 2013).

Person-first vs. identity-first language. Those changes are part of a larger movement among advocates and self-advocates to destigmatize and humanize people with disabilities through the use of language. **Person-first language** began in the 1980s as a way of speaking and acting that avoids sensationalizing, victimizing, or otherwise stereotyping a person because he or she has a disability (People First Language, 2017). An important aspect of person-first language is the practice of putting the person first and the disability second when speaking or writing. This avoids using the disability to define the person. For example, instead of saying "the disabled child," when using person-first language, one would

## Table 13.3   Terminology

| Person-first terminology | Terminology to avoid |
| --- | --- |
| • He has Down syndrome.<br>• She has muscular dystrophy.<br>• He uses a wheelchair.<br>• She competes.<br>• The child has a congenital disability. | • He is afflicted with Down syndrome.<br>• She is a victim of muscular dystrophy.<br>• He is wheelchair-bound or confined to a wheelchair.<br>• She bravely competes despite her disability.<br>• The child has a birth defect.<br>• He bravely overcame his disability. |

Shaw, M., & Harkins Monaco, E. A. (2018). We can't hide: Pop culture and digital media. In E. A. Harkins Monaco, T. Gibbon, & D. Bateman (Eds.), *Talking about sex: Sexuality education for learners with disabilities*. Rowman & Littlefield.

say, "the child with a disability." Emphasizing abilities rather than disabilities or limitations and avoiding terminology that casts a person with a disability in one of the stereotypical categories of victim or hero are also ways to practice person-first language.

In Harkins Monaco et al. (2018), *Talking about sex*, Shaw (2018) defined the examples and non-examples of person-first terminology found in Table 13.3.

It is important to note that many individuals with disabilities, particularly those who are members of the deaf, blind, and autistic communities, view their differences as a part of their identity and prefer not to use person-first terminology. They embrace their differences and their labels and advocate the use of identity-first language. The major difference between use of person-first and use of identity-first language is in how each describes an individual with a disability. For example, users of identity-first language will say "Autistic person" or "Deaf person" instead of "person with autism" or "person with a hearing impairment." The idea being that "Autistic" and "Deaf" are characteristics that are part of one's identity like race, religion, or nationality, and not something negative (Dunn & Andrews, 2015). When using identity-first language in writing, the disability category is capitalized. *(See Chapter 3)*.

There is some controversy among and within disability groups about whether person-first or identity-first language is appropriate. The goals of both are to promote a view of people with disabilities as individuals who have the right to be treated and spoken of with respect and dignity. There is no one way of speaking that is correct, but organizations like the Arc of the United States, Special Olympics, and the American Psychiatric

Association currently advocate the use of person-first language and most schools expect teachers and related service providers to use person-first language. Individual preferences of the person in question should be the determining factor in deciding how one speaks about him or her. Using language that respects the individual being discussed or referred to is one of the first steps in combating stereotypes and promoting respect for people with disabilities.

Despite the widespread push to embrace respectful language and eliminate the use of the word *retarded*, these are new concepts for many in the United States. A Harris poll (2017) found about 40% of adults stated they saw nothing wrong in using the word to describe a thing or situation. In fact, 50% of those polled have heard someone with an intellectual disability called a *retard*.

## Entertainment

> The goal is that everyone should get to turn on the TV and see someone who looks like them and loves like them. And just as important, everyone should turn on the TV and see someone who doesn't look like them and love like them. Because perhaps then they will learn from them. Perhaps then they will not isolate them. Marginalize them. Erase them. Perhaps they will even come to recognize themselves in them. Perhaps they will even learn to love them.
>
> —Shonda Rhimes (Rhimes, 2015)

While progress is being made to improve portrayals, a segment of entertainment media continues to perpetuate stereotypes and stigmatize people with disabilities. The decade of the 2010s ushered in some long-awaited and hoped-for changes in casting and programming for television, internet productions, and big-screen cinema. More productions featured storylines about people with disabilities in realistic (or as realistic as television entertainment gets) situations including romantic and sexual relationships. More actors with disabilities are being cast in roles of characters with disabilities. While the trend is promising, there is great room for improvement. The statistics reflect the immense scope of the problem. In 2019, 20% of the U.S. population had a disability, fewer than 2% of all television characters did, and 95% of TV programs that featured characters with disabilities had them played by nondisabled performers (Woodburn & Kopic, 2016).

In 2008, the movie *Tropic Thunder* received negative attention for insensitive content directed at people with intellectual disabilities, and for repeated use of the word *retard*. A coalition of 22 advocacy groups, including the Special Olympics, the Arc of the United States, and the National Down Syndrome Congress reacted by launching a nationwide boycott of the film (Zeidler, 2008). In spite of the negative attention the film garnered, it achieved box-office success and earned almost 200 million dollars worldwide (*Tropic Thunder,* 2008). *Million Dollar Baby,* released in 2004, and *Me Before You,* released in 2016, are both critically acclaimed films and both contain disturbing storylines suggesting that suicide is preferable to living with a physical disability.

**Entertainment media.** Like spoken language, entertainment media has the power to influence society's perception of groups of people in a positive or a negative way. Advocacy organizations continue to urge popular media to develop realistic characters with disabilities living successful lives and suggest that people with disabilities be included in story development. It appears that some in the entertainment industry have been listening and share those feelings.

**Movies.** In 2005, Johnny Knoxville (of *Jackass* fame) starred in the movie *The Ringer,* as a man who pretends he had a cognitive disability to win the Special Olympics. This film relies on stereotypes of disability by exposing the normalcy of making the person with a disability the butt of jokes and by having nondisabled persons play characters with disabilities (Cherney, 2006). By the 2010s, more believable multidimensional characters began appearing in dramas and comedies in motion pictures and on television, sometimes in title roles, and portrayals seem to be moving away from the stereotypical hero or victim. For example, successful movies like *The Accountant* starring Ben Affleck and *Extremely Loud and Incredibly Close,* with Tom Hanks, feature characters with autism in leading roles. While these two films feature lead characters with disabilities, they both received mixed reviews and criticism from some who cite exploitation and unrealistic portrayals by actors who do not have the same disability as the characters they portray. Some more recent feature films star actors who have disabilities playing characters with disabilities. One notable example is *The Peanut Butter Falcon,* released in 2019 to critical acclaim. The film tells the story of a Mark Twain–like adventure with a lead character who has Down syndrome. The actor who plays him, Zack Gottsagen, also has Down syndrome. Most recently, Zack Gottsagen became the first individual with Down syndrome to present an Oscar award (*The Peanut Butter Falcon,* 2019).

Documentary feature films have also done a great deal to break stereotypes and raise awareness for individuals with autism and intellectual disabilities. *Autism in Love* (2015) is a PBS Independent Lens film chronicling the lives of four adults, all on the autism spectrum, and the challenges they face as they search for love and intimacy (Fuller, 2016). *Monica and David* (2009), an HBO documentary film, follows a newly married couple with Down syndrome through their first year of marriage. Another documentary, *Life Animated* (n.d.), portrays the journey of a young man with autism. In the film, he navigates his first break-up. *Monica and David*, *Autism in Love*, and *Life Animated* have received positive reviews from advocacy groups and are sold as educational DVDs with public performance rights. They provide opportunities for discussion of the complex issues of intimacy, marriage, sex, loss, and love for individuals with autism and IDD, their teachers, counselors, and families. These films also showcase the unique ways in which the disabilities affect the lives of the stars while depicting them as people first. Their challenges and celebrations are ones that an average person can relate to; they are realistic, emotional, and honest.

**Television.** Several notable programs developed for the small screen also include complex characters with disabilities, but while the recent television productions provide thoughtful storylines, none of the actors portraying characters with disabilities have disabilities themselves. *The Good Doctor* and *Atypical*, two series from ABC and Netflix respectively, both feature lead characters on the autism spectrum who are portrayed by neurotypical actors. Many advocates argue that these are not authentic portrayals and fight for changes in hiring, but these shows have addressed dating and romantic relationships in a fairly realistic manner.

There is some progress that can be noted regarding representation. Lauren Potter is an actor and disability rights advocate with Down syndrome. She broke barriers in the early 2000s when she played a recurring character on the TV series *Glee* for six seasons. Her character Becky was a cheerleader who also had Down syndrome. Her romantic feelings were realistically portrayed when she unsuccessfully tried to win the affections of another character. Another notable exception is Micah Fowler, a young actor who has cerebral palsy and starred in the ABC sitcom *Speechless*, which debuted in 2016. He played a character with cerebral palsy who used augmentative and alternative communication (AAC) to communicate. Minnie Driver, who plays Fowler's mother on the show, describes his character, JJ: "He likes girls, wants to try beer for the first time, wants to hang out and get in with the cool kids" (Rovenstine, 2016). In 2019, the character Jack Damon was introduced on the NBC hit series *This Is Us*. The character and the actor who plays him, Blake Stadnik, are both blind. Jack's storyline includes a meaningful romantic relationship. Cole Sibus, an actor with Down syndrome, is featured in an ABC TV drama released in 2019 called *Stumptown*. Sibus's previous television credits include *Born This Way*, an award-winning reality

TV series on the A&E cable network that ended its fifth and final season in 2019. Another new television show, *Everything's Gonna Be OK* on Freeform, stars Kayla Cromer, an actor on the autism spectrum. Her character on the show is also on the autism spectrum (Heasley, 2020).

**Reality television.** While there is controversy surrounding the ethics and accuracy of so-called reality TV, it is this genre that portrays the most characters with disabilities and employs the greatest number of actors with disabilities (Kidd, 2014). At its worst, reality TV exploits its stars and sensationalizes disabilities, but at its best it challenges damaging stereotypes and promotes meaningful discussion by presenting a "normalized" view of the lives of people with disabilities. For example, *Born This Way* followed the lives of seven young adults with Down syndrome and their parents as they react and adjust to challenges and successes in their everyday lives. The show addresses issues such as dating, sex, healthcare, and self-determination. *Born This Way* has been well received by many disability advocates. Randy Rutta (2016), the CEO of Easter Seals, said this about the program:

> *Born This Way* set out to change the way the world views young adults with disabilities and their potential—looking beyond the disability and focusing on the person: a son, daughter, friend, sibling, girlfriend, boyfriend or fiancé. . . . Millennials living with disabilities, those who grew up with the ADA, have high expectations for their future. They want and deserve careers and independence. All they need is an opportunity. And it starts with taking on the stigma. Taking on the inequality. Taking on the challenges that people with disabilities and the disability community face across myriad issues and the landscape of American society.

Research reveals that 50% of polled households support accurate portrayals of characters with disabilities. With a combined spending power estimated at more than 10 billion dollars per month for U.S. households, this opinion has the potential to facilitate real change in the entertainment industry (Woodburn & Kopic, 2016). Regardless of the motives of audiences and producers, documentaries on both the big and small screen have large viewerships and have done much to provide a more accurate look at multidimensional people with disabilities in real-world scenarios involving love, romance, and sexual relationships.

**Beauty pageants.** The early part of the 21st century saw some important "firsts" that have broken barriers for people with disabilities in American pop culture. Women with autism and Down syndrome have competed in the Miss America and Miss USA beauty pageants (Blanchette, 2017; Oldenburg, 2013). In 2007, when a contestant on the autism spectrum finished in fourth place on the hit TV series *America's Next*

*Top Model*, the subject of females with autism became a topic of discussion in the media (Parker-Popedek, 2007). In 2015, Jamie Brewer, best known for her roles in the FX TV series *American Horror Story*, became the first person with Down syndrome to walk the red carpet at New York's Fashion Week (Brewer, 2017).

**Fashion.** Dispelling stereotypes by educating children is one way to help change a culture. There appears to be a trend toward acceptance that is pervasive in pop culture and it is becoming difficult to ignore. In 2019, Mattel introduced the Barbie Fashionistas line in an effort to provide more diverse representations of beauty. Some of these dolls feature realistic removable prosthetic limbs and some come with wheelchairs. The toy company also introduced ramps for the Barbie Dreamhouse. "As a brand, we can elevate the conversation around physical disabilities by including them into our fashion doll line to further showcase a multi-dimensional view of beauty and fashion," Mattel said in a statement (Lou & Griggs, 2019).

Another positive sign of inclusive thinking in the fashion industry is the trend toward providing adaptive clothing that is fashion-forward. Mindy Scheier founded the Runway of Dreams Foundation, a nonprofit dedicated to "bringing inclusion, acceptance, and opportunity to the fashion industry" after she realized that her son, who has muscular dystrophy, had no real choices in adaptive clothing (Allard, 2018). She gave a TED Talk in 2017 explaining how adaptive clothing empowers people with disabilities. Visit https://www.ted.com/talks/mindy_scheier_how_adaptive_clothing_empowers_people_with_disabilities?language=en to listen to Scheier's TED Talk. In an interview in 2018, Scheier was asked how she is bringing adaptive clothing into the mainstream market. This is her response:

> We're introducing the industry to a population that hasn't been recognized until this point, and we're working to educate and dispel common misconceptions. To start, the disability population is not a niche market. There are over one billion people worldwide living with a disability, making up our largest minority group. That results in tremendous buying power—over $175 billion each year. Our goal is to shine a light on the human side of disability, showing that people with disabilities care about how they look and dress just like any other person. (Allard, 2018)

Companies such as Target, Tommy Hilfiger, and Nike are recognizing that market and fashion choices for individuals with disabilities are becoming more and more common. As a result, advertising may no longer avoid featuring people with visible disabilities in marketing campaigns.

**Teaching tools and interventions to reduce minority rhetoric.** One way to reduce minority rhetoric is to incorporate realistic rhetoric directly into K–12 environments with classroom materials, curricula, exhibits, or teacher-provided resources. When this is increased across all subject areas, the wondrous, sentimental, and exotic rhetorics will not be as powerful because students will have had more opportunities to develop positive schemas regarding "other" social identities. For example, in English Language Arts, literature can show (un)realistic and (in) appropriate representation, or various rhetorics in film can be identified and discussed. Science and math courses, which typically do not explore contributions made by multiple minoritized identities, can discuss those contributions or emphasize how technologies have benefited people with disabilities (Bialka, 2017; Harkins Monaco, 2020).

## Digital Media: Risks and Rewards

Another popular misconception involving some people with disabilities is that they are uninterested in forming friendships or romantic relationships and, in the case of those with autism, prefer being alone. In fact, many feel the pain of loneliness and long for meaningful relationships but lack the skills and understanding needed to keep and maintain relationships, and they lack the opportunities to meet and socialize with others in a romantic or sexual way (Bauminger & Kasari, 2003; Mazurek, 2014). Most people with disabilities, like their typical peers, want to date, and often turn to the internet to help them understand and be successful in romantic and sexual relationships. As with typical peers, online dating is gaining in popularity (Roth & Gillis, 2015).

Digital technology has become a vital part of today's culture. Smartphones and tablets are considered necessities by many people and are important tools that can help level the social playing field for those with disabilities. Many have grown up with computers and view them as a familiar, comfortable way to gather information and often as a primary source of entertainment. Digital media represents a myriad of possibilities to expand social capital for people with disabilities, creating new opportunities to interact and communicate with others via email, text, voice, or video chats. There is convincing evidence that using social media can improve social interactions, reduce feelings of loneliness, and provide a sense of well-being for users with disabilities (Chadwick & Wesson, 2016). There are obvious benefits for people who struggle with fast-paced, give-and-take exchanges that make up typical conversations. The ability to make inferences and understand nonverbal language in face-to-face communication is difficult for some with disabilities, and can cause anxiety, which in turn can increase the likelihood of misunderstandings, communication lapses, and social faux pas (Roth & Gillis, 2015). Texting and computer-mediated communication have the potential to eliminate some of those problems. Voice or video chats can provide an option for communication for those who have trouble typing and reading.

Digital devices and internet access can serve as valuable tools for individuals with disabilities who want to learn about, start, and maintain emotional and physical relationships, but they also pose significant threats that should not be ignored (Attwood et al., 2014; Chadwick & Wesson, 2016). Due to deficits in understanding social cues, communication styles, and theory of mind, they may not realize that they are being taken advantage of or made fun of online. They may not understand the difference between flirtatious and threatening language and may not realize that people they meet online could be projecting a false identity. Stalking and harassment are possible problem behaviors that can result from a lack of understanding of social media and texting etiquette (Attwood et al., 2014; Baker, 2013; Roth & Gillis, 2015).

While it is far more common for individuals with disabilities to be victims of sex crimes, there is a real danger for individuals with disabilities to interact with illegal pornography (Attwood et al., 2014). In his book *No More Victims* (2013), Jed Baker uses the popular internet meme *Rule 34:* "If it exists, someone has made porn out of it. No exceptions," to illustrate that even with filters, pornography is easy to access. Google and YouTube searches for characters from television series, cartoons, and video games that are popular with children can lead to pornographic or violent videos and images.

The case of Nick Dubin can serve as a cautionary tale of the dangers that exist for people who do not understand the law, lack social cues and theory of mind, and are not able to recognize dangerous situations. Nick Dubin is a successful writer and was well known as an advocate for people on the autism spectrum. He appeared to be well-grounded and confident. However, he was socially isolated and bullied for most of his life and was not diagnosed with autism until the age of 27. Assessment of Nick's adaptive skills revealed scores in the preadolescent level. He was not sexually active and also lacked basic information about sexuality. Failing to understand the moral, ethical, and legal rules associated with child pornography, Nick downloaded child pornography through the internet. As a result of this naive action Nick was arrested and convicted on a felony count of possession of child pornography. In his book *The Autism Spectrum, Sexuality and the Law,* Nick writes:

After I was arrested, my therapist explained to me that the children in the images I was viewing are victims and I feel great remorse for their degradation. Unfortunately, I was not able to make these connections prior to my arrest and I deeply regret my actions. My greatest sadness is wishing that I knew then what I know now. (Attwood et al., 2014)

## Teaching Tools and Interventions to Promote Safety in Digital Media

Instructing adolescents and adults on the law regarding child pornography, and the dangers to both personal and professional relationships of posting explicit pictures and text, are essential (Attwood et al., 2014; Baker, 2013). Furthermore, they should understand how to avoid being a victim or perpetrator in any of those activities, and what to do if they realize that they have become the victim or the perpetrator. Rules about cyberbullying, emailing, accessing the internet, and viewing online pornography while at work or school should be explicitly taught. Evidence-based social skills programs and teacher-created lessons that include direct instruction, modeling, role-playing, practicing the skill in different settings, and performance feedback can be used to teach some of these skills. The use of games, Social Stories®, Comic Book Conversations, and natural environment teaching is also effective (Attwood et al., 2014).

**Table 13.4    Suggested Topics for Instruction in Internet Safety**

- Risks and consequences of posting explicit images and messages online
- Differences between legal and illegal pornography and the dangers both pose
- Acceptable and non-acceptable images to share via online posts or texts
- Understanding privacy settings and why they are important
- How to safely create a personal profile
- Risks and consequences of posting messages and images impulsively when hurt or angry
- Cyberstalking vs. online flirting
- How to recognize and report cyberbullying and cyberstalking
- Specific language to use and avoid in online conversations
- Email policies of possible employers
- Rules about when and how often to text
- Differences between an online friend and a real-life friend
- The meaning of common terms used in social media
- Clues that an online friend may be using a false identity
- How to unfriend someone on Facebook

Shaw, M., & Harkins Monaco, E. A. (2018). We can't hide: Pop culture and digital media. In E. A. Harkins Monaco, T. Gibbon, & D. Bateman (Eds.), *Talking about sex: Sexuality education for learners with disabilities*. Rowman & Littlefield.

The 5-point scale, developed by Kari Dunn Buron, is especially useful in making the abstract ideas surrounding the use of the internet and social media into visual, concrete rules or guidelines (Buron, 2007).

Shaw (2018) recommends the topics in Table 13.4.

## Summary

Entertainment media, an avenue for promoting (in)accurate information for and about people with disabilities, uses various kinds of minority rhetoric to influence public perception. These rhetorics result in misleading stereotypes and inaccurate portrayals of people with disabilities—individuals with disabilities are rarely depicted in pop culture as wanting romantic relationships or having positive, reciprocal social connections. This is further exacerbated by digital media and its opportunities for social and emotional growth. Too often for those with certain disabilities, its use also results in misinterpretations and negative social and emotional consequences. There are ways to combat these kinds of stereotypes and consequences in K–12 environments with classroom materials, curricula, exhibits, or teacher-provided resources.

## Resources

### Internet Resources

*Digital Citizenship Program from Common Sense:* https://www.commonsense.org/education/digital-citizenship

> Common Sense is an independent nonprofit organization that provides high-quality digital literacy and citizenship programs to educators and school communities. It offers standards-aligned lesson plans by grade and subject, with videos, essential questions, and activities. Topics include internet safety, cyberbullying, relationships, and more.

*eBuddies:* https://bestbuddies.org/

> eBuddies is a division of Best Buddies for people with and without IDD to come together online to form friendships.

*Spread the word to end the word:* http://www.r-word.org/

> Spread the word to end the word offers many resources for raising awareness, including activities, fact sheets, and information on why it is important to stop using hurtful speech and how you or your group can help.

## Books/Articles and Other Resources

Berger, R. J. (2013). *Introducing disability studies.* Lynne Rienner Publishers, Inc.

Harkins Monaco, E. A., Gibbon, T., & Bateman, D. (2018). *Talking about sex: Sexuality education for learners with disabilities.* Rowman & Littlefield.

*No More Victims* by Jed Baker is a small book packed with ideas for instruction in internet safety, written for individuals with ASD but suitable for all learners.

## Suggestions for How to Maintain Current on This Topic

* Remain current on your state laws and policies related to disability rights, social and digital media laws and safety precautions, and sexuality education.
* Advocate for inclusive sexuality education and support with digital media in your school district.
* Seek ways to reduce minority rhetoric in the K–12 and collegiate classrooms.
* Subscribe to Disability Scoop—the nation's largest news organization devoted to coverage of developmental disabilities. https://www.disabilityscoop.com/
* Connect with your local chapter of Best Buddies, the Arc, and Special Olympics.

## Resources to Help You Stay Current

* American Association of Sexuality Educators, Counselors, and Therapists: https://www.aasect.org/
* Kinsey Institute (Indiana University): https://kinseyinstitute.org/
* Society for Disability Studies: http://disstudies.org/

# CHAPTER 14

# Summary and Call to Action
## Thomas C. Gibbon

*At camp it was a whole other world, I had a girlfriend and I was popular.*

—Jim LeBrecht, *Crip Camp*

*When you grow up disabled, you are not considered a man or a woman.*

—Judith Heumann, *Crip Camp*

## Overview

This chapter discusses the need for sexuality education designed specifically for students with disabilities (SWD) and provides a list of actions that students, families, teachers, and administrators may take when working with these students. It reviews major themes covered throughout the book and notes where the reader can find more detail within the text. The chapter concludes with case studies and questions for further consideration to highlight the diversity of concerns that should be addressed by well-designed sexuality education for SWD.

## Advanced Organizer

- SWD deserve the civil right to experience their sexuality as part of being fully human.
- Sexuality education provided in public education settings is not sufficient for the diversity of learning and ability represented by SWD.
- Sexuality education needs to balance the natural drive for intimacy and pleasure with the unfortunate danger of sexual abuse by others.
- There are many barriers to well-planned and delivered sexuality education for SWD.

- Teachers and school administrators need to support SWD and their families through this process.

## Why Students with Disabilities Need Sexuality Education

This text is an attempt to address the competing concepts for teachers to support SWD in multiple contexts to safely express their sexuality. It is a starting point for teachers who are concerned about these issues. The following sections review important conclusions from earlier chapters, the barriers to sexuality education, and what can be done to overcome the barriers. The claims below reflect the core concepts that the contributing authors support through their research and practice. Where appropriate, specific chapters are noted for reference; other topics are covered throughout the text. Readers are encouraged to revisit the chapters indicated for supporting details:

- Sexuality expression is a basic human right and SWD need access to sexuality education in order to appropriately express sexuality and to fully experience their humanity. SWD have the right to self-determination in this area of their lives *(Chapter 5; most chapters)*.
- The historical record of how our society has treated people with disabilities (PWD) through isolation, stigmatization, and demonization informs current thinking and restricts the inclusion of sexuality education as part of the curriculum for SWD *(Chapter 1; Chapter 11)*. Popular culture and media have contributed to negative stereotypes *(Chapter 13)*. Teachers and school administrators need to work to destigmatize sexuality education and reframe it as an important aspect of public education.
- Appropriate sexuality education for SWD combats misinformation acquired through internet sites and uninformed peers and decreases the likelihood of sexually inappropriate and potentially abusive behavior *(Chapter 11)*.
- Sexuality expression should be considered a major life function in order for SWD to achieve their fullest quality of life and, therefore, sexuality education needs to be included in the transition to adulthood section of the IEP *(Chapter 11)*.
- Adolescents with disabilities develop physically and hormonally at similar rates to nondisabled peers *(Chapter 6; Chapter 10)*.
- The intricacies of intersectionality exacerbate the transition to adolescence and adulthood for SWD.
- To the greatest extent possible, SWD should be included with age peers during school-based sexuality education. Sexuality education should not be deferred to the later grades for SWD.

- Sexuality education needs to be comprehensive; consider the life-span, relationship components, and use a team approach *(Chapter 7)*.
- Specialized instruction is needed *(Chapter 9)* to effectively teach sexuality to SWD; there are different needs for students with high- and low-incidence disabilities *(Chapter 5)*.
- The nature of a disability affects how the SWD will understand and learn about sexuality; information processing, language ability, physical function, neurological perception, understanding others' behavior, and more need to be considered.
- A team approach should be used for sexuality curriculum development and IEP management around this topic *(Chapter 7)*; natural supports should be considered for both instruction and practice *(Chapter 10)*.

## Barriers to Teaching Sexuality Education to People with Disabilities

As you have learned reading this text, there are many formidable barriers to teaching sexuality education to SWD in public schools in the United States. These barriers result in adolescents and young adults who are vulnerable, underestimated, and uninformed. Where appropriate, specific chapters are noted for reference; other items are covered throughout the text; you are encouraged to revisit the chapters indicated for supporting details:

- Sexuality education is not comprehensive, nor is it adequate for the needs of SWD.
  - Instructional time, accommodations, direct instruction, and assessment are often missing from sexuality education programs.
  - It does not include information about SWD who may also identify as LGBTQ+ *(Chapter 4)*.
- Sexuality education is often deferred to later grades or not taught at all to SWD.
- Teacher education programs do not teach sexuality education *(Chapter 11)*.
- Media perpetuates popular stereotypes that shape thinking about SWD and sexuality education *(Chapter 13)*.
- PWD continue to be excluded from many aspects of society and therefore are infantilized or marginalized and devalued *(Chapter 5)*.
- It is difficult for all stakeholders to be on the same page due to cultural and religious beliefs *(Chapter 12)*.

- In many states parents must opt in to sexuality education *(Chapter 11).*
- Parent, caregiver, and school personnel attitudes affect whether or not sexuality education will be included in the curriculum either informally or formally *(Chapter 7).*
  - Often the assumption is overprotection because SWD can be both victims and perpetrators of sexual violence.
  - SWD are not always permitted to socialize both in supervised and unsupervised settings.
  - Students miss out on opportunities for development.
- Entrenched thinking and theoretical models argue against sexuality expression or instruction for SWD *(Chapter 2).*
  - Ableism, the idea that there are "normal" and "not normal" bodies and genders, perpetuate the idea that only those who are able should participate.
  - Medical model negates the innate humanity of PWD because it espouses the idea PWD are not well and should be "fixed" to be more like the rest of society.
- Traditional thinking about gender and what is considered appropriate for male and female students should be reconsidered for all individuals, including PWD *(Chapter 4).*
- SWD are controlled by institutions *(Chapter 1)*:
  - Social segregation in our schools can lead to misperceptions that SWD are unworthy to date or are asexual beings, and segregation can lead to potential abuse and violence.
  - Socially segregated housing of adults with disabilities can perpetuate these misperceptions into adulthood.
- Access to sexuality education and the practice of sexuality as a right conflicts with the traditional way of ignoring that PWD have an interest in sex *(Chapter 1).*
- Questions about SWD capacity to consent, understand emotional risks, and long-term consequences of decisions about sexual activity exist *(Chapter 11).*
  - The incorrect assumptions of others about all PWD's capacity for consent.
- Legal and liability about sexuality questions are unclear *(Chapter 11).*
  - Sexuality education is not covered in Perkins or IDEA.
  - Existing legislation is not specific and outdated.

## How to Overcome Barriers

### *What Students Can Do*

- Understand sexuality is a normal part of growing up and being human.
- Communicate with potential partners, trusted adults, and IEP teams.
- Find a trusted and knowledgeable person to answer questions and help with problem solving.

### *What Families and Caregivers Can Do*

- Consider what you want for your child as they move into late adolescence and adulthood.
- Ask your school for help in understanding adolescent development for SWD.
- Start a parents' group to discuss issues related to sexuality education for SWD in your school.
- Listen to your child about issues related to sexuality.
- Consider supported decision making to help your child have a role in self-determination about sexuality and other issues.
- Consult with your IEP team for support about sexuality education; tell the team you want it to be addressed as part of the IEP.
- Embrace the team approach for addressing sexuality issues for your child.
- Recognize that addressing sexuality issues will be a lifelong process.

### *What Teachers Can Do*

- Identify personal bias.
- Listen to students and families about topics related to sexuality.
- Embrace the idea that SWD deserve to learn about sexuality.
- Inform yourself about adolescent development as it relates to sexuality; know that SWD develop similarly to those with no disability.
- Advocate for *all* students to be educated about sexuality over time with age-appropriate teaching; use **specially designed instruction** for SWD when teaching this curriculum.
- Create an accepting environment of appropriate sexual expression within your classroom and school in order to combat stigmatization of SWD.
- Talk with parents about the idea that sexuality education needs to be included on the IEP in relation to the transition to adulthood.

- Teach problem solving, social interaction, self-regulation, socially appropriate touching.
- Support a team approach to developing a sexual education curriculum in your school.
- Seek out existing curricula for teaching sexuality education to SWD that includes the following instructional features and content:
  - Instructional features
    - Explicit, systematic instruction
    - Screening instruments to determine where to start instruction
    - Systematic assessment of learning
    - Understandable language
    - Opportunities for practice and generalization
  - Content
    - Support for social pragmatic skills and executive functioning skills
    - Self-care and hygiene
    - Social and behavioral guidelines
    - Community access skills, including skills related to your specific environment and students
    - Self-determination and self-advocacy
    - The widest understanding of sexual activity, intimacy, procreation, appropriate management of sexual pleasure, dating, safety, sexual violence, and consent

## What Administrators Can Do

- Identify personal bias.
- Listen to students, families, and teachers about topics related to sexuality.
- Invite parents to form a support group around the topic of sexuality education for SWD.
- To the best of your ability, embrace the idea that SWD deserve to learn about sexuality.
- Celebrate diversity of sexual expression; challenge heteronormative assumptions.
- Inform yourself about adolescent development as it relates to sexuality; know that SWD develop similarly to those with no disability.
- Advocate for all students to be educated about sexuality over time with age-appropriate teaching; support the use of specially-designed instruction for SWD when teaching this curriculum.

- Create an accepting environment of appropriate sexual expression within your building or district in order to combat stigmatization of SWD.
- Talk with parents about the idea that sexuality education needs to be included on the IEP in relation to the transition to adulthood.
- Support a team approach to developing sexual education curriculum in your building or district.
- Develop or support building- and district-wide training about sexuality education for SWD; include teachers, paraprofessionals, office staff, drivers, and others in this training.

## What Is Next: Call to Action

Adolescents and adults with disabilities engage in sex. Hopefully, if you have read this far in this chapter or textbook, this will not come as a surprise to you. If you support PWD, this likely was not a surprise to you when you started reading this text. As advocates who want what is best for our students and others with disabilities, we must acknowledge that PWD are not waiting for society to grant permission. Sexuality education for PWD is a social justice issue for our profession.

The current advocacy for specially-designed sexuality education for PWD grows out of a historical progression of advocacy for disability rights and **inclusion.** In the 1960s and 1970s disability advocates promoted inclusion in educational settings and pushed for legislation to mandate inclusion and improve instruction. Later legislation supported physical access to businesses and public settings and attempted to protect the rights of PWD in the workplace.

The idea of including sexuality education in the standard curriculum for SWD is an extension of the ideas of earlier generations of disability advocates who pushed to pass legislation such as Section 504, IDEA, and ADA. Advocates and PWD themselves from those earlier decades were attempting to change public opinion about accessibility to buildings and education for PWD. Now advocates are continuing this idea as it applies to public opinion and public-school curriculum as it relates to sexuality and PWD. The intention is to change the cultural perceptions about sexuality and PWD. An underlying theme in this changing climate is that PWD engaging in sex for pleasure is not aberrant; it is to be expected and celebrated by others and taught about by our profession as exemplified in the film *Crip Camp* and the book *My Body Politic* by Simi Linton. This type of public opinion change will need to include changes in training for teachers, administrators, and paraprofessionals as well as specific support for families.

Families of SWD need our support in understanding the normal progression of adolescence and how they can support their child or young person. As mentioned earlier in this text, families come to this topic from a wide range of cultural perspectives; special education professionals need to listen carefully to the families and SWD with whom we work. Because family members are more likely to support their children over their lifespan, family is key to long-term self-actualization for the PWD. Teachers and support personnel usually only have one or a few years of contact with any specific SWD. For continuity of support, protection of families and SWD's legal rights, and for documentation of specially-designed instruction and progress, our profession has adopted the use of the IEP. Because the IEP is our established means to ensure we deliver what the team recommends, this is one important location where sexuality education needs to be embedded.

The **Council for Exceptional Children** (CEC), the premier organization for special education in the United States, provides standards for special education teacher training programs. Due to the importance of including sexuality education in IEPs, sexuality instruction should be addressed within special education teacher training programs. Currently there is no direct mention of sexuality instruction in the CEC Standards for Professional Practice; however, there are many places where the

---

■■■■■ **TEXTBOX 14.1** ■■■■■

## Key Elements of CEC Standards

1.2 Beginning special education professionals use understanding of development and individual differences to respond to the needs of individuals with exceptionalities.

2.1 Beginning special education professionals, through collaboration with general educators and other colleagues, create safe, inclusive, culturally responsive learning environments to engage individuals with exceptionalities in meaningful learning activities and social interactions.

3.3 Beginning special education professionals modify general and specialized curricula to make them accessible to individuals with exceptionalities.

4.4 Beginning special education professionals engage individuals with exceptionalities to work toward quality learning and performance and provide feedback to guide them.

5.1 Beginning special education professionals consider individual abilities, interests, learning environments, and cultural and linguistic factors in the selection, development, and adaptation of learning experiences for individuals with exceptionalities.

6.3 Beginning special education professionals understand that diversity is a part of families, cultures, and schools, and that complex human issues can interact with the delivery of special education services.

standards support aspects of sexuality instruction. For each standard, CEC delineates several Key Elements to clarify the standard's intent.

Textbox 14.1 delineates several Key Elements of CEC Standards that fit with sexuality instruction.

For the purpose of this chapter, we only selected one Key Element for each Standard to highlight in relation to sexuality instruction for PWD. From this list it is clear that CEC Standards can be applied to sexuality instruction. Our profession supports ethical practice, individualized instruction, modified curriculum, collaboration, cultural awareness, and diversity in the support of SWD. Our profession is organized around the principles of **normalcy** and inclusion for PWD. Accepting these principles means supporting PWD in all aspects of their development; sexuality is an integral part of this development. The CEC standards provide a conceptional foundation for understanding how to address issues related to sexuality education for SWD. The call to action is the ability to apply these concepts in an actionable and meaningful way to enhance the lives of PWD. The following section contains a series of scenarios to help facilitate this application. Please read all the Standards and Key Elements in the Appendix.

## Sexuality Scenarios

A. John is a 35-year-old with IDD and CP who is nonverbal. He lives in the group home run by a nonprofit agency with two other men. John attends a day program where he is part of a work crew that cleans a church and cares for the grounds of various businesses. John is supervised during the day by a job coach and after work by residential staff. Recently John was found in the bed of his roommate, Bob. Bob is approximately 40 years old, is nonverbal, and has IDD. Bob did not seem happy to have John in his bed. As far as the staff can tell, Bob has not indicated any interest in a sexual relationship with John.

- If you were the residential staff in this scenario, what should be your plan of action?
- What immediate steps should you take?
- What secondary steps should you initiate?

B. Bill is one of the students in your high school intensive learning support classroom. Bill is a 17-year-old student with intellectual disabilities and chronic health concerns. As a supportive teacher, you visit Bill during a recent week-long stay in the hospital. When you ask him if he needs anything, Bill asks you to bring him lube so he can masturbate when alone. Bill did not want his mother or the nurses to know about this request.

- What are your responsibilities to Bill regarding his request?
- Does his age matter in your response?
- What are your responsibilities to Bill regarding his request for confidentiality from his mother or the nurses?
- Beyond his specific request, are there longer-term actions you may take based on his question to you?

C. Mary is a 21-year-old woman with Down syndrome who lives in a group home. Recently she has told her residential staff that she wants a boyfriend. At her day program she has begun to show interest in one of the counselors. She asks him what he is doing on the weekend and what he likes to do for fun. She compliments him about the clothes he wears. Even though Mary attends an organized social outing group for adults with intellectual disabilities, she is not interested in dating others from this group.

- What concerns do you have for Mary?
- Is her conversation with her day program counselor within societal norms?
- If you were Mary's residential staff, do you think you need to talk with Mary? Do you have any advice for the day program counselor?
- Is it your responsibility to talk with Mary's parents about any of this?

D. Mike is a 50-year-old man with IDD who lives in a group home. He is a double-leg amputee due to advanced diabetes and uses a wheelchair. Mike is a fall risk so the staff protocol is to keep Mike within visual observation at all times. When Mike wants privacy to masturbate, he closes the door to his private bedroom. The staff are concerned about his safety.

- What should the staff do to protect Mike's privacy and safety?
- Should his family be consulted?
- If Mike's family are no longer available to consult, should you talk with his advocate? Do you expect any differences if you had a family member or a state advocate to consult?

E. In your town, the local sheltered workshop has been in operation for decades. The PWD who attend the workshop do piecework for less than minimum wage. They also celebrate birthdays, have dances, and develop friendships and romantic relationships there. The Workforce Innovation and Opportunity Act of 2014 has made the workshop less popular as a day program for high school graduates with IDD and other disabilities. As an advocate for PWD you support the idea that sheltered work is not the best outcome for PWD; however, you notice that since fewer PWD attend the workshop setting, there are fewer opportunities for the PWD in your community to socialize.

- What steps can you take to address the problem you have noticed in your community?
- Who should be involved in collaborating to work on solutions?
- Should sheltered workshops focus mostly on work skills and supported employment or is socialization their responsibility as well?

F.  Betty is the mother of Sue, a 9th-grader with ADHD with associated impulsivity control behavior. As a child, Sue was the kind of girl who would step off the curb even after Betty got her attention and told her to wait. Recently Sue has been making friends with a group of girls and boys who spend a lot of time together after school and on the weekends. Most of this interaction is supervised by one of the other parents but recently Sue has been asking to go out with her friends to the movies or to the small downtown area without parental supervision. Betty has read up on adolescent development and understands that Sue needs to socialize with friends in both supervised and unsupervised settings at some point, but she is concerned that Sue will not make good decisions when out of her sight.

- Should Betty be more concerned about Sue than any other parent of a 9th-grader?
- Are there ways that Betty can support Sue's steps toward independence in a measured manner?
- What advice do you have for Betty and Sue?

G.  Margot is a college sophomore at a small liberal arts college who has bipolar disorder. She has had an up-and-down academic career so far, depending upon how well her medication is working and her ability to control how much alcohol she drinks. During a hot day in a recent summer session Margot decided to bring a kiddie swimming pool into her residence hall room and fill it with the hose from the janitor's closet. She invited several friends to have a swimming party in her room. When water started to leak out through the room door, the residence life coordinator busted the scene. What she found were several students including Margot with and without swim attire and many beer cans spread around. After a brief hearing, the dean expelled Margot from the college.

- Do Margot or her parents have a case to get her reinstated at the college? Can they claim that her disorder caused her to make this poor decision?
- Is Margot's impulse to cool off with friends associated at all with her disability?

# Resources

## Podcasts/Audio

Disability Visibility Project: https://disabilityvisibilityproject.com/2018/12/03/ep-39-sex-education/

During this episode, Julia Bascom and Robin Wilson-Beattie discuss sex education. Important topics discussed are what inclusive sex education looks like, bodily autonomy, and the right of all disabled to have pleasure and sexual expression.

*Land of Milk and Honey*—Season 3, Episode 77: Your Body, Your Boundaries: Teaching Sexual Health: https://www.lomah.org/podcastseason3/77

In this episode, guest Katie Thun shares foundational concepts we can be teaching our loved ones. These foundational concepts include consent, guidelines, and rules and some everyday gray areas like private and public spaces, compliance vs. appropriate noncompliance, and exploitive vs. necessary touch.

*Land of Milk and Honey*—Season 2, Episode 69: Self-Determination with Complex Communication Needs: https://www.lomah.org/podcast2/69

In this episode, a professor at Kansas University in the Department of Special Education, Karrie Shogren, PhD, speaks about her research on self-determination and support systems for students with disabilities. She further explains her and her team's primary focus on developing effective and realistic strategies of self-determination for teachers, families, and providers to implement across the life span.

*ABA Inside Track*—Bonus Episode 7: Sex Education for Individuals with Developmental Disabilities with Katherine McLaughlin: https://www.abainsidetrack.com/home/2018/3/7/bonus-7-sex-education-for-individuals-with-developmental-disabilities

During this episode, guest Katherine McLaughlin of Sexuality and Developmental Disability Workshops and creator of a sex education curriculum for individuals with disabilities is interviewed. Topics that are discussed include the challenges educators face when having to bring up sex education, why sexuality is being discussed within special education, and McLaughlin's process of developing her curriculum.

NPR Series—*Abused and Betrayed*: https://www.npr.org/series/575502633/abused-and-betrayed

In this series, there are multiple podcasts that provide further information regarding sexual abuse within the population of people with disabilities.

*The eSpecial Needs Podcast*—Episode 4: Sex Education for Individuals with Special Needs with Sex Therapist Nicholas Maio-Ather: https://www.youtube.com/watch?v=FHexJFj-CG0

In this episode, sex therapist Nicholas Maio-Ather discusses the importance and need of talking to children with special needs about sex education, how to help them understand the anatomy of it, and why it is significant to teach your children consent at an early age.

## Internet Resources

Center for Parent Information & Resources—Sexuality Education for Students with Disabilities: https://www.parentcenterhub.org/sexed/

This resource page addresses one aspect of development that is important not to ignore with children with or without disabilities—the development of sexuality. This page provides further information regarding basics of human sexuality, sexuality and disability, the special role of the parent, the content that should be taught, materials on specific disabilities, and commercial products. This site incorporates many links for further information on each of these topics regarding sexuality education for students with disabilities.

Mad Hatter Wellness—Sexuality for All Abilities: https://www.sexualityforallabilities.com/

Mad Hatter Wellness creates comprehensive sexual health education programming that educates, trains, and empowers people with intellectual disabilities and their support systems. Mad Hatter Wellness provides tools for healthy relationships and boundaries, specifically for people with I/DD, education needed to start conversations about health and sexuality, and a community to work with on issues of disability, health, and sexuality.

RespectAbility: Fighting Stigmas. Advancing Opportunities—Sexual Education Resource: https://www.respectability.org/resources/sexual-education-resources/

In coordination with Couwenhoven, RespectAbility released an extensive guide featuring resources for sexual education for children, teenagers, and adults with disabilities, with a focus on those with intellectual and developmental disabilities.

American Psychological Association—Sex and Intellectual Abilities: https://
www.apa.org/monitor/2017/12/seeking-intimacy-sidebar

> This resource provides further information about the lack of sex education that individuals with disabilities receive compared to peers and why it is important for them to receive that information. This resource also discusses the reasoning as to why it is important that individuals with disabilities learn self-advocacy skills.

Elevatus Training—Curriculum: Sexuality Education for People with Developmental Disabilities: https://www.elevatustraining.com/workshops-and
-products/sexuality-education-for-people-with-developmental-disabilities
-curriculum/

> This curriculum has been praised by experts and also has been field-tested. It is designed for teams of self-advocates, staff, and teachers to co-lead an inspiring and engaging sexuality class. The curriculum includes a comprehensive instructor manual that provides tips on how to establish a sexuality education class and how to be an engaging and effective sexuality educator. It outlines common challenges when teaching this topic and offers innovative strategies to help overcome them.

## Videos

Sexuality & Disability—A Seat at the Table with Cheryl Cohen Greene: https://
www.youtube.com/watch?v=gds2RvmCBKE

> In this TEDx, Cheryl Cohen Greene, a certified clinical sexologist/sex educator, discusses how individuals with disabilities are overlooked when it comes to sexuality and sex therapy.

TED: Every Body: Glamour, dateability, sexuality, and disability: https://www
.youtube.com/watch?v=7PwvGfs6Pok

> In this TEDx Dr. Danielle Sheypuk, psychologist and wheelchair dependent since childhood, gets real about sex and disability, unabashedly exploring sexual satisfaction writ large. She encourages curiosity and invites you to shed your preconceived notions of sexual norms in favor of a new reality that just might pique your interest.

Sexuality and Disability: Forging Identity in a World that Leaves You Out | Gaelynn Lea | TEDxYale: https://www.youtube.com/watch?v=akGYugciSVw

> In this TEDx, Gaelynn Lea, a musician from Duluth, Minnesota, recounts the epiphany that empowered her to pursue life, love, and a musical career on her own terms. She also discusses how there were times she felt left out of mainstream dating and beauty culture due to her physical disability.

Undressing Disability | Emily Yates | TEDxYouth@StPeterPort: https://www
.youtube.com/watch?v=fkq3cIgVhR8

> In this TEDx, Emily, a 24-year-old who has cerebral palsy, is an accessibility consultant, Lonely Planet travel writer, and TV presenter currently based

between the United Kingdom and Rio de Janeiro, addresses the issues of sex and relationships for the disabled, and how disabled communities can have access to this, which others usually take for granted. She hopes to one day eliminate the sexual taboo that seems to surround disability and tackle the subject of disability and sex in this revealing open talk.

## Books

*Sexuality Education for People with Developmental Disabilities*—Katherine McLaughlin

This book is designed for high school students and adults with developmental disabilities. The book includes everything you need to get started including a comprehensive instructor manual with tips on how to be an effective sexuality educator, innovative strategies for handling common challenges, 22 lessons, practice skills revolving around various topics; it covers internet safety, social media and communication, gender identity and expression, and abuse prevention skills and techniques.

## Other Resources

Boundaries Flip Book—Mad Hatter Wellness: https://www.sexualityforallabili ties.com/product/flip-book/

These flip books create sentences for discussion on healthy and unhealthy behaviors and touch. This activity helps people explore personal boundaries and appropriate behavior.

*Crip Camp*—Netflix

This 2020 film features a summer camp that galvanizes a group of teenagers with disabilities to help build a movement, creating a new path toward greater equality.

Linton, S. (2006). *My body politic*. University Press of Michigan.

Shapiro, J. (2018, January 9). *For some with intellectual disabilities, ending abuse starts with sex ed*. https://www.npr.org

Collier, L. (2017, December). Seeking intimacy. *Monitor on Psychology, 48*(11), 48.

Anthes, E. (2017, December 7). *Some adults with autism traits reject conventional sexual labels*. https://spectrumnews.org

Griswold, A. (2017, May 3). *Sex and other foreign words*. https://spectrumnews .org

# Appendix
## CEC Standards and Key Elements

## Standard

1.0 Beginning special education professionals understand how exceptionalities may interact with development and learning and use this knowledge to provide meaningful and challenging learning experiences for individuals with exceptionalities.

### Key Elements

1.1 Beginning special education professionals understand how language, culture, and family background influences the learning of individuals with exceptionalities.

1.2 Beginning special education professionals use understanding of development and individual differences to respond to the needs of individuals with exceptionalities.

## Standard

2.0 Beginning special education professionals create safe, inclusive, culturally responsive learning environments so that individuals with exceptionalities become active and effective learners and develop emotional well-being, positive social interactions, and self-determination.

### Key Elements

2.1 Beginning special education professionals, through collaboration with general educators and other colleagues, create safe, inclusive, culturally responsive learning environments to engage individuals with exceptionalities in meaningful learning activities and social interactions.

2.2 Beginning special education professionals use motivational and instructional interventions to teach individuals with exceptionalities how to adapt to different environments.

2.3 Beginning special education professionals know how to intervene safely and appropriately with individuals with exceptionalities in crisis.

# Standard

3.0 Beginning special education professionals use knowledge of general and specialized curricula to individualize learning for individuals with exceptionalities.

## Key Elements

3.1 Beginning special education professionals understand the central concepts, structures of the discipline, and tools of inquiry of the content areas they teach, and can organize this knowledge, integrate cross-disciplinary skills, and develop meaningful learning progressions for individuals with exceptionalities.
3.2 Beginning special education professionals understand and use general and specialized content knowledge for teaching across curricular content areas to individualize learning for individuals with exceptionalities.
3.3 Beginning special education professionals modify general and specialized curricula to make them accessible to individuals with exceptionalities.

# Standard

4.0 Beginning special education professionals use multiple methods of assessment and data sources in making educational decisions.

## Key Elements

4.1 Beginning special education professionals select and use technically sound formal and informal assessments that minimize bias.
4.2 Beginning special education professionals use knowledge of measurement principles and practices to interpret assessment results and guide educational decisions for individuals with exceptionalities.
4.3 Beginning special education professionals, in collaboration with colleagues and families, use multiple types of assessment information in making decisions about individuals with exceptionalities.
4.4 Beginning special education professionals engage individuals with exceptionalities to work toward quality learning and performance and provide feedback to guide them.

# Standard

5.0 Beginning special education professionals select, adapt, and use a repertoire of evidence-based instructional strategies to advance learning of individuals with exceptionalities.

## Key Elements

5.1 Beginning special education professionals consider individual abilities, interests, learning environments, and cultural and linguistic factors in the selection, development, and adaptation of learning experiences for individuals with exceptionalities.

5.2 Beginning special education professionals use technologies to support instructional assessment, planning, and delivery for individuals with exceptionalities.

5.3 Beginning special education professionals are familiar with augmentative and alternative communication systems and a variety of assistive technologies to support the communication and learning of individuals with exceptionalities.

5.4 Beginning special education professionals use strategies to enhance language development and communication skills of individuals with exceptionalities.

5.5 Beginning special education professionals develop and implement a variety of education and transition plans for individuals with exceptionalities across a wide range of settings and different learning experiences in collaboration with individuals, families, and teams.

5.6 Beginning special education professionals teach to mastery and promote generalization of learning.

5.7 Beginning special education professionals teach cross-disciplinary knowledge and skills such as critical thinking and problem solving to individuals with exceptionalities.

# Standard

6.0 Beginning special education professionals use foundational knowledge of the field and their professional ethical principles and practice standards to inform special education practice, to engage in lifelong learning, and to advance the profession.

## Key Elements

6.1 Beginning special education professionals use professional ethical principles and professional practice standards to guide their practice.
6.2 Beginning special education professionals understand how foundational knowledge and current issues influence professional practice.
6.3 Beginning special education professionals understand that diversity is a part of families, cultures, and schools, and that complex human issues can interact with the delivery of special education services.
6.4 Beginning special education professionals understand the significance of lifelong learning and participate in professional activities and learning communities.
6.5 Beginning special education professionals advance the profession by engaging in activities such as advocacy and mentoring.
6.6 Beginning special education professionals provide guidance and direction to paraeducators, tutors, and volunteers.

# Standard

7.0 Beginning special education professionals collaborate with families, other educators, related service providers, individuals with exceptionalities, and personnel from community agencies in culturally responsive ways to address the needs of individuals with exceptionalities across a range of learning experiences.

## Key Elements

7.1 Beginning special education professionals use the theory and elements of effective collaboration.
7.2 Beginning special education professionals serve as a collaborative resource to colleagues.
7.3 Beginning special education professionals use collaboration to promote the well-being of individuals with exceptionalities across a wide range of settings and collaborators.

Council for Exceptional Children. (2015). *What every special educator must know: Professional ethics and standards* (7th ed.). CEC.

# Glossary

**ableism**—An uncritical assertion that particular ways of being and performing are preferable, often privileging the experience of individuals who do not experience disabilities.

**ASD**—Autism Spectrum Disorder.

**asexuality**—When people are not sexually aroused by any gender.

**assigned biological sex**—The anatomical and physical traits of male and female bodies.

**bias**—A preference for or against something or someone.

**bisexuality**—When people are attracted to both sexes.

**body image**—How one perceives their body and its desirability to others.

***Buck v. Bell***—Supreme Court decision from 1927 that upheld a Virginia law providing for sterilization of people considered genetically unfit.

**Carl Perkins Act of 1984**—This law has as its sole purpose to increase the quality of technical education in the United States to help the economy.

**celebration agenda**—Celebrates the integration of disabled people into mainstream society and the cultural development of disability.

**comprehensive sexuality education**—Sexuality education that includes medically accurate information about a broad range of topics such as consent and healthy relationships; puberty and adolescent development; sexual and reproductive anatomy and physiology; gender identity and expression; sexual identity and orientation; interpersonal and sexual violence; contraception, pregnancy, and reproduction; and HIV and other STDs/STIs.

**compulsory able-bodiedness**—The way in which disabled people adopted the terms *gimp* and *crip* in a positive way.

**compulsory heterosexuality**—The way in which gay, lesbian, and transgendered people adopted the term *queer* in a positive way.

**consent**—Consent occurs when one person voluntarily agrees to the proposal or desires of another.

**Council for Exceptional Children**—An international professional organization dedicated to improving the educational success of children and youth with disabilities and/or gifts and talents.

**crip theory**—The way the field of disability studies critiques the "normal" body.

**cultural model of disability**—Encourages people with disabilities to join a community in affirming their identities in a positive way.

**custody**—A court-ordered arrangement providing for the care of a minor child.

**diagnostically overshadow**—When one blames the person's impairment as the cause for the caregiver's stress.

**differentiation of instruction**—Planning and implementing instruction designed to meet the individual needs of students.

**disability**—The inability to perform a personal or socially necessary task because of an impairment or the societal reaction to the impairment.

**disability studies**—A theoretical approach to the perspectives of disability from the social sciences, humanities, medical, rehabilitation, and educational lenses.

**ecological validity**—The extent to which students are able to use knowledge and skills learned in instructional settings outside the classroom in the home and community.

**egalitarian**—A social system in which a family functions where there is decentralized power among family members.

**eternal child**—A presumptive term that individuals with disabilities will not grow or develop past adolescence.

**eugenics**—The practice or advocacy of improving the human species by selectively mating people with specific desirable hereditary traits.

**evidence-based best practice in sexuality and relationship education**—Practices for teaching sexuality education that include the following:

- considering chronological age and developmental level of student,
- utilizing lessons from a variety of programs based on student need,
- utilizing evidenced-based instructional strategies to deliver content, and
- building in opportunities for generalization of skills learned.

**executive functioning**—A variety of cognitive processes that permit individuals to make decisions, organize their thoughts, prioritize tasks, and problem solve.

**exotic rhetoric**—Presents people with disabilities as easy entertainment or promotional.

**expressive language**—Language used to communicate ideas including verbal communication (i.e., speaking and writing) and nonverbal communication (i.e., gestures and facial expressions).

**feminist theory**—Defines gender through social statuses and symbols assigned to women and men through their expression, appearance, and personality traits.

**gender**—Roles, expectations, behaviors, attitudes, and activities that society defines as appropriate for men and women.

**gender binary**—Westernized society's definition of gender based upon whether one has male genitalia or female genitalia.

**gender dysphoria**—The replacement of gender identity disorder.

**gender identity**—Defines gender as inherently diverse and reflects both biological and psychological considerations.

**gender spectrum**—Alternatives to the gender binary that include gender expansive, gender fluid, gender variant, gender creativity, genderqueer, bigender, and agender.

**general education curriculum**—Grade-level curriculum students are taught and expected to master within a school year.

**generalization**—The ability to transfer learning from one setting to another.

**gerontocracy**—A social system in which a family functions where authority is in elders.

**guardianship**—Guardianship, also referred to as conservatorship, is a legal process, utilized when a person can no longer make or communicate safe or sound decisions about their person and/or property or has become susceptible to fraud or undue influence.

handicap—Implies something is inherently wrong and therefore is considered to be an outdated term.

heterosexuality—When one is attracted to people of the opposite sex.

high-incidence disability—Term used to describe the more prevalent disability categories with the Individuals with Disabilities Education Act (IDEA); they tend to be mild and primarily impact learning.

high-leverage practices—Teaching practices intended to address the most critical practices that every K–12 special education teacher should master and be able to demonstrate.

homosexuality—When one is attracted to people of the same sex.

IDD—Intellectual and developmental disabilities.

IDEA—The Individuals with Disabilities Education Act.

identity development—A process through which a person creates a coherent sense of self that incorporates individual traits, values, and goals.

identity-first language—A way of speaking and thinking that views a disability as an inherent part of an individual's identity. It includes the practice of putting the disability category first, before the person, when writing or speaking. It is primarily used by members of the Deaf and Autistic communities.

IEP—Individualized Education Program. The program or plan developed to ensure that a school-aged student with a disability receives specialized instruction and related services.

impairment—The biological or physiological conditions that entail the loss of physical, sensory, or cognitive functioning.

implicit biases—Unconscious feelings or inclinations toward or against people or ideas.

inclusion—The idea that SWD should be taught with their nondisabled peers.

inclusion courses—Classrooms of peers without disabilities in which individuals with disabilities are welcomed into the course.

information processing—Process of taking in, storing, and retrieving information.

institutional discrimination—Recurring political, economic, cultural, and social discrimination.

intersectional pedagogy—The teaching methods that develop awareness around intersectional concepts and the impact this has on students with marginalized identities.

intersectionality—A framework used to understand how multiple overlapping social identities (e.g., race, gender, socioeconomic status, sexual orientation, or disability) impact and oppress certain populations; the problems certain people face stem from the multiplied oppressions that accompany a particular combination of identities.

intersectionality theory—How multiple overlapping social identities oppress certain populations.

IPSE—Inclusive postsecondary education.

key topics of comprehensive sexuality education—The National Sex Education Standards and the American Academy of Pediatrics suggest the following key topics be included in comprehensive sexuality curricula:

- healthy sexual development, including anatomy, physiology, puberty, adolescent development, and body image;
- gender identity and expression;
- interpersonal relationships, including friendship, romantic relationships, consent, affection, intimacy, healthy relationships, and interpersonal violence;
- sexual orientation and identity; and
- sexual health.

**legal custody**—Authority to make decisions regarding a child's medical care, education, and legal rights.

**limbic system**—A set of structures located in the brain that identify positive and negative environmental stimuli and produce emotional responses. These structures include the hippocampus, the hypothalamus, and the amygdala, as well as neurons that connect to other parts of the brain.

**low-incidence disability**—Term used to describe less prevalent IDEA disability categories; these disabilities occur less frequently and have a more significant effect on an individual.

**masturbation**—Stimulating one's own body for the purpose of sexual gratification.

**matriarchal**—A social system in which a family functions where the mother is the authority figure.

**medical model of disability**—Approaches disability through a rehabilitative lens.

**mental retardation**—A term that was replaced by "Intellectual Disability" in the 21st century because it developed a negative connotation.

**modeling**—Modeling allows the learner to observe someone performing a target behavior. Modeling can provide a primer to task completion or serve as a prompt. Modeling works best when used along with prompting and reinforcement.

**National Sex Education Standards**—The National Sex Education Standards in the United States that provide K–12 core content and skills developed by the Future of Sex Initiative. These standards provide clear, consistent, and straightforward guidance for schools with a vision of healthy sexual development for all students.

**natural supports**—Assistance that naturally flows from environments; sources include the family, school, work, and community.

**no promo homo laws**—Laws that ban the "promotion of homosexuality" through teaching.

**normalcy or normalization**—The principle of assuring that PWD have access to the conditions of living that are as close as possible to those available to all people.

**pansexuality**—When one is attracted to all forms of gender expression.

**partnered sexual activity**—Sexual acts engaged in with another person.

**patriarchal**—A social system in which a family functions where the father is the authority figure.

**person-first language**—A way of speaking and acting that avoids sensationalizing, victimizing, or otherwise stereotyping a person because they have a disability. It includes the practice of putting the person first, before the disability, when speaking or writing.

**person-first philosophy**—A way of speaking and acting that avoids sensationalizing, victimizing, or otherwise stereotyping a person because they have a disability. It includes the practice of putting the person first, before the disability, when speaking or writing.

**physical custody**—Right to exercise physical control over a child for a defined period of time.

**physical disability**—A condition that incapacitates skeletal, muscular, and/or neurological systems of the body to a degree that impacts one or more major life functions.

**PLAAFP**—Present levels of academic achievement and functional performance.

**political economy**—The relationship between one's societal contributions and their access to resources.

**politics of appearance**—Blames a lack of desire on someone's physical appearance.

**pragmatic language**—The use and interpretation of language in social situations; involves knowing what to say and how and when to say it; may also involve nonverbal behaviors such as eye contact, facial expressions, and body language.

**pragmatics**—The use of language in social situations.

**prefrontal cortex**—The part of the brain that covers the front part of the frontal lobe and governs self-control, problem solving, risk assessment, and long-term planning.

**prejudgment**—Coming to conclusions before hearing all of the information presented.

**presumed incompetents**—The self-perception of an individual in their capabilities and ability to control their environment and situation. It is how skilled and effective a person perceives themselves to be in a particular situation.

**protection**—Actions taken to reduce the risks associated with engaging in sexual activity.

**puberty**—The stage of human development during which adolescents reach physical maturity and become capable of reproduction.

**queer theory**—Critiques the concept of "normal" sexuality.

**question**—When one may not know who they are attracted to.

**realistic rhetoric**—Presents people with disabilities as "normal" people who are capable of "normal" feelings, thoughts, and actions.

**receptive language**—The ability to understand verbal and nonverbal communication.

**rhetoric**—Subliminal messages.

**Rosa's Law**—A federal law passed in 2010 that changed the term "mental retardation" to "intellectual disability," and references to "a mentally retarded individual" to "an individual with an intellectual disability" in federal health, education, and labor laws and policy. Also known as Public Law 111–256.

**schemas**—Patterns of subconscious thought.

**secondary sex characteristics**—Physical traits associated with sexual maturity: in girls, breast development and growth of body hair; in boys, deepening of the voice, enlargement of the penis and scrotum, and growth of body hair.

**Section 504**—A brief but powerful nondiscrimination law included in the Rehabilitation Act of 1973.

**self-advocacy**—Ability to speak up and represent for oneself; involves the use of social skills, self-determination, and disability awareness.

**self-contained classroom**—A special education classroom that functions separate from peers without disabilities.

**self-determination**—Acting as the primary causal agent in one's life, making choices and decisions regarding the quality of one's life free from undue external influences or interference.

**sentimental rhetoric**—Presents people with disabilities as charitable cases who need money, time, and help from others.

**sex ed**—A shorthand term used to describe sexual education.

**sexual abuse**—Sexual activity in the absence of freely given consent.

**sexual agency**—The ability to define yourself sexually, the ability to choose whether you want to experience sexual activity, the ability to choose how you want to engage in sexual activity, and the ability to stop or refuse any sexual activity.

**sexual arousal**—The physical response to an attraction that leads to sexual behavior.

**sexual behavior**—The physical actions of sexual activity with oneself or with a sexual partner.

**sexual citizenship**—Developing a sexual identity through full access to all legal and social rights.

**sexual intercourse**—Sexual contact that includes penetration.

**sexual orientation**—The attractions, arousal, and behavior as demonstrated through emotional and physical attractions.

**sexuality education**—A program of instruction that includes information about physical maturation and reproduction, sexual identity development, safe and responsible sexual activity, and social-emotional learning for healthy relationships.

**sexuality education curricula**—Sexuality education curricula specifically designed to meet the needs of people with intellectual disabilities and developmental disabilities or other disabilities, such as autism spectrum disorders.

**sexuality**—The capacity to have sexual feelings and desires.

**sexually transmitted infections**—A parasitic, bacterial, or viral infection passed from one individual to another through sexual contact.

**social model of disability**—Emphasizes society's responsibilities in ensuring accessibility and acceptance.

**social narratives**—Social narratives describe social situations for learners by providing relevant cues, explanation of the feelings and thoughts of others in the social situation, and descriptions of appropriate behavior expectations.

Typically, social narratives are short, individualized based upon the needs of the learner, and written from the perspective of the learner.

**social pragmatic skills**—The ability to effectively adjust communication for a variety of purposes with an array of communication partners within diverse circumstances.

**social privilege**—The social power held by identities considered the "norm."

**societal devaluation of disability**—The stigma that portrays disabled people as asexual beings.

**sociopolitical**—Describing a context that combines social and political factors such as policies, laws, practices, traditions, and events.

**specially designed instruction**—Instruction that addresses the unique needs that exist because of a student's disability.

**stereotyping**—Forming an opinion about an individual member of a group based on preconceived ideas about the group, rather than on the specific characteristics of the individual.

**stigma**—Attitude.

**stigmatization**—The action of describing or regarding someone or something as worthy of disgrace or disapproval.

**systematic instruction**—Teaching concepts in a highly structured, sequential means; often referred to as buttons-up instruction.

**systems of supervision**—When people who are considered socially dominant are in charge of personal care decisions of others.

**task analysis**—Task analysis is the process of breaking a skill into smaller, more manageable steps in order to teach the skill.

**team**—A set of individuals who work together to provide effective educational programs and services to students.

**transgender**—Someone whose assigned biological sex is not the same as their gender identity.

**transition**—A results-oriented process focused on improving the academic and functional achievement of the child with a disability to facilitate the child's movement from school to post-school activities, including postsecondary education, vocational education, integrated employment (including supported employment), continuing and adult education, adult services, independent living, or community participation.

**transition services**—A process mandated under the Individuals with Disabilities Education Act for students 14 years old and older focused on improving academic and functional achievement to facilitate their movement from school to postsecondary activities such as postsecondary education, vocational education, and integrated employment.

**visual supports**—Visual supports are concrete cues paired with, or used in place of, verbal cues to provide information about a routine, activity, behavioral expectation, or skill demonstration. Visual supports can include pictures, written words, objects, etc.

**Vocational Rehabilitation Act**—see Section 504.

**wondrous rhetoric**—Shows people with disabilities as heroes when they complete everyday tasks; also known as inspiration porn.

# References

## Chapter 1: Introduction

Allen, G. E. (2012). "Culling the Herd": Eugenics and the conservation movement in the United States, 1900–1940. *Journal of the History of Biology, 46*, 31–72.

Baladerian, N. J. (1991). Sexual abuse of people with developmental disabilities. *Sexuality and Disability, 9*(4), 323–335. https://doi.org/10.1007/BF01102020

Baladerian, N. J., Coleman, T. F., & Stream, J. (2013). *A report on the 2012 national survey on abuse of people with disabilities*. Spectrum Institute.

Baxley, D. L., & Zendell, A. (2005). *Sexuality education for children and adolescents with developmental disabilities: An instruction manual for caregivers of and individuals with developmental disabilities*. Florida Developmental Disabilities Council, Inc.

Blum, R. W. (1997). Sexual health contraceptive needs of adolescents with chronic conditions. *Archives of Pediatrics and Adolescent Medicine, 151*, 290–297.

Brown, F. E., McDonnell, J. J., & Snell, M. E. (2015). *Instruction of students with severe disabilities*. Pearson.

Center for Parent Information and Resources (2018). Sexuality education for students with disabilities. http://www.parentcenterhub.org/repository/sexed/#materials

Harrell, E. (2014). *Crimes against persons with disabilities, 2009–2012 statistical tables*. U.S. Department of Justice.

Krohn, J. (2014). Sexual harassment, sexual assault, and students with special needs: Crafting an effective response for schools. *University of Pennsylvania Journal of Law and Social Change, 17*(1), 2.

Lombardo, P. A. (2012). Return of the Jukes: Eugenic mythologies and internet evangelism. *American Journal of Legal Medicine, 33*(2), 207–233.

Marshall, R. M., & Neuman, S. (2011). *The middle school mind: Growing pains in early adolescent brains*. Rowman & Littlefield.

Murphy, N. A., & Elias, E. R. (2006). Sexuality of adolescents with developmental disabilities. *Pediatrics, 118*(1), 398–403.

Neufeld, J. A., Klingbeil, F., Bryen, D. N., & Thomas, A. (2002). Adolescent sexuality and disability. *Physical Medicine and Rehabilitation Clinics of North America, 13*(4), 857–873.

O'Brien, G. V., & Bundy, M. E. (2009). Reading beyond the "Moron": Eugenic control of secondary disability groups. *Journal of Sociology and Social Welfare, 36*(4), 153–171.

Perkins, D. F., & Borden, L. M. (2003). Positive behaviors, problem behaviors, and resiliency in adolescence. In R. M. Lerner, M. A. Easterbrooks, & J. Mistry (Eds.), *Handbook of psychology: Vol. 6, Developmental psychology* (pp. 373–394). Wiley.

Powell, R. (March/April 2014). Can parents lose custody simply because they are disabled? *GPSolo, 31*(2), 14–17.

Sabornie, E. J., Thomas, V., & Coffman, R. M. (1989). Assessment of social/affective measures to discriminate between BD and nonhandicapped early adolescents. *Monograph in Behavior Disorders: Severe Behavior Disorders in Children and Youth, 12, 21–32.*

Sullivan, P. M., and Knutson, J. F. (2000). Maltreatment and disabilities: A population based epidemiological study. *Child Abuse & Neglect*, 24(10), 1257–1273. https://doi.org/10.1016/S0145-2134(00)00190-3

Thompson, J. (2013). A Historical Earmark. *Nation, 297, 5.*

White House Council on Women and Girls (2014). *Rape and sexual assault: A renewed call to action.* Author.

Wissink, I. B., van Vugt, E., Moonen, X., Stams, G. J., & Hendriks, J. (2015). Sexual abuse involving children with an intellectual disability (ID): A narrative review. *Research in Developmental Disabilities, 36*, 20–35. https://doi.org/10.1016/j.ridd.2014.09.007

## Chapter 2: Disability Studies

Albrecht, M., & Bury, M. (2001). The political economy of the disability marketplace. In G. L. Albrecht, K. D. Seelman, and M. Bury (Eds.), *Handbook of disabilities studies.* Sage.

Aronson, J. (2001). *Sound and Fury.* PBS Documentary.

Bacchi, C., & Beasley, C. (2002). Citizen bodies: Is embodied citizenship a contradiction in terms? *Critical Social Policy, 22*, 324–352. https://doi.org/10.1177/02610183020220020801

Barnes, C., & Mercer, G. (2001). Disability culture: Assimilation or Inclusion? In G. L. Albrecht, K. D. Seelman, and M. Bury (Eds.), *Handbook of disabilities studies.* Sage.

Barton, L., & Armstrong, F. (2001). Disability, education, and inclusion: Cross-cultural issues and dilemmas. In G. L. Albrecht, K. D. Seelman, and M. Bury (Eds.), *Handbook of disabilities studies.* Sage.

Berger, R. J. (2013). *Introducing Disability Studies.* Lynne Rienner Publishers, Inc.

Connor, D. J., & Ferri, B. A. (2007). The conflict within: Resistance to inclusion and other paradoxes in special education. *Disability & Society, 22*, 19–33.

Darling, R. B., & Heckert, D. A. (2010). *Families against society: A study of reactions to children with birth defects.* Sage.

East, L. J., and Orchard, T. R. (2014). Somebody else's job: Experiences of sex education among health professionals, parents and adolescents with physical disabilities in Southwestern Ontario. *Sexuality and Disability, 32*, 335–350. https://doi.org/10.1007/s11195-013-9289-5

Finger, A. (1992). Forbidden fruit. *New Internationalist, 233*, 8–10.

French, S., & Swain, J. (2001). The relationship between disabled people and health and welfare professionals. In G. L. Albrecht, K. D. Seelman, and M. Bury (Eds.), *Handbook of disabilities studies*. Sage.

Gerschick, T. J. (2000). Toward a theory of disability and gender. *Signs: Journal of Women in Culture and Society, 25*, 1263–1268.

Gerschick, T. J., & Miller, A. S. (1995). Coming to terms: Masculinity and physical disability. In D. G. Sabo & David Frederick Gordon (Eds.), *Men's health and illness: Gender, power and the body*. Sage.

Groch, S. (2001). Free spaces: Creating oppositional consciousness in the disability rights movement. In J. J. Mansbridge & A. Morris (Eds.), *Oppositional consciousness: The subjective roots of protest*. University of Chicago Press.

Harkins Monaco, E. A., Gibbon, T., & Bateman, D. (2018). *Talking about sex: Sexuality education for learners with disabilities*: Rowman & Littlefield.

Hernon, J., Brandon, M., Cossar, J., & Shakespeare, T. (2015). Recognising and responding to the maltreatment of disabled children: A children's rights approach. *Social Work & Social Sciences Review, 17*, 61–77. https://doi.org/10.1921/SWSSR.V17I3.799

Jaggar, A. M. (1983). *Feminist politics and human nature*. Rowman and Allanheld.

Jones, L., Bellis, M. A., Wood, S., Hughes, K., McCoy, E., Eckley, L., Bates, G., Mikton, C., Shakespeare, T., & Officer, A. (2012). Prevalence and risk of violence against children with disabilities: A systematic review and meta-analysis of observational studies. *Lancet, 380*, 899–907. https://doi.org/10.1016/S0140-6736(12)60692-8

Kennedy, M. (1996). Sexual abuse and disabled children. In J. Morris (Ed.), *Encounters with strangers: Feminism and disability* (pp. 116–134). The Women's Press Ltd.

Lane, H. (1995). Construction of deafness. *Disability and Society, 10*, 171–189.

Linton, S. (1998). *Claiming disability: Knowledge and identity*. New York University Press.

Lipsky, D. K., & Gartner, A. (1997). *Inclusion and school reform: Transforming America's classrooms*. Paul H. Brookes.

Marchak, L. E., Seligman, M., & Prezant, F. (1999). *Disability and the family life cycle*. Basic Books.

Morris, J. (1997). Gone missing? Disabled children living away from their families. *Disability & Society, 12*(2), 241–258. https://doi.org/10.1080/09687599727353

Murray, M., and Osborne, C. (2009). *Safeguarding disabled children: Practice guidelines*. The Children's Group.

National Child Traumatic Stress Network. (2009). *Sexual development and behavior in children: Information for parents and caregivers*. https://www.nctsn.org/sites/default/files/resources//sexual_development_and_behavior_in_children.pdf

Niles, G. Y. (2018). No one can escape puberty: Physical and cognitive development. In E. A. Harkins Monaco, T. Gibbon, & D. Bateman (Eds.), *Talking about sex: Sexuality education for learners with disabilities.* Rowman & Littlefield.

Nowell, N. L. (2006). Oppression. In G. L. Albrecht (Ed.), *Encyclopedia of disability* (Vol. 3). Sage.

Oakley, A. (1972). *Sex, gender, and society.* Temple Smith.

Papadimitriou, C. (2001). From dis-ability to difference: Conceptual and methodological issues in the study of physical disability. In S. K. Toombs, (Ed.), *Handbook of phenomenology and medicine.* Kluwer Academic.

Payne, D. A., Hickey, H., Nelson, A., Rees, K., Bollinger, H., & Hartley, S. (2016). Physically disabled women and sexual identity: A PhotoVoice study. *Disability & Society, 31*(8), 1030–1049. https://doi:10.1080/09687599.2016.1230044

Pincus, F. (2011). *Understanding diversity: An introduction to class, race, gender, sexual orientation and disability* (2nd ed.). Lynne Rienner.

Rainey, S. S. (2011). *Love, sex, and disability: The pleasures of care.* Lynne Rienner.

*Roe v. Wade,* 410 U.S. 113 (1973).

Saxton, M. (1998). Disability rights and selective abortion. In R. Solinger (Ed.), *Abortion wars: A half-century of struggle, 1950–2000.* University of California Press.

Shah, S. (2005). *Career success of disabled high-flyers.* Jessica Kingsley Publishers.

Shah, S. (2017). "Disabled people are sexual citizens too": Supporting sexual identity, well-being, and safety for disabled young people. *Frontiers in Education, 2.* https://doi.org/10.3389/feduc.2017.00046

Shah, S., Tsitsou, L., and Woodin, S. (2016a). Hidden voices: Disabled women's experiences of violence and support over the life course. *Violence Against Women, 22,* 1189–1210. https://doi.org/10.1177/1077801215622577

Shah, S., Tsitsou, L., and Woodin, S. (2016b). "I can't forget": Experiences of violence and disclosure in the childhoods of disabled women. *Childhood, 23,* 521–536. https://doi.org/10.1177/0907568215626781

Shakespeare, T. (2006). *Disability rights and wrongs.* Routledge.

Shakespeare, T., Gillespie-Sells, K., & Davies, D. (1996). *The sexual politics of disability: Untold desires.* Burns & Oates.

Shapiro, J. P. (1993). *No pity: People with disabilities forging a new civil rights movement.* Times Books.

Shildrick, M. (2013). Sexual citizenship, governance and disability: From Foucault to Deleuze. In S. Roseneil (Ed.), *Beyond citizenship? Feminism and the transformation of belonging* (pp. 138–159). Palgrave Macmillan.

Siebers, T. (2008). *Disability theory.* University of Michigan Press.

Society of Obstetricians and Gynecologists of Canada. (n.d.). *Sexuality and childhood development.* http://www.sexualityandu.ca/parents/sexuality-child-development

Stodden, R. A., & Dowrick, P. W. (2000). Postsecondary education and employment of adults with disabilities. *American Rehabilitation, 25,* 19–23.

Sullivan, P. M., and Knutson, J. F. (2000). Maltreatment and disabilities: A population based epidemiological study. *Child Abuse & Neglect*, 24(10), 1257–1273. https://doi.org/10.1016/S0145-2134(00)00190-3

Taylor, J., Cameron, A., Jones, C., Franklin, A., Stalker, K., & Fry, D. (2015). *Deaf and disabled children talking about child protection*. University of Edinburgh: NSPCC Child Protection Research Centre.

Thomas, C. (2004). Rescuing a social relational understanding of disability. *Scandinavian Journal of Disability Research*, 6(1), 22–36. https://doi.org/10.1080/15017410409512637

Tucker, B. P. (1998). Deaf culture, cochlear implants, and elective disability. *Hastings Center report*, 28, 6–14.

Turner, B. S. (2001). Disability and the sociology of the body. In G. L. Albrecht, K. D. Seelman, and M. Bury (Eds.), *Handbook of disabilities studies*. Sage.

Watson, N. (2002). Well, I know this is going to sound very strange to you, but I don't see myself as a disabled person: Identity and disability. *Disability & Society*, 17, 509–527.

Wendell, S. (1996). *The rejected body: Feminist philosophical reflections on disability*. Routledge.

Westcott, H., & Cross, M. (1996). *This far and no further: Tending the abuse of disabled children*. Venture Press.

World Health Organization. (2012). *Sexual and reproductive health: Gender and human rights*. www.who.int/reproductivehealth/topics/gender_rights/sexual_health/en/

Zola, I. (1982). *Missing pieces: A chronicle of living with a disability*. Temple University Press.

Zuckoff, M. (2002). *Choosing Naia: A family's journey*. Beacon Press.

# Chapter 3: Ethics

Adams, R. (2015). Privacy, dependency, discegenation: Toward a sexual culture for people with intellectual disabilities. *Disability Studies Quarterly*, 35(1). https://dsqsds.org/article/view/4185/3825

American Association on Intellectual and Developmental Disabilities. (2013). Sexuality position statement. https://www.aaidd.org/news-policy/policy/position-statements/sexuality

Arias, B., Ovejero, A., & Morentin, R. (2009). Love and emotional well-being in people with intellectual disabilities. *The Spanish Journal of Psychology*, 12(1), 204–216. https://doi.org/10.1017/S113874160000161X

Azzopardi-Lane, C., & Callus, A. M. (2014). Constructing sexual identities: People with intellectual disability talking about sexuality. *British Journal of Learning Disabilities*, 43(1), 32–37. https://doi.org/10.1111/bld.12083

Barnard-Brak, L., Schmidt, M., Chesnut, S., Wei, T., & Richman, D. (2014). Predictors of access to sex education for children with intellectual disabilities in public schools. *Mental Retardation*, 52(2), 85–97. https://doi.org/10.1352/1934-9556-52.2.85

Beres, M. A. (2007). "Spontaneous" sexual consent: An analysis of sexual consent literature. *Feminism & Psychology, 17*(1), 93–108. https://doi.org/10.1177/0959353507072914

Brodwin, M. G., & Frederick, P. C. (2010). Sexuality and societal beliefs regarding persons living with disabilities. *Journal of Rehabilitation, 76*(4), 37.

Brown, D. (2018). 19 million tweets later: A look at #MeToo a year after the hashtag went viral. *USA Today.* https://www.usatoday.com/story/news/2018/10/13/metoo-impact-hashtag-made-online/1633570002/

Brown, M., & McCann, E. (2018). Sexuality issues and the voices of adults with intellectual disabilities: A systematic review of the literature. *Research in Developmental Disabilities 74,* 124–138. https://doi.org/10.1016/j.ridd.2018.01.009

Castelão, T., Campos, T., & Torres, V. (2010). A new perspective of sexual orientation for adolescents that have mental retardation. *Sexologies 36*(3), 231–248. https://doi.org/10.1007/s11195-017-9508-6

Dinwoodie, R., Greenhill, B., & Cookson, A. (2016). "Them two things are what collide together": Understanding the sexual identity experiences of lesbian, gay, bisexual and trans people labelled with intellectual disability. *Journal of Applied Research in Intellectual Disabilities, 33*(1), 3–16. https://doi.org/10.1111/jar.12252

Ditchman, N., Easton, A. B., Batchos, E., Rafajko, S., & Shah, N. (2017). The impact of culture on attitudes toward the sexuality of people with intellectual disabilities. *Sexuality and Disability, 35*(2), 245–260. https://doi.org/10.1007/s11195-017-9484-x

Esmail, S., Darry, K., Walter, A., & Knupp, H. (2010). Attitudes and perceptions towards disability and sexuality. *Disability and Rehabilitation, 32*(14), 1148–1155. https://doi.org/10.3109/09638280903419277

Gil-Llario, M. D., Morell-Mengual, V., Ballester-Arnal, R., & Díaz-Rodríguez, I. (2018). The experience of sexuality in adults with intellectual disability. *Journal of Intellectual Disability Research, 62*(1), 72–80. https://doi.org/10.1111/jir.12455

Gougeon, N. A. (2009). Sexuality education for students with intellectual disabilities, a critical pedagogical approach: Outing the ignored curriculum. *Sex Education, 9*(3), 277–291. https://doi.org/10.1080/14681810903059094

Greenspan, S. (2002). A sex police for adults with "mental retardation"? Comment on Spiecker and Steutel. *Journal of Moral Education, 31*(2), 171–179. https://doi.org/10.1080/03057240220143278

Greenwood, N. W., & Wilkinson, J. (2013). Sexual and reproductive health care for women with intellectual disabilities: A primary care perspective. *International Journal of Family Medicine, 2013.* https://doi.org/10.1155/2013/642472

Harris, J. E. (2018). Sexual consent and disability. *New York Law Review, 93,* 480–556.

Healy, E., McGuire, B. E., Evans, D. S., & Carley, S. N. (2009). Sexuality and personal relationships for people with an intellectual disability. Part

I: Service-user perspectives. *Journal of Intellectual Disability Research,* *53*(11), 905–912. https://doi.org/10.1111/j.1365-2788.2009.01203.x

Herring, J. (2012). Mental disability and capacity to consent to sex: *A Local Authority v H* [2012] EWHC 49 (COP). *Journal of Social Welfare and Family Law, 34*(4), 471–478. https://doi.org/10.1080/09649069.2012.753733

Isler, A., Tas, F., Beytut, D., & Conk, Z. (2009). Sexuality in adolescents with intellectual disabilities. *Sexuality and Disability, 27*(1), 27–34. https://doi.org/10.1007/s111950099107-2

Lin, Z., & Yang, L. (2019). "Me too!": Individual empowerment of disabled women in the #MeToo movement in China. *Disability & Society, 34*(5), 842–847. https://doi.org/10.1080/09687599.2019.1596608

McDaniels, B., & Fleming, A. (2016). Sexuality education and intellectual disability: Time to address the challenge. *Sexuality and Disability, 34*(2), 215–225. https://doi.org/10.1007/s11195-016-9427-y

Normand, C. L., & Sallafranque-St-Louis, F. (2015). Cybervictimization of young people with an intellectual or developmental disability: Risks specific to sexual solicitation. *Journal of Applied Research in Intellectual Disabilities, 29*(2), 99–110. https://doi.org/10.1111/jar.12163

Parchomiuk, M. (2012). Specialists and sexuality of individuals with disability. *Sexuality and Disability, 30*(4), 407–419. https://doi.org/10.1007/s11195-011-9249-x

Rohleder, P., Braathen, S. H., & Carew, M. T. (2018). *Disability and sexual health: A critical exploration of key issues.* Routledge.

Shogren, K. A., & Wehmeyer, M. L. (2017). Self-determination and goal attainment. In M. L. Wehmeyer & K. A. Shogren (Eds.), *Handbook of research-based practices for educating students with intellectual disability* (pp. 255–273). New York: Routledge.

Silvers, A., Francis, L. P., & Badesch, B. (2016). Reproductive rights and access to reproductive services for women with disabilities. *American Medical Association Journal of Ethics, 18*(4), 430–437. https://ssrn.com/abstract=2791656

Sinclair, J., Unruh, D., Lindstrom, L., & Scanlon, D. (2015). Barriers to sexuality for individuals with intellectual and developmental disabilities: A literature review. *Education and Training in Autism and Developmental Disabilities, 50*(1), 3–16. https://www.jstor.org/stable/24827497

Spiecker, B., & Steutel, J. (2002). Sex between people with "mental retardation": An ethical evaluation. *Journal of Moral Education, 31*(2), 155–169. https://doi.org/10.1080/03057240220143269

Strike, A. W. (2018). Disabled women see #MeToo and think: What about us? *The Guardian.* https://www.theguardian.com/commentisfree/2018/mar/08/disabledpeople-metoo womens-movement-inclusion-diversity

Vehmas, S. (2019). Persons with profound intellectual disability and their right to sex. *Disability & Society, 34*(4), 519–539. https://doi.org/10.1080/0968 7599.2018.1545110

World Health Organization. (2012). *Sexual and reproductive health: Gender and human rights.* www.who.int/reproductivehealth/topics/gender_rights/ sexual_health/en/

# Chapter 4: Intersectionality

American Civil Liberties Union. (2017, March 6). *GG v. Gloucester County School Board.* https://www.aclu.org/cases/gg-v-gloucester-county-school-board

American Psychological Association. (2015). *Diagnostic and statistical manual of mental disorders (DSM-5)* (5th ed.) American Psychiatric Publishing.

Appreciating the Impact of Intersectionality in Education Settings Using the Example of Females of Color. (n.d.). http://smhp.psych.ucla.edu/pdfdocs/ intersect.pdf

Azzopardi-Lane, C., & Callus, A. (2015). Constructing sexual identities: People with intellectual disability talking about sexuality. *British Journal of Learning Disabilities, 43*(1), 32–37. https://doi.org/10.1111/bld.12083

Banaji, M. R., Bazerman, M. H., & Chugh, D. (2003). How (un)ethical are you? *Harvard Business Review, 56–65.*

Bateman, D. F., & Cline, J. L. (Eds.). (2019). *Special education leadership: Building effective programming in schools.* Routledge/Taylor and Francis Group.

Bazerman, M. H., & Tenbrunsel, A. E. (2011). *BlindSpots: Why we fail to do what's right and what to do about it.* Princeton University Press.

Bell, L. A. (2016). Theoretical foundations for social justice education. In M. Adams, L. A. Bell, D. Goodman, & K. Y. Joshi (Eds.), *Teaching for diversity and social justice* (pp. 3–26). Routledge.

Berger, R. J. (2013). *Introducing disability studies.* Lynne Rienner Publishers, Inc.

Bialka, C. S. (2017). Fortifying the foundation: Tools for addressing disability within the multicultural classroom. *Multicultural Perspectives, 19*(3), 172–177.

Bond, J. (2019, August 23). Drag syndrome [Online statement]. https:// www.facebook.com/DragSyndrome/videos/2416826848437614 /?v=2416826848437614

Brown, M. (2007). Educating all students: Creating culturally responsive teachers, classrooms, and schools. *Intervention in School and Clinic, 43*(1), 57–62.

Bryan, J. (2012). *From the dress-up corner to the senior prom: Navigating gender and sexuality diversity in pre-K–12 schools.* Rowman & Littlefield Education.

Carroll, D. W. (2009). Toward multicultural competence: A practice model for implementation in the schools. In J. M. Jones (Ed.), *The psychology of multiculturalism in schools: A primer for practice, training, and research* (pp. 1–16). National Association of School Psychologists.

Choudhury, S. (2015). *Deep diversity: Overcoming us vs. them.* Between the Lines.

Chugh, D., Bazerman, M. H., & Banaji, M. R. (2005). Bounded ethically as a psychological barrier to recognizing conflicts of interest. In D. Moore, D. Cain, G. Loewenstein, & M. Bazerman (Eds.), *Conflict of interest: Challenges and solutions in business, law, medicine, and public policy.* Cambridge University Press.

Cooper, B. (2015). Intersectionality. In L. Disch & M. Hawkesworth (Eds.), *The Oxford handbook of feminist theory.* http://www.oxfordhandbooks .com/view/10.1093/oxfordhb/9780199328581.001.0001/oxfordhb -9780199328581-e-20

Crenshaw, K. (1989). Demarginalizing the intersection of race and sex: A Black feminist critique of antidiscrimination doctrine, feminist theory, and antiracist politics. *University of Chicago Legal Forum, 1989*(1), 139–167.

Crenshaw, K. (2015, September 24). Why intersectionality can't wait. *Washington Post.* http://www.washingtonpost.com/news/in-theory/wp/2015/09/24/ why-intersectionality-cant-wait/

Darling-Hammond, L. (2002). Educating a profession for equitable practice. In L. Darling-Hammond, J. French, & S. P. Garcia-Lopez (Eds.), *Learning to teach for social justice* (pp. 201–212). Teachers College Press.

Dill, B. T., & Zambrana, R. E. (2009). Critical thinking about inequality: An emerging lens. In B. T. Dill & R. E. Zambrana (Eds.), *Emerging intersections: Race, class and gender in theory, policy and practice* (pp. 1–21). Rutgers University Press.

*Disability Drag Show.* (2019). https://www.eventbrite.com/e/disability-drag -show-tickets-71002499387

Gay, G., & Howard, T. C. (2000). Multicultural teacher education for the 21st century. *The Teacher Educator, 36*(1), 1–16. http://dx.doi .org/10.1080/08878730009555246

Harkins Monaco, E. A. (2019). Working with parents. In D. F. Bateman & J. L. Cline (Eds.), *Special education leadership: Building effective programming in schools.* Routledge/Taylor and Francis Group.

Harkins Monaco, E. A. (2020). Intersectional practices in the college classroom. *Journal on Excellence in College Teaching, 31*(3), 71–92.

Harkins Monaco, E. A., Gibbon, T., & Bateman, D. (2018). *Talking about sex: Sexuality education for learners with disabilities.* Rowman & Littlefield.

Harkins Monaco, E. A., & McCollow, M. (2019). Legal brief: Gender identity and disability. *DADD Express Newsletter, 30*(1).

Harrison, M. (2007). Does this child have a friend? *Teaching Tolerance, 32.* https://www.tolerance.org/magazine/fall-2007/does-this-child-have-a-friend

Howard-Hamilton, M. F., Cuyjet, M. J., & Cooper, D. (2011). Understanding multiculturalism and multicultural competence among college students. In M. J. Cuyjet, M. F. Howard-Hamilton, & D. L. Cooper (Eds.), *Multiculturalism on campus: Theory, models, and practices for understanding diversity and creating inclusion* (pp. 2–18). Stylus.

*Gender Spectrum.* (2016). https://www.genderspectrum.org/bathroomfaq/

GLSEN. (2019). https://www.glsen.org/school-climate-survey

Jacobs, J. (2019). Complaint filed after door closes on drag performers with Down syndrome. *New York Times*. https://www.nytimes.com/2019/09/05/arts/drag-syndrome-peter-meijer.html

Kothlow, K., & Chamberlain, K. (2012). *Disrupting heteronormativity in schools* (doctoral dissertation). ProQuest Dissertations and Theses. http://hdl/handle.net.libproxy.Lib.unc.edu/2429/42758

Leins, C. (2019). These states require schools to teach LGBT history. *U.S. News*. https://www.usnews.com/news/best-states/articles/2019-08-14/states-that-require-schools-to-teach-lgbt-history

Linton, S. (1998). *Claiming disability: Knowledge and identity*. New York University Press.

Luterman, S. (2019). A glimpse of freedom, in glittery heels. *Slate*. https://slate.com/human-interest/2019/09/drag-syndrome-performance-republican-controversy.html

Maich, K., & Belcher, C. (2014) Autism Spectrum Disorder in popular media: Storied reflections of societal views. *Brock Education, 23*, 97–115.

Murray Law, B. (2011). Retraining the biased brain: Is it possible to break people of unconscious prejudice? *American Psychological Association, 42*(9), 42.

Museus, S. D., & Griffin, K. A. (2011). Mapping the margins in higher education: On the promise of intersectionality frameworks in research and discourse. *New Directions for Institutional Research, 151*, 5–13. https://doi.org/10.1002/ir.395

National Association of School Psychologists. (2017). *Understanding intersectionality* [handout]. Author.

National Center for Education Statistics. (2017). *Condition of education 2017*. Author.

Niles, G., & Harkins Monaco, E. A. (2017). Supporting gender and sexual diversity through inclusive sexual education for students with IDD. *DADD Online Journal (DOJ), 4*(1), 177–189.

Niles, G. Y., & Harkins Monaco, E. A. (2018). What does it all mean? LGBTQ+. In E. A. Harkins Monaco, T. Gibbon, & D. Bateman (Eds.), *Talking about sex: Sexuality education for learners with disabilities*. Rowman & Littlefield.

Niles, G., & Harkins Monaco, E. A. (2019). Privilege, social identity and autism: Preparing preservice practitioners for intersectional pedagogy. *DADD Online Journal (DOJ), 6*(1), 112–123.

Owen, P. M. (2010). Increasing preservice teachers' support of multicultural education. *Multicultural Perspectives, 12*(1), 18–25. http://dx.doi.org/10.1080/15210961003641310

Planned Parenthood. (2017). Gender and gender identity. https://www.plannedparenthood.org/learn/sexual-orientation-gender/gender-gender-identity#sthash.9xfuo4U7.dpuf.

Proctor, S. L., Kyle, J., Fefer, K., & Lau, C. (2017). Examining racial microaggressions, race/ethnicity, gender, and bilingual status with school psychology students: The role of intersectionality. *Contemporary School Psychology.* Advance online publication. https://doi.10.1007/s40688-017-0156-8

Proctor, S. L., & Meyers, J. (2015). Best practices in primary prevention in diverse schools and communities. In P. L. Harrison & A. Thomas (Eds.), *Best practices in school psychology: Foundations* (pp. 33–47). National Association of School Psychologists.

Proctor, S. L., Simpson, C. M., Levin, J., & Hackimer, L. (2014). Recruitment of diverse students in school psychology programs: Direction for future research and practice. *Contemporary School Psychology, 18,* 117–126. https://doi.10.1007/s40688-014-0012-z

Richards, C., & Barker, M. J. (2015). *The Palgrave handbook of the psychology of sexuality and gender.* Palgrave Macmillan.

Roysircar, G. (2008). A response to "Social privilege, social justice, and group counseling: An Inquiry": Counselors' competence with systemically determined inequalities. *The Journal for Specialists in Group Work 33*(4), 377–384.

Sager, J. (2017, May 16). Why parents of kids with special needs are fighting "bathroom bills." https://www.washingtonpost.com/news/parenting/wp/2017/05/16/why-parents-of-kids-with-special-needsare-fighting-bathroom-bills/?noredirect=on&utm_term=.33cc92030c3d

Scharf, A. (2016). Critical practices for anti-bias education. *Teaching Tolerance.* https://www.tolerance.org/magazine/publications/critical-practices-for-anti bias-education

Sherer, I., Baum, J., Ehrensaft, D., & Rosenthal, S. M. (2015). Affirming gender: Caring for gender-atypical children and adolescents. *Contemporary Pediatrics, 32*(1), 16–19.

Shriberg, D. (2016). School psychologists as advocates for racial and social justice: Some proposed steps. *Commentary: School Psychology Forum, 10,* 337–339.

Sobsey, D. (1994). *Violence and abuse in the lives of people with disabilities: The end of silent acceptance?* Paul H. Brookes.

Sobsey, D., Randall, W., & Parrila, R. K. (1997). Gender differences in abuse of children with and without disabilities. *Child Abuse and Neglect, 21,* 707–720.

Spring, J. (2000). *The intersection of cultures: Multicultural education in the United States and the global economy.* McGraw-Hill Higher Education.

Strauss, V. (2017). What the latest research really says about LGBTQ youth in schools. *Washington Post.* https://www.washingtonpost.com/news/answer-sheet/wp/2017/12/06/what-the-latest-research-really-says-about-lgbtq-youth-in-schools/

Sullivan, P. M., & Knutson, J. F. (2000). Maltreatment and disabilities: A population-based epidemiological study. *Child Abuse and Neglect, 24,* 1257–1273.

Tenbrunsel, A. E., & Messick, D. M. (2004). Ethical fading: The role of self-deception in unethical behavior. *Social Justice Research, 17,* 223–236.

Thiara, R. K., Hague, G., & Mullender, A. (2011). Losing on both counts: Disabled women and domestic violence. *Disability & Society, 26,* 757–771.

U.S. Census Bureau. (2016). Data USA: Special education teachers. https://datausa.io/profile/soc/252050/

Walcott, C. M., Charvat, J., McNamara, K. M., & Hyson, D. M. (2016). School psychology at a glance: 2015 member survey results. Special session presented at the annual meeting of the National Association of School Psychologists.

Weber L. (2007). Foreword. In B. Landry (Ed.), *Race, Gender and Class: Theory and Methods of Analysis* (pp. xi–xiv). Pearson Education.

Wijeyesinghe, C. L., & Jones, S. R. (2014). Intersectionality, identity, and systems of power and inequality. In D. Mitchell, C. Y. Simmons, & L. A. Greyerbiehl (Eds.), *Intersectionality and higher education: Theory, research, and praxis* (pp. 9–19). Peter Lang.

# Chapter 5: Students with High- and Low-Incidence and Physical Disabilities

American Psychiatric Association. (2015). *Diagnostic and statistical manual of mental disorders* (5th ed.). https://doi.org/10.1176/appi.books.9780890425596

Americans with Disabilities Act of 1990, Pub. L. No. 101-336, § 2, 104 Stat. 328 (1991).

Becker, H., Stuifbergen, A., & Tinkle, M. (1997). Reproductive health care experiences of women with physical disabilities: A qualitative study. *Archives of Physical Medicine and Rehabilitation, 78*(12 Suppl.), S26–S33. https://doi.10.1016/S0003-9993(97)90218-5

Boyle, J., & Scanlon, D. (2019). *Methods and strategies for teaching students with high incidence disabilities* (2nd ed). Wadsworth, Cengage Learning.

Bryant, D. P., Bryant, B. R., & Smith, D. D. (2019). *Teaching students with special needs in inclusive classrooms* (2nd ed.). Sage Publications.

Chall, J. S. (1996). *Stages of reading development* (2nd ed.). Harcourt Brace.

Eglseder, K., & Webb, S. (2017). Sexuality education and implications for quality of care for individuals with adult onset disability: A review of current literature. *American Journal of Sexuality Education, 12*(4), 409–422.

Gargiulo, R. M., & Bouch, E. C. (2019). *Special education in contemporary society* (7th ed.). Sage Publications.

Gresham, F. M., & Elliot, S. N. (1987). The relationship between adaptive behavior and social skills: Issues in definition and assessment. *Journal of Special Education, 21*(1), 167–181.

Hallahan, D. P., Kauffman, J. M., & Pullen, P. C. (2019). *Exceptional learners: An introduction to special education* (14th ed.). Pearson.

Harkins Monaco, E. A., Gibbon, T., & Bateman, D. (2018). *Let's talk about sex.* Rowman & Littlefield.

Hunt, N., & Marshall, K. (2015). *Exceptional children and youth* (5th ed.). Houghton-Mifflin.

Individuals with Disabilities Education Act, 20 U.S.C. § 1400 (2004).

Kauffman, J. M., & Landrum, T. J. (2018). *Characteristics of emotional and behavioral disorders of children and youth* (11th ed.). Pearson.

Kedde, H., van de Wiel, H., Schultz, W., Vanwesenbeeck, I., & Bender, J. (2012). Sexual health problems and associated help-seeking behavior of people with physical disabilities and chronic diseases. *Journal of Sex & Marital Therapy, 38*(1), 63–67.

Kroll, K., & Klein, E. K. (2001). *Enabling romance: A guide to love, sex, and relationships for people with disabilities.* No Limits Communications.

Landrum, T. J., Tankersley, M., & Kauffman, J. M. (2003). What is special about special education for students with emotional or behavioral disorders? *Journal of Special Education, 37*(3), 148–156.

McDaniels, B. W., & Fleming, A. R. (2018). Sexual health education: A missing piece in transition services for youth with intellectual and developmental disabilities? *Journal of Rehabilitation, 84*(3), 28–38.

McFarland, J., & Hussar, B. (2019, May). *The condition of special education.* National Center for Education Statistics. https://nces.ed.gov/pubs2019/2019144.pdf

Rowe, D. A., Sinclair, J., Hirano, K., & Barbour, J. (2018). Let's Talk About Sex . . . Education. *American Journal of Sexuality Education, 13*(2), 205–216. https://doi.org/10.1080/15546128.2018.1457462

Sinclair, J., Unruh, D., Lindstrom, L., & Scanlon, D. (2015). Barriers to sexuality for individuals with intellectual and developmental disabilities: A literature review. *Education and Training in Autism and Developmental Disabilities, 50*(1), 3–16.

TASH (The Association for People with Severe Disabilities). (1991). Definition of the people TASH serves. In L. H. Meyer, C. A. Peck, & L. Brown (Eds.), *Critical issues in the lives of people with severe disabilities.* Paul H. Brookes.

Treacy, A. C., Taylor, S. S., & Abernathy, T. V. (2018). Sexual health education for individuals with disabilities: A call to action. *American Journal of Sexuality Education, 13*(1), 65–93.

Tullis, C. A., & Zangrillo, A. N. (2013). Sexuality education for adolescents and adults with autism spectrum disorders. *Psychology in the Schools, 50*(9), 866–875.

University of Michigan Health System. (2010). *Your child.* https://www.mottchildren.org/your-child

Wehmeyer, M. L. (2007). *Promoting self-determination in students with developmental disabilities.* Guilford Press.

Westling, D. L., Fox, L., & Carter, E. W. (2015). *Teaching students with severe disabilities* (5th ed.). Pearson.

Wolfe, P. S., & Blanchett, W. (2003). Sex education for students with disabilities: An evaluation guide. *TEACHING Exceptional Children, 36*(1), 46–51.

## Chapter 6: Physical and Cognitive Effects of Puberty on People with Disabilities

Arbeit, M. R. (2014). What does healthy sexual development look like among youth? Towards a skills-based model for promoting adolescent sexuality development. *Human Development, 57,* 259–286.

Ballan, M. (2012). Parental perspectives of communication about sexuality in families of children with autism spectrum disorders. *Journal of Autism and Developmental Disorders, 42,* 676–684. https://doi.10.1007/s10803-011-1293-y

Bancroft, J. (2002). Biological factors in human sexuality. *Journal of Sex Research, 39*(1), 15–21.

Barnard-Brak, L., Schmidt, M., Chesnut, S., Wei, T., & Richman, D. (2014). Predictors of access to sex education for children with intellectual disabilities in public schools. *Intellectual and Developmental Disabilities, 52*(2), 85–97.

Brandon-Friedman, R. A. (2019). Youth sexual development: A primer for social workers. *Social Work, 64*(4), 356–364.

Brodwin, M. G., & Frederick, P. C. (2010). Sexuality and societal beliefs regarding persons living with disabilities. *Journal of Rehabilitation, 76*(4), 37–41.

Cambridge, P., & Mellan, B. (2000). Reconstructing the sexuality of men with learning disabilities: Empirical evidence and theoretical interpretations of need. *Disability & Society, 15*(2), 293–311.

Centers for Disease Control and Prevention. (2019). *Preventing Sexual Violence.* https://www.cdc.gov/violenceprevention/sexualviolence/fastfact.html

Crugnola, C. R., Ierardi, E., & Canevini, M. P. (2018). Reflective functioning, maternal attachment, mind-mindedness, and emotional availability in adolescent and adult mothers at infant 3 months. *Attachment & Human Development, 20*(1), 84–106. https://doi.org/10.1080/14616734.2017.1379546

Davidson, T. E., & McCabe, M. P. (2006). Adolescent body image and psychosocial functioning. *Journal of Social Psychology, 146*(1), 15–30.

Dryden, E. M., Desmarais, J., & Arsenault, L. (2014). Effectiveness of the IMPACT: Ability program to improve safety and self-advocacy of high school students with disabilities. *Journal of School Health, 84*(12), 793–801.

Emmanuel, M., & Bokor, B. R. (2017). *Tanner Stages.* StatPearls.

Fuhrmann, D., Knoll, L. J., & Blakemore, S. J. (2015). Adolescence as a sensitive period of brain development. *Trends in Cognitive Sciences, 19*(10), 558–566.

Gage, N. A., Lierheimer, K. S., & Goran, L. G. (2012). Characteristics of students with high-incidence disabilities broadly defined. *Journal of Disability Policy Studies, 23*(3), 168–178.

Hartmann, K., Urbano, M. R., Raffaele, C. T., Qualls, L. R., Williams, T. V., Warren, C., . . . & Deutsch, S. I. (2019). Sexuality in the Autism Spectrum

Study (SASS): Reports from young adults and parents. *Journal of Autism and Developmental Disorders, 49*(9), 3638–3655.

Heward, W. L., Alber-Morgan, S., & Konrad, M. (2017). *Exceptional children: An introduction to special education.* Pearson.

Kim, K. M., & Choi, J. S. (2020). Female university students' menstrual-hygiene management and factors associated with genitourinary-tract infections in Korea. *Women & Health, 60*(5), 559–569.

Kim, S. (2010). Personal safety programs for children with intellectual disabilities. *Education and Training in Autism and Developmental Disabilities, 45*(2), 312–319.

Mollborn, S. (2010). Exploring variation in teenage mothers' and fathers' educational attainment. *Perspectives on Sexual and Reproductive Health, 42*(3), 152–159. https://doi.org/10.1363/4215210

Murphy, N. A., & Elias, E. R. (2006). Sexuality of children and adolescents with developmental disabilities. *Pediatrics, 118*, 398–403.

Murphy, N., & Young, P. C. (2005). Sexuality in children and adolescents with disabilities. *Developmental Medicine & Child Neurology, 47*(9), 640–644. https://doi.org/10.1017/S0012162205001258

National Child Traumatic Stress Network. (2009). *Sexual development and behavior in children: Information for parents and caregivers.* https://www.nctsn.org/sites/default/files/resources/sexual_development_and_behavior_inchildren.pdf

Oakes, L. R., & Thorpe, S. (2019). The sexual health needs and perspectives of college students with intellectual and/or developmental disabilities and their support staff: A brief report. *Sexuality and Disability, 37*(4), 587–598.

O'Sullivan, L. F., Cheng, M. M., Harris, K. M., & Brooks-Gunn, J. (2007). I wanna hold your hand: The progression of social, romantic and sexual events in adolescent relationships. *Perspectives on Sexual and Reproductive Health, 39*(2), 100–107.

Paris, N. (2019). The young adolescent state of mind: What neuroscience reveals about our students and how we should respond. *AMLE Magazine, 7*(1), 6–8.

Planned Parenthood. (2020). *Sexual Consent.* https://www.plannedparenthood.org/learn/relationships/sexual-consent

Post, M., Haymes, L., Storey, K., Loughrey, T., & Campbell, C. (2014). Understanding stalking behaviors by individuals with autism spectrum disorders and recommended prevention strategies for school settings. *Journal of Autism and Developmental Disorders, 44*(11), 2698–2706.

Richards, C., & Barker, M. J. (2015). *The Palgrave handbook of the psychology of sexuality and gender.* Palgrave Macmillan.

Robbins, C. L., Schick, V., Reece, M., Herbenick, D., Sanders, S. A., Dodge, B., & Fortenberry, J. D. (2011). Prevalence, frequency, and associations of masturbation with partnered sexual behaviors among US adolescents. *Archives of Pediatric and Adolescent Medicine, 165*(12), 1087–1093.

Ryan, A. M. (2000). Peer groups as a context for the socialization of adolescents' motivation, engagement, and achievement in school. *Educational Psychologist, 35*(2), 101–111.

Shulman, E. P., Smith, A. R., Silva, K., Icenogle, G., Duell, N., Chein, J., & Steinberg, L. (2016). The dual systems model: Review, reappraisal, and reaffirmation. *Developmental Cognitive Neuroscience, 17*, 103–117.

Sinclair, J., Unruh, D., Lindstrom, L., & Scanlon, D. (2015). Barriers to sexuality for individuals with intellectual and developmental disabilities: A literature review. *Education and Training in Autism and Developmental Disabilities, 50*(1), 3–16.

Titus, S., & Hodge, J. (2012). Diagnosis and treatment of acne. *American Family Physician, 86*(8), 734–740.

Tolman, D. L., & McClelland, S. I. (2011). Normative sexuality development in adolescence: A decade in review, 2000–2009. *Journal of Research on Adolescence, 21*(1), 242–255.

Tullis, C. A., & Zangrillo, A. N. (2013). Sexuality education for adolescents and adults with autism spectrum disorders. *Psychology in the Schools, 50*(9), 866–875.

U.S. Department of Health and Human Services, Office of Adolescent Health. (2019). *Reproductive health and teen pregnancy.* https://www.hhs.gov/ash/oah/adolescent-development/reproductive-health-and-teen-pregnancy/index.html

Wang, M.-T., & Sheikh-Kahil, S. (2014). Does parental involvement matter for student achievement and mental health in high school? *Child Development, 85*(2), 610–625.

## Chapter 7: The Team

Areskoug-Josefsson, K., & Gard, G. (2015). Physiotherapy as a promoter of sexual health. *Physiotherapy Theory and Practice, 31*(6), 390–395. http://dx.doi.org/10.3109/09593985.2015.1023876

Bambara, L. M., & Chovanes, J. (in press). Teaming. In L. M. Bambara and L. Kern (Eds.), *Individualized Supports for Students with Behavior Problems* (2nd ed.). Guilford Press.

Bambara, L. M., & Kunsch, C. (2014). Effective teaming for positive behavior support. In F. Brown, J. Anderson, & R. L. De Pry (Eds.), *Individual positive behavior supports: A standards-based guide to practices in school and community-based settings* (pp. 47–70). Paul H. Brookes.

Barnard-Brak, L., Schmidt, M., Chesnut, S., Wei, T., & Richman, D. (2014). Predictors of access to sex education for children with intellectual disabilities in public schools. *Intellectual and Developmental Disabilities, 52*, 85–97. http://dx.doi.org/10.1352/1934-9556-52.2.85

Berman, H., Harris, D., Enright, R., Gilpin, M., Cathers, T., & Bukovy, G. (1999). Sexuality and the adolescent with a physical disability: Understandings and misunderstandings. *Issues in Comprehensive Pediatric Nursing, 22*(4), 183–196. http://dx.doi.org/10.1080/014608699265275

Blanchett, W. J., & Wolfe, P. S. (2002). A review of sexuality education curricula: Meeting the sexuality education needs of individuals with moderate and severe intellectual disabilities. *Research & Practice for Persons with Severe Disabilities, 27*(1), 43–57.

Breuner, C. C., & Mattson, G. (2016). Sexuality education for children and adolescents. *Pediatrics, 138*(2), 1–11. http://dx.doi.org/10.1542/peds.2016-1348

Brock, M. E., & Carter, E. W. (2013). A systematic review of paraprofessional-delivered educational practices to improve outcomes for students with intellectual and developmental disabilities. *Research and Practice for Persons with Severe Disabilities, 38*(4), 211–221. http://dx.doi.org/10.1177/154079691303800401

Carter, E. W., & Hughes, C. (2006). Including high school students with severe disabilities in general education classes: Perspectives of general and special educators, paraprofessionals, and administrators. *Research and Practice for Persons with Severe Disabilities, 31*(2), 174–185.

Ditchman, N., Easton, A. B., Batchos, E., Rafajko, S., & Shah, N. (2017). The impact of culture on attitudes toward the sexuality of people with intellectual disabilities. *Sexuality and Disability, 35*(2), 245–260. https://doi.org/10.1007/s11195-017-9484-x

Ehren, B. J., & Whitmire, K. (2009). Speech-language pathologists as primary contributors to response to intervention at the secondary level. *Seminars in Speech and Language, 30*(2), 90–104. http://dx.doi.org/10.1055/s-0029-1215717

Friend, M., & Cook, L. (2017). *Interactions: Collaboration skills for school professionals* (8th ed.). Pearson.

Gage, N. A., Lierheimer, K. S., & Goran, L. G. (2012). Characteristics of students with high-incidence disabilities broadly defined. *Journal of Disability Policy Studies, 23*(3), 168–178. http://dx.doi.org/10.1177/1044207311425385

Graff, H. J., Moyher, R. E., Bair, J., Foster, C., Gorden, M. E., & Clem, J. (2018). Relationships and sexuality: How is a young adult with an intellectual disability supposed to navigate? *Sex and Disability, 36*, 175–183. http://dx.doi.org/10.1007/s11195-017-9499-3

Greenwood, N. W., & Wilkinson, J. (2013). Sexual and reproductive health care for women with intellectual disabilities: A primary care perspective. *International Journal of Family Medicine, 2013*. https://doi.org/10.1155/2013/642472

Guilamo-Ramos, V., & Bouris, A. (2009). Working with parents to promote healthy adolescent sexual development. *Prevention Researcher, 16*(4), 7–11.

Howard-Barr, E. M., Rienzo, B., Pigg, R. M., & James, D. (2005). Teacher beliefs, professional preparation, and practices regarding exceptional students and sexuality education. *Journal of School Health, 75*(3), 99–104. https://doi.org/10.1111/j.1746-1561.2005.tb06649.x

Individuals with Disabilities Education Act, 20 U.S.C. § 1400 (2004).

King-Sears, M. E., Janney, R., & Snell, M. E. (2015). *Collaborative Teaming* (3rd ed.). Paul H. Brookes.

Knackendoffel, A. (2007). Collaborative teaming in the secondary school. *Focus on Exceptional Children, 40*(4), 1–20.

Knackendoffel, A., Detmer, P., & Thurston, L. P. (2018). *Collaborating, Consulting, and Working in Teams for Students with Special Needs* (8th ed.). Pearson.

Krantz, G., Tolan, V., Pontarelli, K., & Cahill, S. (2016). What do adolescents with developmental disabilities learn about sexuality and dating? A potential role for occupational therapy. *Open Journal of Occupational Therapy, 4*(2), 1–15. http://dx.doi.org/10.15453/2168-6408.1208

Kuff, R. M., Greytak, E. A., & Kosciw, J. G. (2019). Supporting safe and healthy schools for lesbian, gay, bisexual, transgender, and queer students: A national survey of school counselors, social workers, and psychologists. *Gay, Lesbian and Straight Education Network (GLSEN)*. https://www.glsen.org/research/supporting-safe-and-healthy-schools-national-survey-mental-health-providers

McDaniels, B., & Fleming, A. (2016). Sexuality education and intellectual disability: Time to address the challenge. *Sex and Disability, 34*, 215–255. http://dx.doi.org/10.1007/s11195-016-9427-y

Murza, K. (2019). Think beyond you: Activate the power of your school treatment team. *ASHA Leader, 24*(8), 46–55. http://dx.doi.org/10.1044/leader.ftr1.24082019.46

Pugach, M. C., & Winn, J. A. (2011). Research on co-teaching and teaming: An untapped resource for induction. *Journal of Special Education Leadership, 24*(1), 36–46.

Rafoth, M. A., & Foriska, T. (2006). Administrator participation in promoting effective problem-solving teams. *Remedial and Special Education, 27*(3), 130–135.

Romano, J. L., & Kachgal, M. M. (2004). Counseling psychology and school counseling: An underutilized partnership. *The Counseling Psychologist, 32*(2), 184–215.

Rowe, D. A., Sinclair, J., Hirano, K., & Barbour, J. (2018) Let's Talk About Sex … Education. *American Journal of Sexuality Education, 13*(2), 205–216. http://dx.doi.org/10.1080/15546128.2018.1457462

Saxe, A., & Flanagan, T. (2014). Factors that impact support workers' perceptions of the sexuality of adults with developmental disabilities: A quantitative analysis. *Sex and Disability, 32*, 45–63. http://dx.doi.org/10.1007/s11195-013-9314-8

Schaafsma, D., Kok, G., Stoffelen, J. M. T., & Curfs, L. (2015). Identifying effective methods for teaching sex education to individuals with intellectual disabilities: A systematic review. *Journal of Sex Research, 52*(4), 412–432. http://dx.doi.org/10.1080/00224499.2014.919373

Sinclair, J., Kahn, L. G., Rowe, D. A., Mazzotti, V. L., Hirano, K. A., & Knowles, C. (2017). Collaborating to plan and implement a sex education curriculum for individuals with disabilities. *Career Development*

*and Transition for Exceptional Individuals, 40*(2), 123–128. http://dx.doi
.org/10.1177/2165143416670136

Solone, C. J., Thornton, B. E., Chiappe, J. C., Perez, C., Rearick, M. K., &
Falvey, M. A. (2020). Creating collaborative schools in the United States:
A review of best practices. *International Electronic Journal of Elementary
Education, 12*(3), 283–292.

Staples, K. E., & Diliberto, J. A. (2010). Guidelines for successful parent
involvement: Working with parents of students with disabilities. *TEACH-
ING Exceptional Children, 42*(6), 58–63.

Sullivan, A., & Caterino, L. C. (2008). Addressing the sexuality and sex education of individuals with autism spectrum disorders. *Education & Treatment
of Children, 31*(3), 381–394.

Treacy, A. C., Taylor, S. S., & Abernathy, T. V. (2018). Sexual health education
for individuals with disabilities: A call to action. *American Journal of Sexuality Education, 13*(1), 65–93. http://dx.doi.org/10.1080/15546128.2017
.1399492

Walker, V. L., Douglas, K. H., & Brewer, C. (2020). Teacher-delivered training to promote paraprofessional implementation of systematic instruction.
*Teacher Education and Special Education, 43*(3), 257–274. http://dx.doi
.org/10.1177/0888406419869029

Wolfe, P. S., Wertalik, J. L., Domire Monaco, S., Gardner, S., & Ruiz, S. (2019).
Review of sociosexuality curricular content for individuals with developmental disabilities. *Focus on Autism & Other Developmental Disabilities,
34*(3), 153–162. http://dx.doi.org/10.1177/1088357618800040

# Chapter 8: Individualized Education Program and Sexuality Education

*Endrew F. v. Douglas County School District* Re-1, 137 S.Ct. 988, 580 U.S.
(2017).

Goran, L., Harkins Monaco, E. A., Yell, M. L., Shriner, J., & Bateman, D. F.
(2020). Pursuing academic and functional advancement: Goals, services, and measuring progress. *TEACHING Exceptional Children, 52*(5),
333–343.

Graves, J. C., & Graves, C. (2013). Parents have the power to make special education work: An insider guide. Jessica Kingsley.

Harkins Monaco, E. A., Gibbon, T. C., & Bateman, D. F. (2018). *Talking
about sex: Sexuality education for learners with disabilities.* Rowman &
Littlefield.

Harmon, S., Street, M., Bateman, D. F., & Yell, M. P. (2020). Developing present levels of academic achievement and functional performance statements
for IEPs. *TEACHING Exceptional Children, 52*(5), 320–332.

Hedin, L., & DeSpain, S. (2018). SMART or not? Writing specific, measurable
IEP goals. *TEACHING Exceptional Children, 51*(2), 100–110. https://doi
.org/10.1177/0040059918802587

IDEA regulations, 34 C.F.R. § 300 (2012).

Winegarden, B. J. (2005). *Writing instructional objectives*. https://training.nwcg .gov/pre-courses/m410/Writing_Instructional_Objectives.pdf

# Chapter 9: Comprehensive Sexuality and Relationship Education Curriculum and Teaching Strategies

AAIDD. (2008). Sexuality: Joint position statement of AAIDD and the Arc. http://aaidd.org/news-policy/policy/position-statements/sexuality#.U2O5 JFdhvzo.

Anderson, D. L., Lubig, J., & Smith, M. (2012). Meeting the needs of all students: How student teachers identify individualization. *Education Research and Perspectives, 39*, 1–23.

Archer, A. L., & Hughes, C. A. (2011). *Effective and efficient teaching*. Guilford.

Barnard-Brak, L., Schmidt, M., Chesnut, S., Wei, T., & Richman, D. (2014). Predictors of access to sex education for children with intellectual disabilities in public schools. *Intellectual and Developmental Disabilities 52*, 85–97. https://doi.org/10.1352/1934-9556-52.2.85

Blanchett, W. J., & Wolfe, P. S. (2002). A review of sexuality education curricula: Meeting the needs of individuals with moderate to severe intellectual disabilities. *Research & Practice for Persons with Severe Disabilities, 27*, 43–57. https://doi.org/10.2511/rpsd.27.1.43

Breuner, C. C., & Mattson, G. (2016). Committee on adolescence and committee on psychosocial aspects of child and family health. *Pediatrics 138*(2), e20161348. https://doi.org/10.1542/peds.2016-1348

Bridges, E., & Alford, S. (2010). Comprehensive sex education and academic success: Effective programs foster student achievement. *Advocates for Youth*. https://advocatesforyouth.org/wp-content/uploads/2019/09/compre hensive_sex_education_and_academic_success.pdf

Bridges, E., & Hauser, D. (2014). Building an evidence- and rights-based approach to healthy decision-making. *Advocates for Youth*. https://www .advocatesforyouth.org/resources/fact-sheets/sexuality-education-2/

Centers for Disease Control (CDC). What works: Sexual health education. https://www.cdc.gov/healthyyouth/whatworks/what-works-sexual-health -education.htm

Council for Exceptional Children & CEEDAR Center. (2019). Introducing high-leverage practices in special education: A professional development guide for school leaders. *Council for Exceptional Children & CEEDAR Center*. www.highleveragepractices.org

Curtiss, S. L. (2018). The birds and the bees: teaching comprehensive human sexuality education. *TEACHING Exceptional Children, 51*, 134–143. https://doi.org/10.1177/0040059918794029

Davis, L. A. (2009). *People with intellectual disabilities and sexual offenses*. http://www.thearc.org/page.aspx?pid=2456

Eyres, R., Williamson, R. L., Hunter, W., & Casey, L. (2016). Providing comprehensive sexuality education to students with intellectual and developmental disabilities: Preparing the trainer. *Division on Autism and Developmental Disabilities Online Journal, 3*(1), 160–171.

Finnerty, M., Jackson, L. B., & Ostergren, R. (2019). Adaptations in general education classrooms for students with severe disabilities: Access, progress assessment, and sustained use. *Research and Practice in Severe Disabilities, 44*(2), 87–102. https://doi.org/10.1177/1540796919846424

Franzone, E. (2009). Overview of task analysis. *National Professional Development Center on Autism Spectrum Disorders*, Waisman Center, University of Wisconsin.

Future of Sex Education Initiative. (2020). *National sexuality education standards: Core content and skills, K–12* (2nd ed.). http://www.futureofsexeducation.org/documents/josh-fose-standards-web.pdf

Gray, C. (2010). *The new social story book: Over 150 social stories that teach everyday social skills to children with autism or Asperger's syndrome and their peers* (10th ed.). Future Horizons.

Healy, E., McGuire, B. E., Evans, D. S., & Carley, S. N. (2009). Sexuality and personal relationships for people with an intellectual disability. Part I: Service-user perspectives. *Journal of Intellectual Disability Research, 53,* 905–912. https://doi.org/10.1111/j.1365-2788.2009.01203.x

Hume, K., Wong, C., Plavnick, J., & Schultz, T. (2014). Use of visual supports with young children with autism spectrum disorders. In J. Tarbox, D. R. Dixon, P. Sturmey, & J. L. Matson (Eds.), *Handbook of early intervention for autism spectrum disorders* (pp. 375–402). Springer. https://doi.org/10.1007/978-1-4939-0401-3

Individuals with Disabilities Education Act, 20 U.S.C. § 1400 (2004).

Janney, R., Snell, M. E., & Elliot, J. (2000). *Modifying schoolwork*. Paul H. Brookes.

Kirby, D. (2007). *Emerging answers: Research findings on programs to reduce teen pregnancy*. National Campaign to Prevent Teen and Unplanned Pregnancy.

Lafferty, A., McConkey, R., & Simpson, A. (2012). Reducing the barriers to relationships and sexuality education for persons with intellectual disabilities. *Journal of Intellectual Disabilities, 16,* 29–43. https://doi.org/10.1177/1744629512438034

McConkey, R., & Ryan, D. (2001). Experiences of staff in dealing with client sexuality in services for teenagers and adults with intellectual disability. *Journal of Intellectual Disability Research, 45,* 83–87. https://doi.org/10.1111/j.1365-2788.2001.00285.x

McDowell, L. S., Gutierrez, A., Jr., & Bennett, K. D. (2015). Analysis of live modeling plus prompting and video modeling for teaching imitation to children with autism. *Behavioral Interventions, 30*(4), 333–351. https://doi.org/10.1002/bin.1419

Multnomah County Health Department (2018). *In their own words: Guidelines for supporting the sexual health of young people experiencing intellectual/developmental disabilities.* https://multco.us/file/73965/download

National Professional Development Center on Autism Spectrum Disorders. (2014). *Evidence-based practices for children, youth, and young adults with autism spectrum disorder: A comprehensive review.* University of North Carolina, Frank Porter Graham Child Development Institute, Autism Evidence-Based Practice Review Group, Chapel Hill. https://autismpdc.fpg .unc.edu/sites/autismpdc.fpg.unc.edu/files/2014-EBP-Report.pdf

National Research Council. (2001). *Educating children with autism.* National Academies Press. https://doi.org/10.17226/10017

Saxe, A., & Flanagan, T. (2014). Factors that impact support workers' perceptions of the sexuality of adults with developmental disabilities: A quantitative analysis. *Sexuality and Disability, 32*, 45–63. https://doi.org/10.1007/ s11195-013-9314-8

Saxe, A., & Flanagan, T. (2016). Unprepared: An appeal for sex education training for support workers for adults with developmental disabilities. *Sexuality and Disability, 34*, 443–454. https://doi.org/10.1007/s11195-016-9449-5

Schaafsma, D., Kok, G., Stoffelen, J. M. T., & Curfs, L. (2015). Identifying effective methods for teaching sex education to individuals with intellectual disabilities: A systematic review. *Journal of Sex Research, 52*(4), 412–432. http://dx.doi.org/10.1080/00224499.2014.919373

Schaafsma, D., Kok, G., Stoffelen, J. M. T., & Curfs, L. M. G. (2017). People with intellectual disabilities talk about sexuality: Implications for the development of sex education. *Sexuality and Disability, 35*, 21–38. https://doi .org/10.1007/s11195-016-9466-4

Schaafsma, D., Stoffelen, J. M. T., Kok, G., & Curfs, L. M. G. (2013). Exploring the development of existing sex education programmes for people with intellectual disabilities: An intervention mapping approach. *Journal of Applied Research in Intellectual Disabilities, 26*, 157–166. https://doi .org/10.1111/jar.12017

Sexuality Information and Education Council of the United States (SIECUS; 2004). *Guidelines for comprehensive sexuality education* (3rd ed.). https:// siecus.org/wp-content/uploads/2018/07/Guidelines-CSE.pdf

Sinclair, J., Unruh, D., Lindstrom, L., & Scanlon, D. (2015). Barriers to sexuality for individuals with intellectual and developmental disabilities: A literature review. *Education and Training in Autism and Developmental Disabilities, 50*, 3–16.

Slocum, V., & Eyres, R. M. (2018). The birds and the bees, round 2: The curriculum. In E. A. Harkins Monaco, T. Gibbon, & D. Bateman (Eds.), *Talking about sex: Sexuality education for learners with disabilities.* Rowman & Littlefield.

Snell, M. E., & Brown, F. (2011). *Instruction of students with severe disabilities.* Pearson Education, Inc.

Swango-Wilson, A. (2008). Caregiver perceptions and implications for sex education for individuals with intellectual and developmental disabilities. *Sexuality and Disability, 26,* 167–174. https://doi.org/10.1007/s11195-008-9081-0

Swango-Wilson, A. (2009). Perception of sex education for individuals with developmental and cognitive disability: A four cohort study. *Sexuality and Disability, 27,* 223–228. https://doi.org/10.1007/s11195-0099140-1

Thompson, J. R., Walker, V. L., Shogren, K. A., & Wehmeyer, M. L. (2018). Expanding inclusive educational opportunities for students with the most significant cognitive disabilities through personalized supports. *Intellectual and Developmental Disabilities, 56,* 396–411. https://doi .org/10.1352/1934-9556-56.6.396

Travers, J., & Tincani, M. (2010). Sexuality education for individuals with autism spectrum disorders: Critical issues and decision making guidelines. *Education and Training in Autism and Developmental Disabilities, 45,* 284–293.

Travers, J., Tincani, M., Whitby, P., & Boutot, A. E. (2014). Alignment of sexuality education with self-determination for people with significant disabilities: A review of research and future directions. *Education and Training in Autism and Developmental Disabilities, 49*(2), 232–247.

Wilkenfeld, B. F., & Ballan, M. S. (2011). Educators' attitudes and beliefs towards the sexuality of individuals with developmental disabilities. *Sexuality and Disability, 29,* 351–361. https://doi.org/10.1007/s11195-011-9211-y

Witmer, S., Ysseldyke, J., & Salvia, J. (2017). *Assessment in special and inclusive education* (13th ed.). Cengage Learning.

Wolfe, P. S. (2020). *Teaching decision-making in sex education to students with developmental disabilities.* Paper presented at the International Conference of Council for Exceptional Children, Sarasota, FL.

Wolfe, P. S., Condo, B., & Hardaway, E. (2009). Socio-sexuality education for persons with autism spectrum disorders using principles of applied behavior analysis. *TEACHING Exceptional Children, 42,* 50–61. https://doi .org/10.1177/004005990904200105

Wolfe, P. S., Wertalik, J. L., Domire Monaco, S., & Gardner, S. (2019). Review of curricular features of socio-sexuality curricula for individuals with developmental disabilities. *Sexuality and Disability, 37,* 315–327.

Wolfe, P. S., Wertalik, J. L., Domire Monaco, S., Gardner, S., & Ruiz, S. (2019). Review of instructional strategies used in socio-sexuality education for individuals with developmental disabilities. *Education and Training in Autism and Developmental Disabilities, 54,* 186–195. https://doi.org/10.1007/s11195-019-09585-4

## Chapter 10: Transitional Considerations

Anderson, A. (2019). Guardianship: A violation of the Americans with Disabilities Act and what can we do about it. *University of St. Thomas Journal of Law and Public Policy, 13*(2), 117–138.

Blanchett, W. (2001). Importance of teacher transition competencies as rated by special educators. *Teacher Education and Special Education, 24*, 3–12.

Galea, J., Butler, J., Iacono, T., & Leighton, D. (2004). The assessment of sexual knowledge in people with intellectual disability. *Journal of Intellectual & Developmental Disability, 29*(4), 350–365, htttps://doi.org/10.1080/13668250400014517

Gleit, R., Freed, G., & Frederick, E. M. (2014). Transition planning: Teaching sexual self-management. *Contemporary Pediatrics, 31*(4), 16–22.

Henley, A. (2017). Why sex education for disabled people is so important. *Teen Vogue*. https://www.teenvogue.com/story/disabled-sex-ed

Individuals with Disabilities Education Act, 20 U.S.C. § 1400 (2004).

Institute on Disability. (2019). *2018 Annual report on people with disabilities in America*. University of New Hampshire: Institute on Disability.

Joiner, T. E. (2005). *Why people die by suicide*. Harvard University Press.

Justia. (2020). *Difference between custody and guardian*. http://www.circuit7.net/familycourt/parentplan/custody-guardianship.aspx

Kavale, K. A., & Mostert, M. P. (2004). Social skill interventions for individuals with learning disabilities. *Learning Disabilities Quarterly, 27*(1), 31–43.

Kroll, K., & Klein, E. L. (2001). *Enabling romance: A guide to love, sex, and relationships for people with disabilities*. No Limits Communications.

Louis-Jacques, J., & Samples, C. (2011). Caring for teens with chronic illness: Risky business? *Current Opinion in Pediatrics, 23*(4), 367–372. https://doi.org/10.1097/MOP.0b013e3283481101

McDaniels, B. W., & Fleming, A. R. (2018). Sexual health education: A missing piece in transition services for youth with intellectual and developmental disabilities? *Journal of Rehabilitation, 84*(3), 28–38.

Morningside, M., Turnbull, A. P., & Turnbull, H. R. (1995). What do students with disabilities tell us about the importance of family involvement in the transition from school to adult life? *Exceptional Children, 62*(3), 249–260.

Murphy, N. A., & Elias, E. R. (2006). Sexuality of children and adolescents with developmental disabilities. *Pediatrics, 118*, 398–403. https://doi.org/10.1542/peds.2006-1115

Newman, L., Wagner, M., Knokey, A., Marder, C., Nagle, K., Shaver, D., & Wei, X. (2011). *The post-high school outcomes of young adults with disabilities up to 8 years after high school. National Longitudinal Transition Study-2* (Report No. NCSER 2011-3005). SRI International.

Rainville, C. (2013). *Legal consent in sexual assault cases involving teens with intellectual disabilities*. American Bar Association. https://www.americanbar.org/groups/public_interest/child_law/resources/child_law_practiceonline/child_law_practice/vol_32/july-2013/legal-consent-in-sexual-assault-cases-involving-teens-with-intel/

Rowe, D. A., Sinclair, J., Hirano, K., & Barbour, J. (2018). Let's Talk About Sex ... Education. *American Journal of Sexuality Education, 13*(2), 205–216. https://doi.org/10.1080/15546128.2018.1457462

Sexuality Information and Education Council of the United States (SIECUS). (n.d.). *Guidelines for comprehensive sexuality education* (3rd ed.). http://sexedu.org.tw/guideline.pdf

Siebers, T. (2012). A sexual culture for disabled people. In R. McRuer & A. Mollow (Eds.), *Sex and disability* (pp. 37–53). Duke University Press.

Sinclair, J., Kahn, L. G., Rowe, D. A., Mazzotti, V. L., Hirano, K. A., & Knowles, C. (2017). Collaborating to plan and implement a sex education curriculum for individuals with disabilities. *Career Development and Transition for Exceptional Individuals, 40*(2), 123–128. http://dx.doi.org/10.1177/2165143416670136

Sinclair, J., Unruh, D., Lindstrom, L., & Scanlon, D. (2015). Barriers to sexuality for individuals with intellectual and developmental disabilities: A literature review. *Education and Training in Autism and Developmental Disabilities, 50*(1) 3–16.

Thompson, V. R., Stancliffe, R. J., Broom, A., & Wilson, N. J. (2016). Clinicians' use of sexual knowledge assessment tools for people with intellectual disability. *Journal of Intellectual & Developmental Disability, 41*(3), 243–254.

Tice, C., & Harnek Hall, D. M. (2008). Sexuality education and adolescents with developmental disabilities: Assessment, policy, and advocacy. *Journal of Social Work in Disability and Rehabilitation, 7*(1), 47–62, https://doi.org/10.1080/15367100802009749

Travers, J., & Tincani, M. (2010). Sexuality education for adolescents and adults with autism spectrum disorders: Critical issues and decision-making guidelines. *Education and Training in Autism and Developmental Disabilities, 45*(2), 284–293.

Treacy, A. C., Taylor, S. S., & Abernathy, T. V. (2018). Sexual health education for individuals with disabilities: A call to action. *American Journal of Sexuality Education, 13*(1), 65–93. https://doi.org/10.1080/15546128.2017.1399492

Weitlauf, A., White, S., Yancy, O., Rissler, C. N., Harland, E., Van Tran, C., Bowers, J., & Newsom, C. (2013). *The healthy body kit.* Vanderbilt Kennedy Center.

Westling, D. L., Fox, L. L., & Carter, E. W. (2015). *Teaching students with severe disabilities* (5th ed.). Pearson.

Wolfe, P. S., & Blanchett, W. (2003). Sex education for students with disabilities: An evaluation guide. *TEACHING Exceptional Children, 36*(1), 46–51.

## Chapter 11: Sexuality Education Policy

Bateman, D. F., & Bateman, C. F. (2014). *A principal's guide to special education* (3rd ed). Council for Exceptional Children. Co-Published by the National Association of Elementary School Principals and the National Association of Secondary School Principals.

Brady, K. P., Russo, C. J., Dietrich, C. A., Osborne, A. G., & Snyder, N. D. (2020). *Legal issues in special education: Principles, policies, and practices.* Routledge.

*Buck v. Bell,* 274 U.S. 200, 47 S. Ct. 584; 71 L. Ed. 1000.

Carl D. Perkins Vocational and Applied Technology Education Act, 20 U.S.C. §2301 et seq. (2018). https://www2.ed.gov/policy/sectech/leg/perkins/index.html

Cohen, A. (2016). *Imbeciles: The Supreme Court, American eugenics, and the sterilization of Carrie Buck.* Penguin Books.

Individuals with Disabilities Education Act, 20 U.S.C. §§ 1400 *et seq.* (2006 & Supp. V. 2011).

Kaelber, L. (2014). Eugenics/Sexual sterilizations in North Carolina. https://www.uvm.edu/~lkaelber/eugenics/NC/NC.html

National Conference of State Legislatures. (2016). State policies on sex education in schools: Why is sexual education taught in schools? https://www.ncsl.org/research/health/state-policies-on-sex-education-in-schools.aspx

Prince, A. M. T., Plotner, A. J., & Gothberg, S. E. (2019). Current special education legal trends for transition-age youth. In D. F. Bateman & M. L. Yell (Eds.), *Current trends and legal issues in special education* (pp. 72–91). Corwin.

Section 504 of the Rehabilitation Act of 1973, as amended, 29 U.S.C. 794.

U.S. Department of Education. (2020). 504 FAQ. http://www2.ed.gov/about/offices/list/ocr/504faq.html#protected

Yell, M. L. (2019). *The law and special education* (5th ed.). Pearson.

# Chapter 12: Family Interactions and Culture

Corona, L. L., Fox, S. A., Christodulu, K. V., & Worlock, J. A. (2016). Providing education on sexuality and relationships to adolescents with autism spectrum disorder and their parents. *Sexuality and Disability, 34*(2), 199–214. https://doi.org/10.1007/s11195-015-9424-6

Dupras, A., & Dionne, H. (2014). The concern of parents regarding the sexuality of their child with a mild intellectual disability. *Sexologies, 23*(4). https://doi.org/10.1016/j.sexol.2013.09.002

Frank, K., & Sandman, L. (2019). Supporting parents as sexuality educators for individuals with intellectual disability: The development of the Home B.A.S.E curriculum. *Sexuality and Disability, 37*(3), 329–337. https://doi.org/10.1007/s11195-019-09582-7

Hemsley, B., Shane, H., Todd, J. T., Schlosser, R., & Lang, R. (2018, May 22). It's time to stop exposing people to the dangers of Facilitated Communication. *The Conservation.*

Isler, A., Beytut, D., Tas, F., & Conk, Z. (2009). A study on sexuality with the parents of adolescents with intellectual disability. *Sexuality and Disability, 27*(4), 229–237. https://doi.org/10.1007/s11195-009-9130-3

Klein, J. D., Sabaratnam, P., Pazos, B., Matos, M., Graff, C., & Brach, M. (2005). Evaluation of the "parents as primary sexuality educators" program. *Journal of Adolescent Health, 32*(2), 165. https://doi.org/10.1016/s1054-139x(02)00699-7

Mathewes, C. T. (2010). *Understanding religious ethics.* Wiley-Blackwell.

Nichols, S., & Blakeley-Smith, A. (2009). "I'm not sure we're ready for this . . .": Working with families toward facilitating healthy sexuality for individuals with autism spectrum disorders. *Social Work in Mental Health, 8*(1), 72–91. https://doi.org/10.1080/15332980902932383

Pownall, J. D., Jahoda, A., Hastings, R., & Kerr, L. (2011). Sexual understanding and development of young people with intellectual disabilities: Mothers' perspectives of within-family context. *American Journal on Intellectual and Developmental Disabilities, 116*(3), 205–219. https://doi.org/10.1352/1944-7558-116.3.205

Rowe, B., & Wright, C. (2017). Sexual knowledge in adolescents with intellectual disabilities: A timely reflection. *Journal of Social Inclusion, 8*(2), 42. https://doi.org/10.36251/josi.123

Schuster, M. A., Corona, R., Elliott, M. N., Kanouse, D. E., Eastman, K. L., Zhou, A. J., & Klein, D. J. (2008). Evaluation of talking parents, healthy teens, a new worksite based parenting programme to promote parent-adolescent communication about sexual health: Randomised controlled trial. *BMJ, 337.* https://doi.org/10.1136/bmj.39609.657581.25

## Chapter 13: Entertainment and Social Media

Allard, J. (2018, February 1). *Meet the mom bringing style to adaptive clothing: Mindy Scheier wants to make fashion more inclusive for all.* https://www.shondaland.com/inspire/a15898543/mindy-scheier-style-to-adaptive-clot

American Psychiatric Association. (2015). *Diagnostic and statistical manual of mental disorders: DSM-5.* American Psychiatric Association.

Attwood, T., Henaut, I., & Dubin, N. A. (2014). *The autism spectrum, sexuality and the law.* Jessica Kingsley Publishers.

Baker, J. (2013). *No more victims: Protecting those with autism from cyberbullying, internet predators and scams.* Future Horizons Inc.

Barnes, C., (1992) *Disabling imagery and the media: An exploration of the principles for media representations of disabled people.* British Council of Organisations of Disabled People and Ryburn Publishing Limited.

Bauminger, N., & Kasari, C. (2003). Loneliness and friendship in high-functioning children with autism. *Child Development, 71*(2), 447–456. https://doi.org/10.1111/1467-8624.00156

Berger, R. J. (2013). *Introducing disability studies.* Lynne Rienner Publishers, Inc.

Bialka, Christa. (2017). Fortifying the foundation: Tools for addressing disability in the multicultural classroom. *Multicultural Perspectives,19*(3), 172–177. https://doi.org/10.1080/15210960.2017.1335077

Blanchette, A. (2017, April 22). Woman with Down syndrome to compete in Miss Minnesota USA pageant. *Minneapolis Star Tribune.* http://www.startribune.com/first-woman-with-down-syndrome-to-compete-in-miss-minnesota-usa-pageant/420145783/

Buron, K. (2007). *A 5 is against the law! Social boundaries: Straight up! An honest guide for teens and young adults.* Autism Asperger Publishing Company.

Chadwick, D., & Wesson, C. (2016). Digital inclusion and disability. In A. Attrill & C. Fullwood (Eds.), *Applied cyberpsychology.* Palgrave Macmillan. https://doi.org/10.1057/9781137517036_1

Cherney, J. L. (2006). Book and film reviews: The Ringer. *Disability Studies Quarterly, 26*(3).

Dunn, S., & Andrews, E. (2015). Person-first and identity-first language: Developing psychologists' cultural competence using disability language. *American Psychologist, 70*(3). https://psycnet.apa.org/doiLanding?doi=10.1037%2Fa0038636

Fuller, M. (2016). *Autism in love.* www.pbs.org/independentlens/films/autism-in-love/

Garland-Thomson, R. (2002). The politics of staring: Visual rhetorics of disability in popular photography. In S. L. Snyder, B. J. Brueggemann, & R. Garland-Thomson (Eds.), *Disability studies: Enabling the humanities* (pp. 56–75). Modern Language Association.

Harkins Monaco, E. A. (2020). Intersectional practices in the college classroom. *Journal on Excellence in College Teaching, 31*(3), 71–92.

Harris Poll. (2017). *R-Word* (Data file). http://media.theharrispoll.com/documents/HarrisPoll_RWord_CompleteResults.pdf

Heasley, S. (2020). *Actress with autism to debut in new TV comedy.* https://www.disabilityscoop.com/2020/01/06/actress-with-autism-to-debut-in-new-tv-comedy/27598/?fbclid=IwAR00LfbEYkKhYAMkYnnBbZJgEPm3LHXH3YzR_5Ff4vo6ME3nae2AXewljTI

"Jamie Brewer." (2017). *The internet movie database.* https://www.imdb.com/name/nm4661932/?ref_=fn_al_nm_1

Kidd, D. (2014). *Pop culture freaks: Identity, mass media, and society.* Westview Press.

Lester, P., & Ross, S. (2003). *Images that injure: Pictorial stereotypes in the media* (2nd ed.). Greenwood Publishing Group.

*Life Animated.* (n.d.). https://www.lifeanimateddoc.com/

Lou, M., & Griggs, B. (2019, February 12). *Barbie introduces dolls with wheelchairs and prosthetic limbs.* https://www.cnn.com/2019/02/12/us/barbie-doll-disabilities-trnd/index.html

Mazurek, M. (2014). Loneliness, friendship, and well-being in adults with autism spectrum disorders. *Autism, 18*(3), 223–232. https://doi.org/10.1177/1362361312474121

*Monica and David.* (2009). http://www.monicaanddavid.com/

Norden, M. (1994). *The cinema of isolation: A history of physical disability in the movies.* Rutgers University Press.

Oldenburg, A. (2013, January 11). *Miss Montana: First autistic Miss America contestant*. USA Today. https://www.usatoday.com/story/life/people/2013/01/11/miss-montana-first-autistic-miss-america-contestant/1827539/

Parker-Popedek, T. (2007, December 4). Asperger's syndrome gets a very public face. *New York Times*. http://www.nytimes.com/2007/12/04/health/04well.html

*Peanut Butter Falcon*. (2019). *The internet movie database*. https://www.imdb.com/title/tt4364194/

People first language. (2017, July 11). In *Wordsense.eu—dictionary*. http://www.wordsense.eu/people-first_language

Reynolds, T., Zupanick, C. & Donbeck, M. (2013). *History of stigmatizing names for intellectual disabilities continued*. https://www.mentalhelp.net/intellectual-disabilities/history-of-stigmatizing-names-for-intellectual-disabilities-continued/

Rhimes, S. (2015). *Year of yes: How to dance it out, stand in the sun and be your own person*. Simon & Schuster.

Roth, M., & Gillis, J. (2015). Convenience with the click of a mouse: A survey of adults with autism spectrum disorder on online dating. *Sexuality and Disability, 33*(1), 133–150. https://doi.org/10.1007/s11195-014-9392-2

Rovenstine, D. (2016, September 20). *Speechless: Micah Fowler is the breakout star*. Explore Entertainment. https://ew.com/article/2016/09/20/speechless-micah-fowler-breakout-star/

Rutta, R. (2016, July 26). *Entertainment that's helping society gain new perspective on disability* [Web log comment]. https://www.huffpost.com/entry/entertainment-thats-helpi_b_11186436

*Tropic Thunder*. (2008). *The internet movie database*. https://www.imdb.com/title/tt0942385/

Woodburn, D., & Kopic, K. (2016). The Ruderman white paper on employment of actors with disabilities in television [Web log comment]. https://rudermanfoundation.org/blog/article/the-ruderman-white-paper-employment-of-actors-with-disabilities-in-television

Young, S. (2012). We're not here for your inspiration. *Ramp Up: Disability, Discussion, Debate*. http://www.abc.net.au/rampup/articles/2012/07/02/3537035.htm

Zeidler, S. (2008, August 11). Advocates for disabled to protest *Tropic Thunder*. Reuters market news. http://www.reuters.com/article/us-boycott-disability-idUSN1029346220080811

# Index

Page numbers in italics refer to figures, tables, and textboxes.

## About the Editors

**Thomas C. Gibbon** is associate professor and chair of the Educational Leadership and Special Education Department at Shippensburg University. In addition to teaching, he coordinates a school-to-work partnership between local school districts and the university for high school students with disabilities.

**Elizabeth A. Harkins Monaco** is assistant professor of special education and disability studies at William Paterson University. With more than 15 years' experience supporting individuals with autism and developmental disabilities, Dr. Harkins's research centers on the critical importance of social justice pedagogy alongside educational excellence for all students.

**David F. Bateman** is professor of special education at Shippensburg University of Pennsylvania. He is a former classroom teacher and a former due process hearings officer.

## About the Contributors

**Jacquelyn Chovanes** is assistant professor of special education at Shippensburg University. She has 20 years of experience as a K–12 special education teacher and educational consultant.

**Ruth M. Eyres** is assistant professor of special education at Henderson State University. She was a teacher in K–12 special education for more than 20 years prior to teaching in higher education. Her research focus is on sexuality education for students with intellectual disabilities and autism.

**Amy Finn** has worked in the field of counseling since 1998 and has served in her role as a school psychologist since 2008. She holds a BA in psychology with a minor concentration in art therapy from Mercyhurst University, an MA in counseling from Indiana University of Pennsylvania, and an MSEd in child psychology with a certificate of advanced graduate study in school psychology from Duquesne University.

**Lisa Goran** is the director of teacher education and director of undergraduate studies in special education at the University of Missouri. She has 20 years of experience in education as a speech-language pathologist, special educator, and teacher preparation faculty member.

**Sara Baillie Gorman** is associate professor and director of the graduate programs in education at Trinity Christian College. She is licensed as both a special education and elementary education teacher as well as a board-certified behavior analyst. She has been working in the field for more than 15 years, with the last seven years being in higher education.

**Heather Hess** has taught special education K–12 since 2004 and is currently teaching K–6 pull-out emotional support and pull-out learning support. She holds a BA in elementary education K–6 and special education N–21 from Indiana University of Pennsylvania and her MEd in special education and supervisor of special education certification from Shippensburg University of Pennsylvania.

**Anne O. Papalia** is assistant professor at Shippensburg University in the Department of Educational Leadership and Special Education. She teaches courses on instructional methods for students with high-incidence disabilities, students with low-incidence disabilities, and collaboration. Her research interest includes service dogs in schools, the impact of therapy dogs on students with disabilities, and suicide prevention for people with disabilities. Dr. Papalia has worked as a special educator for students with high- and low-incidence disabilities in grades K–12, coordinated prereferral intervention teams, and served as a school counselor.

**Willa Papalia-Beatty** is a physical education teacher for the Kenosha Unified School District. She has a BS in kinesiology with an emphasis in exercise science. She has a MEd from Concordia University in physical education, adaptive physical education, health education, coaching, and alternative education. Her interests include coaching, urban education, and inclusive physical education.

**Christine Scholma** is assistant professor of special education and the director of the Center for Special Education at Trinity Christian College. She worked for more than a decade as a high school special education teacher and has supported preservice teachers in higher education for seven years.

**MaryAnn Shaw** is assistant professor at Saint Francis University in Pennsylvania, where she teaches special education courses and oversees community outreach programs. She is a blogger for News 2 You and a consultant for Joey's Foundation, which supports research, innovation, and education related to children with brain injury.

**Victoria Slocum** is the director of academic accessibility resources at Asbury University. She taught special education for 20 years prior to receiving her PhD in special education from the University of Kentucky.

**Rebecca Smith-Hill** is a second-year doctoral fellow in special education and coordinator for CarolinaLIFE at the University of South Carolina. Her research interests include increasing equity in transition outcomes for students with disabilities, enhancing teacher cultural competency, and increasing access to IPSE programs for students from varied socio-economic backgrounds.

**Chelsea VanHorn Stinnett** is a research assistant professor and the director of CarolinaLIFE at the University of South Carolina. Her research interests include postsecondary education for students with IDD, particularly how these programs assist students in building agency across life domains.

**Pamela S. Wolfe** is associate professor of special education at Penn State University. Dr. Wolfe's research centers on empirically based instruction, socio-sexuality education, and advocacy strategies for individuals with developmental disabilities. She serves as coordinator of the Penn State Autism Spectrum Disorders (ASD) certificate at Penn State.